Rescuing the Children

Rescuing the Children

A HOLOCAUST MEMOIR

Vivette Samuel

Translated and with an introduction by
Charles B. Paul, *one of those children*

Foreword by
Elie Wiesel

The University of Wisconsin Press

The University of Wisconsin Press
1930 Monroe Street, 3rd Floor
Madison, Wisconsin 53711-2059
uwpress.wisc.edu

3 Henrietta Street
London WC2E 8LU, England
eurospanbookstore.com

Printed in the United States of America

Library of Congress Cataloging-in-Publication Data
Samuel, Vivette, 1919–
[Sauver les enfants. English]
Rescuing the children : a Holocaust memoir / Vivette Samuel ;
translated by Charles B. Paul.
256 pp.   cm.
Includes bibliographical references (p.) and index.
ISBN 0-299-17740-8 (Cloth : alk. paper)
1. Samuel, Vivette, 1919–
2. Jews—France—Biography.
3. Jews—Persecutions—France.
4. Holocaust, Jewish (1939–1945)—France—Personal narratives.
5. Jewish children in the Holocaust—France.
6. World War, 1939–1945—Jews—Rescue—France.
7. Œuvre de secours aux enfants (France)
8. France—Ethnic relations.   I. Title.
DS135.F9 S2913   2002
940.53'18'092—dc21   2001005416

ISBN 978-0-299-17744-7 (pbk. : alk. paper)
ISBN 978-0-299-17743-0 (e-book)

Contents

Illustrations

FIGURES

MAP

Foreword
Rescue the Children—but the Others?
Elie Wiesel

This testimony by Vivette Samuel is important not only because its author describes dramatic events that took place during the occupation of France but also because the document brings to light insufficiently known facts about an organization—the Œuvre de secours aux enfants (OSE)—whose devotion to human causes does honor to humanity.

When one evokes the tragedy of the Jewish people under the rule of Hitler's Germany, steeped in the darkness and cold-blooded madness of the Nazi system, what is most distressing is the fate of more than a million children. All of them were condemned. Was it because they represented the innocence and future of the Jewish people? Or was it because the killers saw in them future avengers? We can never speak enough about the fear and silent tears that accompanied their last hours. One weeps when reading in history books the chapter that describes their departure from the deportation camp of Drancy.

Some of them escaped the executioner thanks to charitable Christians who, at the risk of their own lives, gave them refuge. There were not many such rescuers. We called those saved the "hidden children." Silent for a long time, they are no longer, and we should be grateful to them for finally speaking up: their story too is part of remembrance. Others, who were luckier, succeeded in illegally crossing the Swiss or Spanish border, helped by clandestine organizations like the OSE.

The daughter of immigrants, intending to pursue a university teaching career, Vivette found herself, at the end of 1940, at Toulouse, where, ironically, she helped for a while in the preparation of someone else's thesis on forgiveness. But she herself sought a more active life. Contacted by a leader of the OSE, she worked for that organization until the liberation of France. Her tasks were those of a social worker at Rivesaltes, a notorious camp where foreign Jews were locked up by the Vichy police, in appalling conditions, while awaiting deportation. Suffering from the "illness of hunger," from the cold, from the constant humiliation, and from anguish in the face of the unknown, the Jewish families put their hope in Vivette and in her friends. She remembers: "The distinction between guards and internees became clearer every day. Contempt seemed to have transformed the guards into jailers. To them, the internee was no longer a human being." Vivette followed the advice of Dr. Joseph Weill, one of the OSE leaders: "Look into misery the way a physician looks into illness."

And time was running short. The antisemitic laws, bearers of violence and menace, turned increasingly malevolent. The OSE worked desperately hard at protecting the children, then at placing them in eighteen secular and religious homes located in the center of the country. There were heart-rending scenes; a mother with several children had to decide which one to entrust to Vivette. All the children were provided with forged documents. The OSE moved heaven and earth, mobilized sympathizers and allies, knocked on every door; several of them opened. An archbishop, pastors, priests, all admirable in their compassion and their generosity, were ready to provide baptismal certificates; an entire Protestant village, le Chambon-sur-Lignon, opened its heart to uprooted children; frontier runners were hired. The OSE struggled against all types of police, all the gendarmes, all the Gestapo agents: one child, then one more, was snatched from them; several were sent to Palestine. The enemy was not always victorious.

Vivette gives numbers that simply take our breath away. How well known is the fact that Switzerland, so often criticized nowadays, took in fifteen hundred children who had been rescued by the OSE? Or that 750 children ages three to eighteen lived in eleven OSE homes in France in 1945? To be more precise: "11,600 Jewish children in France had been deported, all of whom perished in the camps, but 72,400 under eighteen years of age survived." Vivette Samuel continues: "About sixty-two thousand were able to stay with their parents or were directly entrusted by them to institutions or to non-Jewish families. It was possible to save between eight thousand and ten thousand children, generally of foreign origin, thanks to Jewish organizations."

All this warms the heart. But, an instant later, one thinks of the others, of all those who were not rescued because there was no OSE where they lived, no courageous young militants like Vivette, and one is seized by melancholy.

I confess that I read this book with a great deal of emotion, because I owe so much to the OSE. It was the OSE that, in June 1945, took charge of the four hundred "children of Buchenwald." I met Vivette here and there; I knew her husband, Julien Samuel, an impressive man of enormous courage and intelligence; I met their daughter Françoise, a brilliant university professor, and their son-in-law André Elbaz, an inspired painter whose work is suffused with remembrance, and I find it significant that their daughter Judith helped her grandmother compose this work, so rich, so abundant, so grave.

I found in it, and the reader will discover, a powerful appeal to fraternity.

Translated by Charles B. Paul

A Reminiscence

Judith Elbaz

I am helping Vivette Samuel, my grandmother, arrange her archives, and I am typing her text, knowing that I am now as old as she was when she arrived at Rivesaltes.

Snatches of vague and imprecise family memories, things told over and over but never remembered, all suddenly take on the precise outline of history.

As a child I knew that my grandfather had jumped off the train that was taking him [to a German concentration camp]; that incident had left him with fragile vertebrae. I knew that Nelly, his sister, had died with her children. I knew that my great-grandfather had been unable to escape from the Milice. But for me there was no date, no chronology, no link between these events.

As my grandmother's story unfolds, the real events become more precise and echo my own. I assume responsibility for the "I" when I too am twenty-two years old and live in the apartment that had sheltered her as a young woman, that had witnessed the secret meetings of young Zionist militants around my great-grandfather, and that had been requisitioned during the war.

We pursue together the work of remembering and mourning my great-grandmother, her mother, who, after the war, undertook for her husband what she called a "tomb of paper." He was Nahum, for whom this year [1994] marks the fiftieth anniversary of his death after deportation.

I often ask my grandmother whether it was courage or lack of awareness that led her to voluntary internment in the camp of Rivesaltes in 1941 as a nondeclared Jew, to marriage and pregnancy at the height of the war, and to the cruel but saving certainty of a single command—at any price separate the children from their parents so that the former might live. And, in the midst of all this, the heart-rending events she endured: the deportation of her father, for whose return she would wait such a long time; the arrest of her husband, whom she had to save with all the cunning at her command, leaving her baby [Françoise], my mother, hidden with a [Protestant] pastor, under a false name during the bombings; the death of her sister-in-law, pregnant, killed with her children because she was unable to separate herself from them (Nelly, always on my mind, as if I obscurely felt that I was living for her).

She answers me that it certainly must have been lack of awareness.

Memory is here to remind her of it. Certain details have held up against time: the name of a street, a witticism, the color of a coat, as if the sharpness of small memories sometimes screened out the worse ones, as if they were the counterparts of monumental omissions: that of roundups of children taking place in the next town—she no longer remembers whether she had been aware of them.

Awareness of the horror would have threatened her with mental paralysis.

I myself sometimes know this threat—a terrible bitterness toward history. My grandmother, however, seems to have been spared this anguish. But I felt it go through me like the visceral fear that gripped me when I was eight years old, in a class temporarily transferred to a winter resort at Chamrousse [in the French Alps]. It felt like doom. They had torn me away from my parents, I was no longer to see them. I kept hearing in my mind the histories of the Œuvre de secours aux enfants (OSE), of the war, of Nelly. I've always thought that it was an aberration for children to live without their parents. I emptied myself of all substance, of all my tears. I watched the children in the street with the envious eyes of an orphan. Long afterward, I learned that the children who had been sheltered at Chamrousse during the war were those whose parents had been deported and who had been brought there secretly.

These were children who had been removed from their families, then collected, then again separated from one another and hidden all over France, and once more separated from their new families. How did they get accustomed to changing circumstances? How did they remake themselves with new identities, always, everywhere? I think of the incredible faith they must have had in life in order to survive.

Soon one will think of this human drama, already fifty years old, as if it were a story from the preceding century. Today the rescued children are grandparents all over the world. We have difficulty believing in the horror, seeing it as an actual event. We undoubtedly prefer to think of those who fought against it, struggling relentlessly in organizations like the OSE (from the verb *oser*—to dare—for me, from the beginning), and of the extraordinary courage and willpower of those who dared to understand that separation alone could guarantee life, and who did everything to save the children.

March 1995

Introduction
Charles B. Paul

A little four-year-old boy hid in a doghouse. "But what are you doing, my little man?"—"I'm a dog. They don't deport dogs!"

—Overheard by a nurse at the deportation camp of Drancy

This book is the autobiography of an extraordinary woman who in her early twenties wrested numerous children (including my sister) from certain death. It deals with the internment or concentration camps set up in France by the French (*not* by the Germans), a practice that was denied by successive French governments until 1995 and ignored by most of the French population. It shows, in vivid and harrowing detail, how the French Vichy government handed over children to the German Nazi government for deportation to extermination camps in eastern Europe. It deals with numerous organizations, some Jewish and some non-Jewish, that performed, first legally, then illegally, the incredibly difficult task of rescuing children from deportation. It deals with an organization, the Œuvre de secours aux enfants (OSE [Society for Assistance to Children]) that until a few years ago I did not know had saved my life three times during World War II. Above all, this book reveals the heroic work of one woman, Vivette Samuel, née Hermann. As her granddaughter Judith Elbaz reminds us in the reminiscence, her grandmother voluntarily interned herself, at the tender age of twenty-two, in the camp I was to be liberated from four days later by the OSE, for the specific purpose of separating parents and children so that the latter would live. Vivette Samuel carried out this rescue work, like all the other work she performed the last three years of the war, despite the arrest of her father and her husband by the Gestapo and the need to safeguard her newborn daughter. And more than four hundred children did live, thanks to her extraordinary efforts.

When the war in France began in earnest in the spring of 1940, there were about eighty-four thousand Jewish boys and girls in France (out of a total population of forty-two million). Of these, seventy-two thousand survived, most of them through the efforts of numerous organizations, like the OSE, for which Mme. Samuel worked during the war. This rescue work, as Dr. Marion Michel Oliner, one of the surviving children, put it in her review of *Sauver les enfants,* "is still relatively unknown."[1] But even less known, because deliberately concealed by successive French governments for decades after the war, is the role played by the French Vichy government, independent of the German Nazis, in deporting the remaining twelve thousand children, and far more Jewish adults, to their deaths in Nazi death camps. A kind of government censorship had thus concealed the news of the Vichy complicity in genocide. But there was also a kind of internal censorship that had, for many postwar years, made it difficult for Mme. Samuel and the surviving children (including myself) to look back at these terrible years. It is only since the 1980s that we have expressed a renewed interest in our wartime roots. And because we belong to the last two generations of World War II survivors (I was born in Belgium in 1931), I feel compelled to honor her parting words, to recognize that her "book has taken on today the importance of an inheritance. Yes, this is certainly the issue, a patrimony to pass on, a history to transmit."

I therefore view my translation of Vivette Samuel's book as both a duty and a labor of love. I brought to this task the combination of being both a survivor of the events she describes and a professional French historian studying and commenting on these events. I translated her book, partly as a way of better understanding the most harrowing period of my life but mainly to inform English-speaking readers of events in recent history that are very little known or badly understood.

The events that Vivette Samuel describes in her autobiography touched my life in so many ways that the book cries out for some sort of commentary on my part. I realize that I cannot assume that people who did not live in western Europe in the 1930s and 1940s will be as familiar with those events as I am. Hence, I preface my translation with a brief historical background intertwined with a condensed account of my life up to 1946.

When Vivette Samuel was born in Paris in 1919 to a Jewish family that had immigrated from the Ukraine, France had officially been a republic since 1873. It also had been a haven for the oppressed from all over Europe since the French Revolution of 1789 had proclaimed liberty as its major principle. Vivette was also born a few months after the armistice that ended the four-year-long World War I, which had killed about 1.4 million Frenchmen and permanently disabled about 1.5 million. Germany, which had suffered an even larger number of casualties than France, had, moreover, lost that war. In addition, Germany had been compelled by the Versailles peace treaty of June 1919 to pay extensive reparations, lose territories in Europe, Africa, and Oceania, and, more humiliating yet, bear the sole responsibility for having started the war. The desire to avenge the "humiliation of Versailles," as well as the Great Depression, which started in 1929, created the conditions that led to the triumph of the Nazi party in Germany in 1933. Its leader, Adolf Hitler, lost no time in instituting a totalitarian regime and beginning a program of rearmament. He also passed a series of laws that turned Jews into third-class citizens and put many of them, along with Gypsies, Communists, intellectuals, and Jehovah's Witnesses, into concentration camps.

In the meantime, France, hit by the Great Depression in 1931, was paralyzed by a spirit of defeatism and by the rise of antirepublican extremism. Among the French governments that succeeded one another in rapid succession during this period, the most famous (and, for the Right, the most infamous) was led by the Popular Front, a coalition of leftist and centrist parties headed by the Socialist (and highly educated native Jew) Léon Blum between June 1936 and April 1938.

My political education began during the ominous year of 1938. Blum's government and Great Britain stood by when the Nazis and the Italian Fascists helped consolidate Francisco Franco's successful rebellion against the legitimate government of Spain. France and Britain also did not prevent Germany from annexing Austria and from implementing in that country the discrimination, persecutions, street assaults, and imprisonment of Jews that had plagued Germany since 1933. Among the people who fled Austria were two of my mother's sisters and one of her brothers and two of my father's brothers—all with their spouses and children. Only two of these families survived intact. Except for most of my cousins, an uncle who survived Auschwitz, and my sister and myself, my entire family, including my parents and three of my mother's sisters, perished in the Holocaust.

Snatches of conversation overheard from my relatives, as well as screaming newspaper headlines (we were too poor to own a radio), informed us of the German seizure, first of the Sudetenland, then of the remainder of Czechoslovakia. Up to that point, the western powers of France and Great Britain had done nothing to stop this aggression. But when Germany and its temporary ally the Soviet Union attacked and conquered Poland, the two western powers, on 3 September 1939, declared war on Germany, thus initiating World War II in Europe.

Poland was defeated on 27 September, but neither France nor Great Britain engaged in any major fighting for eight months following their declaration of war, except for a few naval engagements. Instead, what occurred was what the French call the *drôle de guerre* (the funny war), the British and the Americans the phony war, and the Germans the *Sitzkrieg* (the sit-down war). Rather than waging a *Blitzkrieg* (lightning war), as they had done in Poland, the German soldiers sat behind the Siegfried line of fortifications in western Germany, while French soldiers sat behind the Maginot line of fortifications in eastern France. Then, in April 1940, Germany occupied Denmark in one day and Norway in a few weeks.

War came directly to us in the early morning of 10 May 1940, when I was startled out of sleep by a number of explosions punctuated by a series of citywide alarm sirens. The Germans had invaded the Netherlands, Belgium, and Luxembourg and were bombing the harbor of my native town of Antwerp, one of the biggest in Europe. Hearing about the rapid German advance, my parents decided to flee to France with their three children—my sister Mira or Martha, born in 1925, my brother David, born in 1937, and myself—in the hope that the French would be able, as in World War I, to stop the German juggernaut. We packed our most essential belongings in a few suitcases and bundles and were lucky enough to catch a train going south.

We left on 13 May—just in time. The Dutch army capitulated on 14 May and the Belgian army on 28 May. *Blitzkrieg,* a war waged with rapidity and great strength by a combination of air forces and mechanized ground forces, had done its job all too well. It panicked the civilian population of the Low Countries and northern France, leading about ten million civilians (including fifty thousand Jews from Belgium) to flee to southern France by any means available. I remember that we traveled in a cattle car that packed together people of both sexes and of all ages, all eating, drinking, and relieving themselves in close proximity. What in normal times would have been at most a two-day journey lasted six days.

While France was overrun by civilian refugees, the German armies bypassed the Maginot line and drove through Belgium and northern France at top speed. They overwhelmed the French armies and forced the British troops to withdraw from the continent at Dunkirk. By mid-June, France faced an unprecedented military disaster. On 14 June, the triumphant Germans marched under the Arc de Triomphe in

Paris into the Champs Elysées. Two days later, the leadership of the French government was handed over to Marshal Philippe Pétain, the eighty-four-year-old hero of the Battle of Verdun in World War I, and on 22 June the majority of the cabinet sued for an armistice. The terms of the armistice imposed by the Germans were onerous. They included a heavy indemnity that exceeded tenfold the costs of the occupation, the retention in Germany of two million French prisoners of war, and the division of most of France into two major zones: northern France and the entire Atlantic coast were occupied by the Germans, and the remainder (and poorer part) of France stayed in French hands. The French also retained their navy and their empire.

Totally overwhelmed by this unparalleled defeat, the Parliament voted 569 to 80 to give full powers to Pétain, thus ending the sixty-seven-year-old Third Republic. Pétain's authoritarian government, now installed in the spa town of Vichy in unoccupied France, set about reorganizing France through a program it called a "National Revolution." It abolished such republican features as the party system, free elections, and labor unions and replaced them with an authoritarian regime largely directed by civil servants and a corporative system roughly modeled on that of Fascist Italy.

Because France's defeat had been so catastrophic, most Frenchmen were too stunned to offer any resistance to either the occupying power or the Vichy regime for at least one year. Many of them rejoiced at the fall of the Republic; many more embraced Pétain as a presumed shield against further German demands. The majority of the French, as H. R. Kedward explained it, "turned further away from the war and concentrated single-mindedly on day-to-day survival and the search for some return to a semblance of acceptable normality."[2]

But for foreign Jews like us, there was no semblance of normality. From 19 May to the middle of October, we lived, with some other Belgian refugees, in an abandoned farmhouse in the village of St. Félix, near Toulouse in southwestern France. My parents received a small allowance from a source that neither my sister nor I has been able to identify. For a few weeks I was placed in the village school, but that schooling did not take, both because I did not speak French at that time and because I was an alien to the teacher and students: they had never seen a Jew in the flesh before. (Two boys once surrounded me in a field and tried to strip me, curious to know what circumcision entailed.) I do not remember what we slept on, but I distinctly remember the absence of electricity in the farmhouse and the ants that tormented us.

From the outside world, news reached us intermittently of the defeat of France, the armistice signed by the Pétain regime, and Great Britain standing alone against the overwhelming might of Nazi Germany. I felt a kind of freedom in wandering about the village, but I also sensed my parents' rootlessness and the fearful suspense that marked our lives for five months. Then we moved again. Pétain's regime, in its august malevolence, was locking up foreign Jews in camps.

The Jews were only the most reviled group in a large category that the Vichy regime dubbed "internal enemies." In addition to Jews, that category included Freemasons, Communists, trade unionists, enemy aliens, and Gypsies.

Antisemitism was not a new phenomenon in France, far from it, but it had been at odds with the tradition of equality and religious freedom that grew out of the eighteenth-century Enlightenment and the Revolution of 1789 and that legally prevailed in the nineteenth and early twentieth centuries. The antisemitic feelings expressed by a sizable portion of the population had been exacerbated by the presence of numerous foreign Jews in France and by two major scandals, or *affaires*. The first was the Dreyfus Affair, in which a French army officer of Jewish ancestry was wrongly found guilty of treason and spent five years on Devil's Island (1894–1899). The second was the Stavisky Affair of 1934, in which a foreign Jew was involved in a far-reaching scandal that implicated politicians and the police; worse, it led to the February 1934 riots in Paris that nearly toppled the republican regime.

Much of the antisemitic legislation crafted by the Vichy government was an imitation of Nazi decrees, but much of it also grew out of native French traditions. At the end of August 1940, the government repealed a 1939 law that had forbidden the press from writing racist and antisemitic articles, thus unleashing a flood of slanderous and scurrilous news articles, films, and exhibits. In October, the Vichy regime issued the First Statute of the Jews, whose quotas and exclusionary laws turned native French Jews into second-class citizens (see chapter 2).

Foreign Jews suffered an even worse fate because they were both foreign and Jewish. The general distrust was aggravated after the fall of France by the arrival of eighty thousand Jews from abroad: some had fled from the Low Countries and from Alsace and Lorraine, while others had been deported from the western German regions of Baden and the Palatinate bordering eastern France. Because most of these Jews were without resources, could not obtain decent jobs in wartime France, and were considered security risks, they were accused by many of their non-Jewish neighbors of living in idleness and by the Vichy government of being parasites or "superfluous to the national economy." Hence their internment in French camps.

A few camps had been created by the French government in late 1939 to intern foreign nationals or refugees from the civil war in Spain, but their number greatly increased in 1940. The most notorious of these camps were Noé, Gurs, Vénissieux, Rivesaltes, and Le Vernet (which is described by the famous writer Arthur Koestler, who was interned there for a short time, in *The Wretched of the Earth*). No matter what the camp, the detainees were deprived of freedom, dignity, and nearly all the basic necessities of life. (See the remarkable description of the camp of Rivesaltes in chapter 4; it confirms and vastly elaborates my recollections of my own experience there.)

At the end of October 1940, we found ourselves in the camp of Brens, near Gaillac, which is fourteen miles from the famous city of Albi, in southwestern France. My memories of Brens, in comparison to those of the next camp, are very sketchy. I don't remember whether the camp was surrounded by barbed wire, as was the camp of Rivesaltes. What I distinctly remember is that the food was meager and monotonous and mostly vegetarian, so that we subsisted on tomatoes for weeks on end, then on rutabaga for other weeks, and on garbanzos or chickpeas for still other weeks. I also recall that we slept in a wooden barrack, which was heated by a kind of stove. Thus we idly spent the winter until February 1941, when the camp was emptied and most of its internees were transferred to Rivesaltes, the largest concentration camp in Vichy France.

Rivesaltes had once served as a military base for the colonial Senegalese soldiers who had shed their blood for the "mother country" of France. For a number of weeks, I clearly heard the bugler sound reveille in the morning and taps at night. The camp also contained Indochinese workers and interned Gypsies, as well as interned Spaniards, who had fled from the victorious Franco's vengeance. The Jews' barracks were grouped into two areas: one for men sixteen years and older, where my father stayed and worked emptying latrine cans (until he escaped, was caught, and was sent to the camp of Gurs), and the so-called women's quarters, containing, among the mobs of women and children, my mother, older sister, younger brother, and myself, then nearly ten years old.

Vivette Samuel's detailed account of the material conditions at Rivesaltes and of the internees' state of mind in chapter 4 can hardly be improved. Still, I need to add a few details of my own nine-month experience there to give her account even greater immediacy.

From the distance of sixty years, my sense of the sanitary and nutritional conditions of the camp is one of unrelieved misery. The barracks where women and children slept in close quarters were dark and unheated. As at Brens, the food was scanty and lacked variety. Many of us suffered from cachexia, the wasting away of the body because of malnutrition and disease. Medical care was virtually nonexistent. (My brother died there from appendicitis.) Outside relief organizations, as described by Mme. Samuel, did their best to alleviate these abysmal conditions resulting from neglect and indifference, but such help could only temporarily improve the overall wretchedness. I remember being inoculated against typhus and also standing in a line of children to receive a cup of watered condensed milk.

The psychological state of the internees was hardly better than their material condition. It was compounded of boredom, a sense of futility, and deep anxiety about the future. Rumors and real news about the German invasion of the Soviet Union in June 1941 and about some camps in eastern Europe only added to the hopelessness we felt. Nothing of these news reports could be verified, for we were cut off from the outside world. Indeed, my only reading material consisted of French colored comic strips that unhygienically served me as toilet paper.

As described in chapter 4, various rescue and relief organizations were able to pressure the Vichy regime in 1941 to take the Jewish children under sixteen (but not the adults) out of the camps and to place them in either foster homes or children's homes. A few were able to emigrate to the United States. The most active of these rescue organizations was the OSE, which for that purpose in November 1941 selected Vivette Hermann (later Samuel) to be its social worker in Rivesaltes in charge of taking as many children as possible out of the camp. She arrived at the camp only three days before the OSE liberated me on 7 November. Along with other children, I was brought to a bus, said good-bye to my mother and sister, and was driven to a sanitarium called Palavas-les-Flots.

I felt the separation deeply but dared not express it. I felt abandoned and watched in agony in the succession of children's homes where I was subsequently lodged from 1941 to 1946, as some of my comrades received mail from a surviving parent, or even a small gift on their birthdays. I attached myself emotionally to substitute parents—guardians in the homes, especially teachers—and worked hard to make myself noticed by them. And so deeply buried was this agony of separation and abandonment that I was unable to grieve when I received my last card from my mother on the eve of her departure for Auschwitz in the summer of 1942.

For six days I stayed at the sanitarium of Palavas, where I partly recuperated from the shock of separation and where I received the very best food that wartime conditions allowed. Most important, care from adults and camaraderie with other children replaced the apathy that had prevailed in Rivesaltes.

On 13 November we were taken by train to a shelter in Lyon and regaled with a visit to a neighborhood movie house, where we saw a film starring Fernandel, France's most famous cinematic comedian. The next day, we were at the Château des Morelles, near the tiny village of Brout-Vernet, only a few miles from the capital city of Vichy. I was to stay there until January 1944. Some of the children in that OSE home had been liberated from the camps, but many were native French children whose parents had either gone into hiding or been interned (and later deported).

As described by Gaby Cohen,[3] who worked there at the end of 1942, the Château des Morelles was "a peaceful house with trees, a garden and flowers. About a hundred children" lived there at any one time. It was the size of a large mansion. In addition to a huge dining hall, a kitchen, a downstairs bathroom, and a basement containing coal, potatoes, and other supplies, it also held the office of the director, rooms for the staff, and at least four dormitories—two for the girls and two for the boys.

The food we ate there was composed largely of bread of varying quality and non-rationed vegetables indigenous to France. This sparse diet was occasionally supplemented by dishes of meat and some canned food acquired both legally and on the black market. On our way to school, we children often picked fruit off the branches hanging over the road that was rotting for lack of labor to gather it. (One must remember that nearly two million men were still prisoners of war in Germany.)

The Château des Morelles was one of four OSE homes that sheltered children described as "observant" of the Hebrew faith. Yet I do not know precisely why I was chosen for that home. My guess is that it was either because, as the reports stated, I was very studious or because my mother had insisted that I be sent there, though my parents were observant only in the sense of their very loosely observing the Sabbath and the high holidays. The two Swiss homes I stayed in between 1944 and 1946 were also religious, but I ceased being so as soon as I came to the United States in May 1946. Like the other boys, I was taught to read the Hebrew Bible in the original language. The itinerant rabbi of the OSE, whose name I've forgotten, was a born storyteller and regaled us on cold winter evenings with stories drawn from Jewish history and legends.

We also attended the public school in the nearby village of Brout-Vernet, where I attended the "middle class" of children ages nine to twelve (I believe), run by

Mme. Bonnet. She taught us French spelling, grammar, dictation, oral recitation of poetry, literature, history, geography, arithmetic, and a little bit of natural science and singing. She was a remarkable teacher who, I'm convinced, inspired me with the ambition of becoming a teacher—without my fully realizing it until much later. She was able to give each student the attention and dose of learning he or she was capable of absorbing. She did all this in spite of the fact that her husband was for four years a prisoner of war in Germany and their only child, a boy, was retarded. (I learned after the war that her husband had returned from captivity and that they had become the parents of twins of normal intelligence.) I internally gloried in my excellent scholastic performance, for I was otherwise timid and without any particular athletic skill except running. After mid-1942, I was also without a family, except for my sister, who was liberated from Rivesaltes in early 1942 by Mme. Samuel and hidden in a convent in Brive-la-Gaillarde in west-central France.

Despite the deportation of foreign Jews to eastern Europe in the summer of 1942 and the threat of deportation that hung over the heads of all Jews after that, our guardians, themselves potential victims of roundups, managed to sustain our morale. They made sure that each one of us was kept busy, either going to classes, studying, doing housework, singing, listening to stories, going for a swim in the Sioule river, or taking long walks in a countryside that in the summer burgeoned with berries, cherries, and plums ripe for the taking.

We were saved from deportation and certain death because, as Mme. Samuel explains in chapter 5, the OSE refused to give out the names and locations of children under its care whom the Vichy authorities wanted to deport with their parents. Even before the Germans occupied the Southern Zone in November 1942, the government of Marshal Pétain and Pierre Laval voluntarily handed over foreign Jews within and outside the camps to the Nazis for deportation. Some Jews managed to escape into the Italian zone in southeastern France, where they were safe from deportation until the Germans seized it too in September 1943.

The irrefutable fact that the Vichy police handed over to the Nazis thirty-three thousand Jews (including my parents and other adult relatives) between July and September 1942 has for decades been attributed to German pressure or, more frequently, been passed over in silence. The excuse of German pressure, however, has successfully been refuted by a host of scholars, including Robert Paxton and Michel R. Marrus in *Vichy France and the Jews*. Indeed, without the help of the French police and later of the French Milice, the thinly stretched German police force would never have been able to carry out its program of genocide in France. The Milice was a forty-five-thousand-member paramilitary organization of Fascists and pro-German sympathizers founded by Joseph Darnand to help the Nazis stamp out the resistance against the German occupation and the Vichy government, as well as to hunt down Jews and other "undesirables."

The sight of children being deported led to a small change in French public opinion about the Nazi occupation and the Vichy government, and to the first open protests by some members of the Catholic hierarchy. A greater change of opinion resulted from news about the German defeats in Egypt and the Soviet Union, from the occupation of the Vichy zone by the German army in November 1942; and especially from the implementation of the Service du travail obligatoire (STO [Service of Obligatory Labor]) in February 1943. The latter was a policy initiated by Laval that compelled a large number of able-bodied Frenchmen to work in Germany in exchange for the return of a smaller number of French prisoners of war. This extremely unpopular policy led numerous young men to join the Maquis (the rural Resistance). The predictable consequences of the growth of the Maquis were the increased repression exerted by the occupying powers and the accelerated program of roundups and deportations of Jews and political enemies.

For a short time, we at the Château des Morelles lived in a kind of cocoon, despite the fact that we were located less than twenty-five miles from the capital city of Vichy. The non-Jews in the village of Brout-Vernet never resorted to the cowardly practice of anonymously denouncing us as Jews (which they knew we were). Imagine, therefore, our consternation when, one morning in the late summer or early fall of 1943, a company of the Wehrmacht (German army troops) surrounded the chateau. In fear of our lives but astounded that an army company should be used for roundups where the German and French police would have sufficed, we held our collective breath until we heard about the purpose of the German visit. They were after the man who was supplying us with black market goods; they found him, arrested him and his family, took them away, and sealed their room, leaving all the remaining children and adults in peace. By what exemption or miracle we had been saved I have never been able to discover, not even from Mme. Samuel when I asked her that question in 1996. The Wehrmacht raid, however, was an omen.

Starting in 1943, we kept hearing about the sinister complicity of the Milice in aiding the Gestapo and the SS (Schutztaffel), the Nazi elite corps, in their work of genocide. It was then, especially from the fall on, that the OSE accelerated its program of placing children of the Château des Morelles and other homes with non-Jewish families or of moving them clandestinely into the neutral countries of either Spain or Switzerland. Early in 1944, I was moved temporarily to a children's home near Limoges for a month and then to another home in that region for only a week. Nine of us boys were being prepared for escape into Switzerland via the Swiss branch of the Garel network, which was headed by Georges Loinger.

In this way the OSE saved my life for the third time. The Garel network was a form of resistance created by the OSE, and one of its most effective. Indeed, resistance in France took many forms. It included, along with overt and covert fighting against the enemy, "the gathering of intelligence, internal lines of transit, military preparations and innumerable services which would equip resisters with false papers and ration books, look after the safety of their families, penetrate the Vichy administration and eventually establish rural hiding places and encampments for those who were on the run or who refused the compulsory labour service in Germany."[4]

Early in March 1944, the eight boys and I were carefully prepared for the illegal crossing into Switzerland. We were given false identity cards with new names, a trumped-up excuse for our journey (we were going to the French Alps for our health as we convalesced from tuberculosis), and an adult escort who accompanied us on the journey. On the train that took us from the Limoges region to Lyon, we sat in a car not far from a company of German soldiers without their ever bothering us. In Lyon, we changed trains and escorts and got off at the small town of Annemasse near the Swiss border.

We assembled in a recreation center where we ate and rested. When the sun began to set, three boys at a time, accompanied by a *passeur* (frontier runner), who was highly paid for this extremely dangerous job, walked on a road parallel to a forest, followed at some distance by another group with a second *passeur,* and, last, by my group of three boys with a third *passeur.* As night came upon us, the six boys and two adults ahead of me disappeared from view, and suddenly our *passeur* pointed to the left into the forest and said to us: "This way, run!" With very light packs on our backs, we ran into the forest, jumped over a very low fence, and crossed the few yards of the no-man's land, when I was confronted with what looked to me like a monstrously high barbed-wire fence. I slowly climbed to the top where I got stuck. I began to weep and heard the sound of the barking dogs that accompanied the German patrol on its rounds, when suddenly there loomed in front of me what in the dark looked like a soldier dressed in a German uniform. It turned out to be a Swiss soldier, who grabbed me, threw me to the ground, and walked with me some distance before we were put into a military truck and driven to an interrogation station. Each of the children was interrogated in turn, while the rest of us waited in the anteroom, frightened, hungry, and especially very sleepy. Having passed the examination, we were driven to the OSE headquarters in Geneva. After staying there for a few weeks, we were separately placed in children's homes throughout Switzerland.

Along with a few of the boys who crossed the frontier with me, I was sent to the OSE children's home in the town of Tavannes, nestled in the Jura mountains not far from Basel. The home, appropriately called the Châlet, was perched on a small hill at the edge of the town and a short distance from a larger hill crowded with forests of pine trees, which we hiked through fairly often. The setting, especially in the winter, was out of an illustrated fairytale. After the experiences I had just undergone in France under the threat of arrest, deportation, and death, it was an enormous relief to live in a neutral country, away from the immediacy of the war and the Holocaust.

The food, although rationed, was more plentiful than in France, more appetizing, and not adulterated with peculiar ingredients to make it look more substantial. As at the French Château des Morelles, housework was assigned to each of the children. And the adult staff that had been hired by the OSE to oversee us was simply marvelous. The paucity of formal class sessions we received was made up for with class visits to local factories: the lumber and the electric bulb factories stick in my mind.

It was while we reveled in our return to sanity that we heard of the Allied landings in Normandy on 6 June 1944, the liberation of Paris at the end of August, and the massing along the French side of the Rhine of Allied armies, whose cannonades we could occasionally hear fifty miles away. Because the OSE office in Geneva kept files on most of its wards, I was able to renew my correspondence with my sister and even to meet her once at the Franco-Swiss frontier. After having been concealed in a convent for two years, she was placed after the liberation of France in the Hebrew Scouts' home at Moissac in southwestern France. As for me, since the OSE decided to group the refugee children according to final destination after the war, I was transferred, along with some other children, to the Institut Ascher at Bex-les-Bains (Vaud), located south of Montreux at the foot of the Alps.

Since 1946, I've always associated the Châlet at Tavannes with joy, freedom, and camaraderie; in contrast, I've always associated the Institut Ascher with restrictions and a religious piety that verged on the mechanical and the joyless. The cause of my deep discontent was partly the sarcastic character of our director, partly the fact that many of us children had reached our rebellious teens, and partly that we surmised that the Institut was only a relay station to our final destination, whether in western Europe, Palestine, or the United States. When we had lived in France, our anxieties had focused on survival in the terrible present. In Tavannes we had felt no anxiety at all. But in Bex-les-Bains our anxieties were focused on the uncertain future. We were all tired of orphanages, of displacements, of the absence of relatives and decent family homes, of living communally with hordes of children and adults in dormitories and dining halls.

I continued my Hebrew lessons, did my household chores, and learned the elements of drafting and carpentry, but my heart was not in any of these activities. The war had ended in Europe in May 1945 and in the Pacific in August, so why were we still refugees and stateless, presumably forgotten by the world? No wonder that one day in the winter of 1946, two French boys at the Institut clandestinely decamped and returned to France.

My despondency, but not my restlessness, came to an end in late 1945 or early 1946. I was sent by train to two offices in Zürich. In one I was given an extensive medical examination and in the other I answered questions asked by two ladies (of the OSE?) and filled out some forms. And then, one fine day in March, I was provided with documents that enabled me to go to the United States: boat and train tickets, a medical certificate attesting to my good health, a few dollars, and a *certificat d'identité* issued by the Swiss government. This multipaged document allowed me to cross various countries on the way to Antwerp, where I was to take a ship to New York. This document was to be filled out and stamped in Switzerland, France, Luxembourg, and Belgium.

On 4 March 1946 I joined several children and adults at the rendezvous point in Lausanne, Switzerland, and we all traveled by train until we reached Antwerp. But we stalled there, as the passenger ships were taking only demobilized American G.I.s and war brides to the United States. For about two weeks I stayed at the home of a plumber, his wife, and three children, who had been acquaintances of my parents before the war and who recognized me as I was wandering the streets of my native town. After six years' absence, I roamed the city I had roamed before the war as a youngster of seven and eight, but I couldn't go home again. Some of the physical landmarks I had been very familiar with had been bombed out of existence, and certainly most of the people I had known had vanished in death camps. (I also learned much later that my maternal grandparents, who had been hidden for four years by a non-Jewish family in Brussels, had been killed by an American bomb that had missed its target.) I met two or three friends from the orphanages and the uncle who had survived Auschwitz (though his wife and child had not). Then, and only then, did I feel most acutely the human losses I had sustained during the war. I was rescued from this deep despondency by staying for three weeks with my favorite aunt, who with her two sons and a female ward had survived the war in Brussels. She gave me some of the warmth and human closeness I had been missing for so long.

Only at the end of April did we take a train first to Paris, then to the port of Le Havre, which was barely standing up after years of bombardment. We boarded a ship of the Holland America Line, slept in the steerage, and arrived in New York on 8 May 1946, one year exactly after the signing of the armistice that ended World War II in Europe. After going through customs, I was greeted by the one surviving sister of my mother, who, with the help of the OSE, had finally and officially adopted me—but only after filling out countless documents, all explained in chapter 8 of Mme. Samuel's book. My sister arrived in the United States a few months later under the sponsorship of our mother's brother, and also with the aid of the OSE.

All in all, the OSE, from November 1941 to May 1946, made it possible for me to keep body and soul together. That organization, of which Mme. Samuel was an outstanding representative, had not only saved my sister's life and my life three times. It had also seen to it that for more than four years I was fed, clothed, housed, educated, entertained, socialized, and kept healthy, sometimes under the most adverse conditions.

Vivette Samuel's extraordinary work can best be judged in the context of both a horrible war and an unspeakable holocaust. (The record shows that the Nazis had killed nearly six million Jews, a large proportion of the Gypsies, and countless Slavs, intellectuals, Jehovah's Witnesses, Communists, homosexuals, and resistants from all the occupied countries of Europe.) Her wartime work, mostly with the OSE, forced her to move all over southern France, first by herself, then with her husband (an important official of the OSE), and then with her oldest daughter. The story of these activities, nearly always for the purpose of saving children from certain death, is told with unbelievable restraint, only occasionally punctuated by almost unbearable moments of poignancy. In fact, she often lets others—workers in the rescue of children and the surviving children themselves (in the chapter called "Children's Odysseys")—speak for the incredibly ingenious efforts carried out to save thousands of lives. Marion

Michel Oliner is absolutely right when she insists in her review of the book that its "most moving aspect is the total absence of self-congratulation. A tone of humility permeates the book as Vivette Samuel recounts the success of saving lives. . . ."[5] This humility extends to lesser matters, as well, such as her linguistic fluency (in French, Spanish, German, and English) and her ability to negotiate the byzantine complexities of the French bureaucracy.

Although Mme. Samuel is unusually reticent about her remarkable efforts in rescuing children from death, she is forthright in denouncing those who, unlike the Righteous Gentiles, chose to do nothing. She would like to have heard from those people as to why "they had shown no reaction when tens of thousands of persons, especially children, were swallowed up in unspeakable ordeals." Elie Wiesel, the Nobel Peace Prize laureate, whom she met after the war as a survivor of Buchenwald in the OSE home of Écouis, is even harsher in his judgment, since he refers here not only to tens of thousands from France but to nearly six million in Europe. "The victims perished not only because of the killers but also because of the apathy of the bystanders. . . . What astounded us after the torment, after the tempest, was not that so many killers killed so many victims, but that so few cared about us at all."[6]

It should be clear from the preceding pages that I, both as a historian and as one who owes his life to the OSE, have special reasons for wanting this book to be read by non-French speakers. My debt to Vivette Samuel and the OSE will obviously never be fully paid, but I hope that my translation will be accepted as partial payment. Indeed, this book is an exciting narrative. Parts of this dramatic story are uplifting, some are depressing, but nearly all are suffused with extraordinary yet understated heroism.

I wish to thank my wife, Janina H. Paul, for spotting and correcting the gallicisms that at first disfigured my translation; Professor Susan Zuccotti, for painstakingly going over my manuscript and correcting the stylistic lapses and historical errors that had crept into it; François Cusset and Lisa Rounds, of the French Publishers' Agency of New York, and especially Genya A. Markon, of the United States Holocaust Memorial Museum, for doing their utmost to help me in my search for a publisher for this translation; and Raphael Kadushin, acquisitions editor at the University of Wisconsin Press, and his staff for steering the manuscript to publication.

Above all, I wish to express my utmost gratitude to Mme. Vivette Samuel herself and to her granddaughter Judith Elbaz for encouraging me to pursue the translation, approaching M. Cusset and Elie Wiesel on the feasibility of publishing the translation, and sending me copies of pertinent documents from the OSE files that enlightened me about obscure byways of my wartime odyssey.

No words, of course, can do justice to Mme. Samuel's efforts in rescuing hundreds of children from the camp of Rivesaltes. One of these children was my sister, who has been able to live past the age of seventy instead of being killed before reaching the age of seventeen.

Rescuing the Children

As the shepherd rescues two legs, or a piece
of an ear from the mouth of the lion, so shall
the people of Israel . . . be rescued.

Amos 3:12 (RSV)

1

Odessa to Paris

1889–1919: MY PARENTS

My parents were both born in 1889: my mother at Yarmolinsk, my father at Tchargorod, two Jewish townships in the Ukraine that no longer exist. Both of them studied in Odessa during the same time period. My father, Nahum Hermann, was then engaged to Rivka, a young sister of my mother. During the war of 1914–1918, my parents met again in Paris. They were married in 1918. My mother at that time was pregnant with me. In a book written "for her children and grandchildren," Rachel Spirt, my mother, described her parents as "national Jews," who (she says) celebrated the Jewish holidays more from tradition than from religious fervor.

My mother, the oldest of seven children, three girls and four boys, was her father's favorite. Of her brothers and sisters I knew only the two youngest, refugees in Paris in the 1920s and 1930s: Charlotte, married to a non-Jew, who survived the Holocaust, and Isaac, who dreamed of becoming a physician but perished in an extermination camp. As for Rivka, I learned long after the war of her deportation to Auschwitz and of her death in 1944, in the same month as my father's.

People in the township of Yarmolinsk lived in total destitution but were famous for their annual fair in July. As my mother remembered, "Everything was done for this fair: the rooms were whitewashed, women dolled themselves up in honor of the merchants who came there for the occasion. The township, which was steeped in poverty all year long, suddenly took on a respectable appearance."

At Yarmolinsk my mother studied Russian with the son of an Orthodox priest. The boy made a special trip from a neighboring village, covering the distance "of six kilometers [about four miles] on foot, his shoes slung over his shoulders. At the end of the lesson he received as salary a glass of sweetened tea with white bread and some small change." Soon, however, she found this teaching inadequate. "I wanted to learn more," she wrote, "always to know more. I wanted to know Hebrew, but how was one to go about it? There was no instructor who taught it. I therefore followed a course in religious instruction. Since the *cheder* (Jewish religious school) was reserved for boys, the instructor came to our home at nine in the evening, after having spent a hard day with inattentive students. He was tired and hungry. During the lesson he often nodded off. . . ."

Undoubtedly encouraged by her own mother, according to whom it was better "to have something in the head than on the head," she decided to leave her village for Odessa. She lived there in modest circumstances by giving private lessons to children from well-to-do homes. After completing secondary school, she would have liked to study medicine but was unable to do so because of the *numerus clausus* [university quota system] imposed upon Jews; she therefore enrolled in the faculty of sciences. She earned a teaching diploma, attended Zionist meetings, and decided to teach Hebrew. Having departed for what she called "an excursion in Palestine," then under Turkish domination, she learned of the declaration of war as she got off the ship in Haifa after a stopover in Istanbul.[1] The group of students, unable to return to Russia, broke up, and my mother was welcomed as an au pair for a family in Petah Tikvah for the purpose of teaching Hebrew to the children. She then left Palestine for Port Said, where she continued to teach Hebrew. Then she departed for Paris, via Alexandria and Genoa.

Once in France, she was unable to fulfill the promise of her youth, no doubt because of my birth. My father, on the other hand, reached the limit of his potential.

In his native town of Tchargorod, he, too, had known poverty and a hostile environment. At the age of sixteen he participated in the actions of several Jewish self-defense groups and, with weapons in hand, defended a synagogue during a pogrom. A militant Zionist, he was a brilliant student at an Odessa *yeshiva*,[2] where, in addition to the traditional religious instruction, he received instruction in secular subjects. He finished his secondary schooling as a nondeclared major and, like my mother, hoped to pursue higher learning. Unfortunately, the doors of the university remained closed to him because of the *numerus clausus*. He decided to leave for Paris, "city of light," while many of his friends chose Berlin or the United States.

My father was then twenty-three years old. Enrolled at the Sorbonne [the University of Paris], he gave private lessons for a living. After earning his degree in history and geography, he was appointed nominal student in the department of religious studies at the École pratique des hautes études.[3] Having become a journalist, a correspondent for the *Morning Journal* of New York and the *Davar* of Jerusalem, he continued to join Jewish groups, notably a Zionist youth group that recruited its members among the recent arrivals from eastern Europe. When World War I broke out, communication between nations became difficult, and he then wrote for the French Zionist newspapers *La Renaissance juive* and *Le Peuple juif.* Very active, he participated in numerous debates and in the development of the Zionist organization.

I believe that my parents met in Paris at the height of the war, in 1916. France was to them "the land of liberty and the rights of man." They shared a Russian childhood, Zionist aspirations, and generally the same interests. They both spoke Russian, Hebrew, Yiddish, and French fluently. This commonality of history and thought undoubtedly brought them together while both of them were living in exile. They sought to assimilate into French culture, without, however, giving up their Jewish identity, and they were naturalized after the war.

My father was put in charge of the column on Russian politics in *Le Temps* (the forerunner of *Le Monde* [the most prestigious French newspaper]), as well as its coverage of Zionism. He set up financial operations to help in the establishment of the Jewish state and became French director of the Keren Hayessod (National Association for Reconstruction). While performing all these activities, he also worked as an insurance agent in order to support his family.

1919–1936: THE INTERWAR PERIOD

I was born in May 1919, a few months after the armistice, at the maternity hospital of Port-Royal. My mother, hospitalized for forty days following an episode of phlebitis, suffered a great deal from the xenophobia and contempt she met at the hospital. Deprived of all family support and badly prepared for her role, she was an anxious mother. One day, on the boulevard Saint-Michel, when I fell asleep in her arms, she thought I had died.

My sister José was born in 1924. We then moved into a larger apartment in the Latin Quarter, whose windows looked out on the cathedral of Notre-Dame. My father paid the rent on this apartment until its requisition in 1943, even though we had left Paris three years earlier. Optimistically, he said, "We'll therefore find it in the same shape at the end of the war." Did he really believe what he said?

[The Franco-Prussian War and] the First World War, which took place before I was born, left their imprint on my entire childhood. I heard about patriots who, in 1872, had exiled themselves "into the interior of the country" in order to remain French, while others were fighting "over there" against German assimilation.[4] With tears in my eyes, at school I studied "The Last Class," in Alphonse Daudet's *Les Contes du lundi.* Throughout my childhood, I was brought up on war stories: Big Bertha, whose cannonballs posed a threat to Paris; the battle of Verdun; the taxis of the Marne; [Generals] Foch and Pétain, "who gave us victory"; Alsace-Lorraine, annexed by the German state in 1872 but later returned; the Treaty of Versailles, resented by the Germans but also unsatisfactory to the French, who had been battered by the loss of nearly a million and a half of their own.

I was a well-behaved little girl, and I felt a great deal of admiration for my father, but, as long as I can remember, I seem to have always been at odds with my mother. I found her strange, too different from my friends' mothers, and undoubtedly not French enough. Because she worried a great deal about our health, she insisted that my sister and I swallow a daily spoonful of cod liver oil every winter of our childhood and that we eat raw horsemeat. I was sorry that she was not as good a housewife as my friends' mothers. She went to auctions and brought back furniture and objects whose value I did not appreciate; she took up silk painting, she was a vegetarian. She told us biblical stories, while I preferred the [children's] books of the comtesse de Ségur. Her originality disturbed me. Now I can understand the extent to which her life must have seemed frustrating, and how ahead of her time she was in her search for intellectual and artistic activities.

Having become a follower of Isadora Duncan [American modern dance pioneer (1878–1927)] in the 1930s, my mother often took us on weekends to a castle near Meudon run by naturists. My father did not really believe in these ideas, but he accompanied us. In this castle we had to dress in Greek tunics and thongs. I felt very ill at ease there. I also remember a vacation spent in children's homes that were inspired by the Coué method [a method of allegedly healing by autosuggestion], which was fashionable at that time. In the evenings, before going to sleep in the large dormitories, we recited as a prayer lines whose overall contents I've forgotten but that ended with the sentence "Day by day in every way, I am getting better and better." None of my friends went to that kind of place. I didn't like feeling different. I was Jewish, and that was already a big deal. I would have preferred not to be so.

The privileged relationship I had with my father was indispensable to me. It was a relief from the guilt I felt for having, by my unplanned birth, prevented my mother from pursuing her studies. To my father, in contrast, my arrival had awakened a new energy. He assumed the responsibility of supporting his family with a dynamism that fueled his personal and professional life.

THE LIMITS OF EXCLUSION

I have clearer memories of the period that began in 1933. Even if I was unable to imagine the danger posed by the accession of Hitler to power, I discerned the uneasiness of the people around me. Little by little I understood that the coming war was not going to be like those I had studied in class. The Germans' desire to avenge the "*Diktat* of Versailles" and the passivity of the democratic states was apparent. Persecution of the Jews was intensifying.

A voyage undertaken with my mother and sister to Palestine, then under British mandate, left me in a genuine state of shock. At the age of fourteen, I had never left France. In the holds of the ship, en route to Haifa [the leading port of Palestine], were young immigrants fleeing Germany. Their lives seemed hard; they were forbidden to ascend to the bridge reserved for first- and second-class passengers. Yet they never stopped singing and dancing. A huge gulf separated me from them; I found it impossible to identify with these youngsters bound for the Promised Land. Resolutely French, I insisted on being secure in my identity. France was viscerally my country, nothing could separate me from it. Nothing?

Only much later did I understand the meaning of the long road followed by these immigrants, despite the difficulties, traps, and restrictive quotas they faced. For the moment, I refused to identify with these youngsters, who, hardly older than I, had left an inhospitable fatherland. Upon my return, I even stopped studying Hebrew.

Our apartment in Paris was open to everyone. My parents frequently invited militant Zionists, students arriving from Palestine and the United States, and those who had fled Nazi Germany. I listened to the lively discussions that took place in the evenings, but, being too young, I took no part in them. Through them I discovered an unknown world of persecutions and exclusions. The names of several of the families who were friends of my parents were to become familiar to historians of the [German] Occupation. Some survived, like Marc Jarblum, Joseph Fischer, Ruven Grimberg. Others perished, victims of Nazism, like Leo Glaeser and David Rapoport.

Of course, news circulated differently than it does today. Television did not exist, and we hardly listened to the radio. I rarely used the telephone. I grew up without worrying too much about what was happening in the outside world.

I continued my studies at the *lycée* Fénelon without noticeable brilliance, but I studied hard. Discipline was strict there. Each of us wore knee socks (ankle socks and stockings were forbidden), a long apron that hid our clothes, and, when we went outdoors, a beret that I dared not take off until I got home.

My sister had difficulty living up to the part of younger sister. By nature less submissive than I, she often found herself in conflict and had difficulty in finding her place in the regular school system. My parents consulted a Dr. Robie, who advised them to send her as a boarder to the medical secondary school at Annel, near Compiègne [about eighty-two kilometers, or fifty miles, from Paris], whose director, Robert Préaut, was a physician. His wife was an instructor of physical education. I visited my sister there during school holidays. They stressed teaching in small groups, life out of doors, gymnastics, and swimming. The bedrooms were named after flowers and looked out on a vast park where races were held. In the evenings, after dinner, we recited the "Our Father" and the "Shema Israel." At Annel I went to church for the first time, on Christmas eve. It was at Annel that I learned to respect the rules, to balance rights against duties, and to be tolerant. When Dr. Préaut invited me to be assistant au pair during the vacation, I also learned to entertain a group of children.

As a student in the class of *philosophie*,[5] I again felt excluded. We had to discuss the influence of certain childhood events on the formation of our character. My friend Charlotte wrote an essay, a copy of which I kept.

Her parents left Russia to study in Germany, but the war of 1914–1918 and the [Russian] Revolution of 1917 prevented them from returning home. Charlotte, who was born in Berlin, was thirteen years old in 1933. One day at school, while the students were singing the "Horst Wessel Lied" [the anthem of the Nazi party], the singing teacher turned to her and said, "You should not sing our song; you're not German." It is this episode that Charlotte relates in her essay.

> "You're not German," and suddenly it seemed to me that the room had darkened, my fellow students had become strangers, the teacher had moved away, and I felt the redness of shame rising in my cheeks. "You're not German"—it was as if, right in the middle of the class, I had been called a thief. It was as if they had said to me, "You cherish your parents, you love them, you admire them, but they're not your parents, you're

the daughter of a drunkard and a madwoman, or you're a bastard child, or. . . ." What! I am not German? I should have laughed, I should have answered, I should have said that I was as much German as I was a blond, that this belonging to a country that I considered mine was my decision; but I kept quiet. Is it forbidden to choose one's own fatherland? Several months later, I left for France. I could have loved France because it is a beautiful country, because it is the land of the Rights of Man, but I no longer want to. I've suffered too much, I'm too fearful of the fact that, one day, I'll be forbidden to sing the national anthem by having it thrown into my face that "you're not French." I'm not Russian, I'm not German, I'm not French, I have no country, I am a child without a country, the way others are children without parents; but since one must be something, I'm therefore Jewish. Amid all these negations there still remains something positive. In short, for me to be Jewish means this community of destiny, being the victim of the ancient malediction, an allegory of sorrow, the symbol of humanity forever on the move toward an unlikely liberation, ever maimed and suffering but incessantly picking oneself up and advancing anew.

I became acquainted with the situation in Fascist Italy through a classmate who wrote to us from Rome. She sent us a juicy account, and, it should also be said, one that described enthusiastically the changes taking place in that country. But only in 1936, with the Popular Front, did I begin to feel concerned about the political situation: the Germans occupied the Ruhr, the war began in Spain.[6] The German refugees with whom we kept in contact were certain that France was bound to intervene soon. My father, like many of his friends, thought that Léon Blum should not have accepted the position of prime minister: a Jew should not have accepted that office.

My admission to the Sorbonne coincided with the beginning of the war in Spain. I chose to specialize in philosophy, but I applied myself particularly to the study of psychology and sociology, which, at that time, were taught within the context of that discipline. I intended these studies to make me financially independent. In trying to avoid the route taken by my mother, I finally embodied what she had wished to be.

In 1937 my mother took my sister and me to Austria for a summer vacation. I adored the land and its people. I was later shocked to learn of its return to Germany by the *Anschluss* [annexation] on 12 and 13 March 1938, and of the cheers that accompanied the annexation. There was not a shadow of resistance, and none of the signatories to the Treaty of Versailles, which had proclaimed the autonomy of Austria, reacted. But how could one be opposed to the principle of national self-determination?

During this time, my father appeared more confident than anxious.

I spent the summer of 1938 with a family in Oxford, England. Meeting the English made me realize the gravity of the danger. Everyone seemed convinced of the imminence of war. Gas masks were being passed out to the population.

Hitler lay claim to the Sudetenland, an area of German-speaking people that bordered the Third Reich. Was there to be another surrender? During the night of 29–30 September, the prime ministers of Great Britain and of France signed the Munich Pact [with Hitler].[7] When I returned to Paris at the beginning of October, I was struck by the atmosphere of "cowardly relief." I, too, was relieved. And then life went on.

The majority of the students at the Sorbonne were Leftists, mostly Communists. As for me, I felt no need to join a party. At that time, I was more worried about the situation in Spain than about that in Germany. From 1936 on, the anti-Fascist character of the Spanish war became clear to me when I saw young people, both French and German, enlisting in the International Brigade to fight on the side of the Republican army. Sensitized to the rise of Fascism and to the appalling powerlessness of the Popular Front to stem it, I was "of the left," assuming vaguely, as I heard my father say, that at the age of eighteen one can only be a Socialist. Today it seems ridiculous to me to have driven through the Latin Quarter in an open taxi, with clenched fist, yelling, "Fascism will not pass. *No passarán.*"

Newsreels kept us abreast of the Spanish situation. I also read Juliette Parry's book *My 126 Kids* and worried about the fate of children. Along with a group of Sorbonne students, I decided to join an organization formed to collect milk for Spanish children. The French government obviously was trying to avoid war and decided to impose an arms embargo on Spain. Leftist students collected money for the children; I was elected to join a delegation to be sent to Barcelona. I very quickly understood that I owed my election to my "apolitical" status: since the Communists were trying to broaden their support, it was important for them to have a representative who was not a party member.

I became involved in this deed out of humanitarianism, as we say today, and it was the first time that such a responsibility had befallen me. I was happy to have been chosen for the mission, but, paradoxically, I had doubts about whether I wanted to go.

How should I announce the news to my parents? I certainly would not go in opposition to my father's wishes. His opinion on the matter was essential to me: I was neither rash nor adventurous. In fact, my parents were not opposed to my going; they even felt great pride in seeing their daughter—so well behaved and submissive—launch herself into a commitment that must have reminded them of their own youth. After all, it was only a question of a week in Barcelona. Hence, they encouraged me to leave.

JANUARY 1939: BARCELONA

We were eight students—six boys and two girls—invited by the government of Barcelona in order to thank us "for bringing aid to Spanish youth." A reception committee brought us to an abandoned luxury hotel, which was without water and electricity and where I discovered what it means to be hungry.

We had brought food from Paris (bread, coffee, chocolate), but when we reached the frontier, Spanish students who had come to meet us convinced us to leave everything to them; they would bring our possessions to our place of residence. We never heard of our possessions again. Everything must have been sold on the black market.

At Barcelona we thus became acquainted with hunger, the panic one feels during bombings and as one seeks refuge in an air-raid shelter. At the end of our planned eight-day stay, we were told that we could not return: the frontiers were sealed. The French embassy would see to our repatriation, but it was short of planes. No news from my family reached me during this compulsory residence. Oblivious and as if anaesthesized, I was, I believed, able to keep my composure. I felt protected, as if nothing could harm me.

From Barcelona we were transferred to Valencia by sea. I can see myself again, curled up in a blanket under the ship's bridge, refusing to descend into the ship's hold. Planes were flying over our embarkation: friends or foes? Was I afraid, and of what? More than the eventual bombings, I undoubtedly feared the eagerness of some soldiers to approach the very young woman that I was.

The waiting began at Valencia. Because I was a girl, I could have taken advantage of the first departures, but I turned down such a privilege. It's possible that I meant to live this adventure to the very end.

We were hungry. All we could find were Valencia and mandarin oranges. The odor of olive oil floated over the city. In our walks, we saw churches that had been bombed: they had been converted into munition depots. Only after being transferred to Madrid in February, at the end of six weeks, were we able to fly back to Paris.

Upon our return, a meeting was held at the Mutualité [a meeting-hall in Paris].

The audience expected revelations from us. I was waiting my turn to speak when a Communist student came over and advised me to say that the churches [in Spain] were the targets of pro-Franco planes. I corrected him: "These churches serve as munition depots, and it is for this reason that they are bombarded; I can speak of bombed churches only if I am precise on this matter." I was not asked to speak, and I took away from this the unpleasant feeling of having been manipulated. From that moment on, I was inoculated against Communism.

After this first political experience, I renewed my studies at the Sorbonne and selected the subject of my philosophy degree: "Bitterness, a Social-Psychological Study." But during this time I was marked by my Spanish experience, which had made me aware, perhaps more than it did my friends, of the difficulty of reconciling a longing for peace with solidarity with the victims of Fascism. We had no control over events. Perhaps the anxiety we felt, the fear of bombardment, the buried memories of stories from the previous war, with their procession of horrors, all prevented us from trying to understand.

As I had ever since the Popular Front came to power, I left for my vacation, which I spent in youth hostels, where I had the chance to become acquainted with workers who were benefiting from the first paid vacations[8] and with anti-Fascist refugees from Germany and Austria. We sang "Ma blonde, entends-tu dans la ville," "Il va vers le soleil levant notre pays," we discovered the poems of Prévert and the works of Giono,[9] we learned about coeducation from experience. I loved the meeting places of young people, who, according to Léo Lagrange, minister of sports and leisure of the Popular Front, would "prepare the real unity of a new world."

In 1939, the war in Spain ended with Franco's victory. By the tens of thousands, entire families, Spanish Republicans, and soldiers of the International Brigade flooded the border region seeking refuge in France. It was only much later that I learned of the fate that awaited them.

2

War, Exodus, and Occupation

SEPTEMBER 1939: WAR

What did war mean to me in 1939? In September, I returned to Paris after a vacation that is inscribed in my memory as one with the vacations of my childhood: a healthy lifestyle, the sun, camping in pine forests, midnight swims on the shore of Sainte-Marguerite island off the coast of Cannes. During the two months when we had been cut off from everything, we had not known about the German–Soviet nonaggression pact signed on 23 August 1939 and intended to last for a period of ten years.[1] Undoubtedly, we would have interpreted the pact only as a guarantee of peace.

In riding back to Paris as a hitchhiker, I heard someone bring up the risks of an imminent war. Yet the concessions offered to avoid it had been innumerable. From 1935 to 1939, Hitler had broken the security lock of the 1919 Treaty [of Versailles], reestablished compulsory military service, and remilitarized the Rhineland, without meeting any resistance. It was the same in 1938 when he annexed Austria. Eager for peace, a part of the French population joined those who proclaimed, "Better Hitler than Stalin," that is, tyranny rather than war. The social democrats [of the Left] and the neopacifists of the nationalist Right had one thing in common: they were not ready to risk another war. On 15 March 1939, German troops entered Czechoslovakia. On 23 August, the German–Soviet nonaggression pact proclaimed a division of zones of influence between Germany and the Soviet Union; it preceded by one week the invasion of Poland. Only then did the British and the French decide to intervene, while Hitler and Mussolini sealed their pact.[2]

How did one pass from peace to war? During the last night of peace, I walked the streets of Paris with a friend I had met in the youth hostels. The capital was plunged in darkness. The windows were camouflaged, the streets deserted. We walked along the Seine, and I held my breath at the beauty of the sleeping city.

War was declared on 3 September. With it came the general mobilization, the commotion of departures, the fear of bombings, the evacuation of children from Paris.

My mother, my sister, and I took the train to Normandy, where we lodged at the house of a local resident. I offered my services to the city hall to help with the reception of refugees.

At the end of a fortnight, reassured by the absence of bombings, we returned to Paris.

The men were guarding the borders. My father, who was fifty years old, was exempt from the draft. He joked, "Just think how lucky you are! Your future husband is certainly mobilized, but since you don't know him, you don't have to worry about him."

It was in October that the secondary school at Annel, now transferred to Orléans, called on me to take the place of a mobilized instructor three days a week. This job made it possible for me to be financially independent. My father encouraged me in this, saying, "Who knows what may happen?" The rest of the week I prepared my thesis in philosophy.

Fully absorbed in my work, I took little notice of the events around me. Still, some news did reach me: the partition of Poland, the fall of Warsaw on 26 September, the Soviet Union's attack on Finland on 30 November, followed by the peace treaty of 12 March 1940. The Soviet Union had become our enemy for the same reasons as Germany. The French Communists were barred from the Chamber of Deputies, which voted their exclusion on 20 January 1940. Denmark and Norway were invaded by the German forces on 10 April 1940. Then, on 10 May, it was the turn of Belgium and the Netherlands [as well as Luxembourg].

I defended my thesis four days after the entrance of the German army into Belgium, on 14 May 1940. Here is its conclusion:

> There is a problem we have not studied, namely the role of bitterness in international relations. We cannot, however, refrain from mentioning it at the end of our paper, if only to skim the surface of an issue that is in the forefront of today's news. From themes we have expounded in our psychological and sociological study, we can derive an indication for the future. Tomorrow we shall have to make a peace that we hope will be definitive. It seems essential to us not only to come out victorious but also to try to establish a peace that excludes bitterness and the desire for revenge. As Christians meant

to realize the union of men through the love of a common God, so let us hope that the love of a common ideal of justice gives rise to the peace toward which the most profound aspirations of humanity are yearning.

I received my diploma of higher studies with distinction.

At the end of the month of May, I left Paris to return to the *collège* at Annel. As for my parents, they rejoined my sister, who, since the opening of the school year, had been living near Vichy, at the *lycée* of Cusset, and they were easily able to find lodgings.

MAY–OCTOBER 1940: ON THE ROADS BY THE THOUSANDS

The German advance, the capitulation of the Dutch and Belgian armies on 15 and 28 May, drove tens of thousands of people onto the highways—men, women, and children, as well as adolescents separated from their parents, who feared the young men would be conscripted into the German army. It was a continuous wave of people to which were added refugees from northern France fleeing before the enemy. [Marshal] Pétain was named vice-premier on 17 May.

On 13 June, Paris was declared an open city, and the government left for Tours. We felt some relief at the thought that our capital would not be destroyed, but it was also the first, and painful, sign of the defeat. The Germans entered Paris on 14 June.

The few children remaining at Annel had to be evacuated. Our four cars crossed the bridge over the Loire at Orléans just before the French blew it up, as they did the other bridges, to impede the German advance—the last one was blown up on 17 June.

We were privileged on two counts: first, because our director had had the foresight to stock gasoline for weeks, and then because we were ahead of the refugees on the French roads. All along our journey we stayed with friends or strangers who, the next day, would in turn join the road of exodus.

About crowds fleeing on the highways, bombardments, cars abandoned for lack of gasoline, and lost children, I learned only much later, through films or writings that recounted these events. I lived these days in this chaotic way, more preoccupied with the few children entrusted to me than with the news that was reaching me.

I nevertheless noticed the violent reactions and the displays of Anglophobia that followed the withdrawal and reembarkment of the English troops that had been encircled by the Germans in the Dunkirk salient.[3]

Powerless, we witnessed these events, all the while experiencing a feeling of unreality. The memory of the well-organized evacuation of Paris in September 1939 stood out in sharp contrast to the rout of May–June 1940. We had the impression of being governed by no one and, especially, of being abandoned by everyone. It became more and more difficult to separate rumors from reality and, especially, to believe anything whatever. Faced with this cataclysm, we were overwhelmed by fear and despair.

[Prime Minister] Paul Reynaud had declared, "We will win because we are the strongest," and here we were, ready for any kind of surrender. The idea of defeat had already been internalized by each one of us. The die was cast; we expected the armistice to demobilize the soldiers, without having any idea that their absence would continue for many years.

The growing panic, the fear of bombings, the unceasing exodus, the very idea of a war that we no longer wanted, led most of us to breathe an enormous sigh of relief as we listened to the speech delivered by Marshal Pétain on 17 June: "It is with a sinking heart that I announce today the cessation of fighting." The armistice was signed at Rethondes on 22 June.

There were some people who at that time had the courage to leave France to continue the struggle, and there were those who, like myself, hoped to remain linked to France even in defeat. My parents received an emergency visa for the United States, as did my sister and I. But, because we refused to leave, they decided not to use it.

We arrived at Saint-Jean-de-Luz on 29 June and learned that the government was leaving Bordeaux for Vichy, via Clermont-Ferrand. In the meantime, the children of the *collège* of Annel had found a haven.

THE ENEMIES OF THE NATION

At that time I did not know that, for several months, southern France had become the land of camps. Names of villages until then unknown—Argelès, Barcarès—are now recorded in history books. Since March 1939, Spanish Republicans, fleeing before the advance of the pro-Franco troops, had been confined to those beaches, then sent to the camp of Rivesaltes. And, from the very first days of September 1939, the belligerent countries had been locking up enemy citizens who happened to be on their respective territories. The great obsession of our government was the infiltration of spies: "Attention, enemy ears are listening." The very concept of "enemy subject" was complicated by the presence of political refugees. The government had failed to find on time a genuine fifth column (the presumed German spies); hence, it arrested without further investigation a large number of [German] anti-Nazis, the very people who had had to leave their country because they were no longer considered citizens there. Among these anti-Nazi refugees, the first ones to be affected were men from eighteen to fifty-five years old. Persuaded that such an investigation was due to take place in our land of law and liberty, they showed up at the summons, were interned, and endured a long winter in the cold and idleness, while those of the fifth column slipped out between the meshes of the net. The children were the first ones to suffer the consequences of this situation. While the Frenchman became soldier, hero, defender of the fatherland, the refugee was considered an enemy of the nation. Moreover, a new decree, issued in May 1940, ordered the internment of women. Even if mothers were generally released immediately, these few days—even few hours—of absence sufficed to leave an imprint on the children and to tarnish their sense of justice.

To these enemies of the nation were added foreigners on the margins of the economy,[4] Belgian refugees fleeing before the German advance. The families moved from rest center to rest center, from assigned place to assigned place, before winding up in the camp of Rivesaltes. In October 1940, seven thousand Jews expelled from the [German] provinces of Baden and the Palatinate were interned in the camp of Gurs. Paradoxically, Jewish children from Germany,[5] whose families had sent them on alone to France after 1938, were "privileged." In fact, they had already been "evacuated" and settled in the center of the country, in the children's homes of the OSE (Œuvre de secours aux enfants [Society for Assistance to Children]).[6]

Like most of my contemporaries, I had no idea of the confusion these children experienced; they had been expelled from their fatherland and had lived through the war alone or beside parents "deprived" of their nationality.

17

THE STATUTE OF THE JEWS

On 27 September 1940, a statute enacted by the Germans ordered that a census be taken of the Jewish population in the Occupied Zone. It was promulgated by the Führer's orders, which led many non-Jews to say that the government of Marshal Pétain had nothing to do with it. On 3 October 1940, the Vichy government promulgated the Statute of the Jews, which was applicable in both zones and which instituted a system of racial discrimination, forbidding French Jews access to public positions (except for some Jewish veterans, and then only at the lower levels) and imposing a strict *numerus clausus* in all professional jobs. On 4 October, another law granted the prefects the power to intern "foreigners of the Jewish race" over the entire territory. On 7 October, the Jews of Algeria, to whom the Crémieux decree of 1870 had granted French citizenship, were deprived of their nationality and subjected to a system of exclusion.[7]

A second German statute, made public on 18 October, dealt with Jewish "economic enterprises," to which trustees were provisionally assigned; the statute was designed to keep such enterprises under both observation and German guardianship. According to this statute, the term "economic enterprise" comprised any industrial or commercial enterprise, any bank, insurance company, law firm, money exchange, or real estate office. And for a company to be considered Jewish, it was sufficient for it to include a Jewish associate, or a Jewish director, or a Jewish administrator working for a corporation. "In addition, a company is considered Jewish," reads the text, "if it is notified by the prefect of the district in which it resides that it is under a preponderantly Jewish influence." All these companies had to make detailed statements as to their activity, stock turnover, and assets. Jews, and even non-Jews married to Jews, were required to make public the stocks or shares they owned. Any violation was severely punished with imprisonment and confiscation. This statute created a veritable panic. Jewish industrialists decided simply to abandon their companies in order to avoid any difficulties that might arise from these draconian measures. Groups were formed with the purpose of buying up the Jewish companies; this led to the ruin of numerous families and constituted a tremendous blow to the French economy.

In general, foreign Jews asked their consulates for instructions on what action to take. The U.S., Soviet, Spanish, and Greek consulates advised their nationals not to register for the census. Many Jewish natives of Bessarabia and the Baltic states found themselves de facto under the protection of the Soviet Union.[8] All Jewish companies, whether French or foreign, were required to post the statute, but the foreign Jews made sure to add a special notice of protection signed by their consulates. As a result, it was especially native Jewish companies that found themselves without protection.

Between 15 October and 1 November of the same year, 1940, I resided in Paris. From Paris I moved once more to Vichy, where I wrote two essays undoubtedly meant for my father or Professor Meyerson [her thesis director at the Sorbonne]. They dealt with the anti-Jewish measures taken by the German authorities in the Occupied Zone as they were understood in Paris at that time.[9]

> During the first days, the Jews hesitated to register at the police station of their district or at the *préfecture* of their *département*. They felt themselves humiliated by this decree. But the reaction of non-Jewish circles was such that the Jews, feeling a wave of sympathy, look on the bright side of things. The attitude of the twenty police chiefs of Paris is so comforting that the Jews, who walk shamefacedly into the police stations, leave them with their heads high. Paris has not lost its sense of humor. Thus, all the students at a Parisian *grande école*, whether Jewish or not, had themselves registered for the census. ("One never knows," they say laughingly, "about a grandmother.") An entire convent of nuns of Jewish ancestry stood on line at the police station to have themselves registered. On 20 October the registration is closed and from the 22 on registered people are recalled to have the word "Jew" or "Jewess" stamped in big red letters on their identity cards. One should likewise note that all the newspapers, with the exception of two, publish this statute without comment (it is a well-known fact that the Parisian newspapers are conforming, *gleichschaltet*).[10]

Concerning a statute that dealt with the wearing of the "armband,"[11] I wrote in November 1940:

> It appears that the ordinance already exists, but its application has been put off. Why? It seems that a similar measure has had little success in Antwerp; the majority of the non-Jewish residents of that city have in fact gone out on the street wearing an armband, thus showing their sympathy for the Jews and their sense of solidarity. One would hope that quite a few Frenchmen would follow this example. . . . Let us note also that the statutes listed above deal only with the Occupied Zone. No census of Jewish persons or goods has taken place in the Unoccupied Zone. The government of Mar-

shal Pétain, for the moment, has merely adopted the Statute of the Jews and stressed in its declaration that it cannot do anything for the persons and possessions of the Jews in the Occupied Zone. Here is some cheerful news: of their own free will, non-Jewish university students in Paris have interceded with their professors, asking that their Jewish friends be allowed to prepare for the competitive examination for the *agréga-tion*.[12] If, according to the statute, they are not permitted to become teachers, at least they will be able to carry the title *professeur agrégé*, and to hold out some hope. . . . The professors, moved by this display of solidarity, acceded to their demands. In another instance, the Algerian Jews who are already *agrégés* and who cannot obtain the position of instructor are given research grants.

Racial discrimination was thus applied in stages. On 2 June 1941, a second Statute of the Jews barred Jews almost completely from work in any professional job or business, as well as from enrolling in institutions of higher learning. That same month, the census of Jews was made obligatory in the Unoccupied Zone. In July 1941, a law dispossessed Jews of all movable and immovable goods. In June 1942, all Jews over the age of six were required to wear the yellow star. Finally, on 11 December 1942, in the so-called Unoccupied Zone which had in fact been occupied [by the Germans] as a result of the Allied landings in North Africa, a new census was followed by the stamping of the word "Jew" on identity cards and ration cards. French Jews could not understand how a legitimate government headed by Marshal Pétain could take such measures against World War I veterans, citizens integrated into the French community—"assimilated," as it was then termed—often the children of mixed marriages who, it should be emphasized, felt very little kinship with the Jews of eastern Europe.

Would the newly immigrated Jews have been more prescient about the antisemitic ordinances? I rather think that they would have had faith in that France which, in spite of the Dreyfus Affair, remained in their eyes the land of the Rights of Man, where justice was able to triumph. They registered for the census in order to stay within the confines of legality. . . .

From my father I remember this sentence about the expulsion of Jews from the civil service: "It is a violation of contract." In his mouth it tolled like the death knell of France, "a nation of law."

As for me, my refusal was visceral. I did not register with the census because I did not understand anything that would compel me to note my religious preference on an official record; that information belonged to the exclusive, private domain on which the identity of any human being is based. Yet it did not even occur to me, in June 1941, to try to escape in this way the terrifying juggernaut of which no one had yet any conception.

PARIS UNDER THE OCCUPATION

However difficult it is to define who is Jewish and on what basis, it's certainly as such that I reacted to the anti-Jewish laws. Yet I was also, and perhaps above everything else, a young Frenchwoman, twenty-one years old, who found her native city occupied.

France was divided into two zones: one, in permanent contact with the enemy, was daily subjected to its laws, while the other zone was controlled only by the French authorities. The two zones were sharply separated. It was only with great difficulty that one could obtain from the Germans a pass allowing one to move from one zone to the other, and only by waiting several days on line. There was no possibility of maintaining a correspondence between the two zones beyond the use of the family postcard, a newly instituted printed card that permitted one to give news of one's health and to cross out any items that did not apply.[13] News from one zone to the other arrived only through foreign intermediaries, generally via Geneva. The Occupied Zone, entirely cut off from news abroad, received information only by radio. Journalists were not permitted to quote their colleagues from the other zone. It appeared that the Parisian public rarely read newspapers; it was considered bad taste to unfold a newspaper in public. Labels stuck on the walls of Paris spoke volumes: "Tell me who authorizes you, I'll tell you whom you serve."

Of course, the organs of propaganda were in the hands of the Germans, who requisitioned all printing paper so that no newspaper, no review, no book could appear without their authorization. In order for an article to be published, it was enough for it to contain a sentence against England or against the Jews and foreign-born French. The two truly antisemitic newspapers were Doriot's *Le Cri du peuple*[14] and *Le Pilori*; the others contented themselves with publishing the documents transmitted to them. Those that were read anyway, for example to find out the exact date when one could collect one's ration cards, were *Le Matin, Paris-Soir*, and *L'Œuvre*. The others were not taken seriously. A story was told, for example, that *Le Pilori* published the names of ten Jewish persons whom it left to the judgment of the public. Nine of these ten people were not Jewish, so the newspaper was compelled to publish a correction and to offer its apologies.

A big competition was held to encourage the public to read newspapers and to listen to Radio-Paris. All the newspapers simultaneously printed a sentence (generally directed against the English or the Jews) taken from a well-known work or play, and the first ten people to identify the source of that sentence were each to receive one hundred francs. The next day, Radio-Paris read the extract from which the sentence had been taken and identified its author. Yet no one ever saw the list of winners of this competition. Is that because no one participated in it?

Of course, the radio was in the hands of the Germans, and Parisians were forbidden to listen to foreign stations (those of Germany and Italy were not considered foreign).

American and English films were no longer shown in Parisian movie houses. Moreover, the German newsreels did not fail to provoke hostile demonstrations, following which some movie houses were closed. From the beginning of the Occupation, Jews had been removed from positions in movie production, as well as from movie direction. Now they even hesitated to go into the movie houses for fear of being taken for demonstrators and being punished as such.

The Germans continued their work of expurgation. History and geography could no longer be taught. All the old textbooks were withdrawn from circulation, and new ones were prepared. It should be mentioned that a significant number of German children, from families of officers or of civil servants, attended French schools, severely limiting teachers' freedom of expression, especially in the higher grades.

Theaters, too, were "purified." Jewish artists were no longer permitted to perform; those who belonged to theaters subsidized by the state nevertheless continued to receive their salaries. Generally, few people went to the theater: the French stayed home, while the Germans preferred the casinos and cabarets, where they spent a good part of the night.

The French people's state of mind underwent a change. At the beginning of the Occupation, they looked upon the Germans with complacence. The actual war had been too short in duration to arouse any deep hatreds. Twenty years of pacifist propaganda had borne fruit, and everybody genuinely desired a rapprochement. The German soldiers, young, well-dressed, behaving with the utmost correctness, displayed some sympathy for the population. Moreover, the Occupation authorities showed some solicitude for the needy, distributing soup and food among the people. All this contributed to creating a favorable impression of the Germans. People went as far as to agree to the idea that France had been wrong in following the lead of Britain. But it is in the very logic of things that an extended occupation ends by weighing heavily on the occupied people. The German occupation was not only military; it was also a methodical infiltration by the occupying power into all the branches of national activity. The Germans brought into France not only their military and Gestapo agents but also a swarm of civil servants who were placed—at the expense of the occupied—in banks, courthouses, factories, fiscal offices, radio stations, and so on, and, of course, each one of them came with his family ("the German cities have been bombed," we were told).

The elegant neighborhoods of Paris experienced a veritable invasion. The Jewish apartments were requisitioned first, then the others. Few German soldiers lodged in Paris; instead, they only passed through it. But the villas and chateaux of the suburbs, provided with all the modern comforts, were in high demand. Some houses were spared because the owners had spread false rumors that they had been occupied by people with tuberculosis. So that "they" would not live in them, the interiors of the houses were frequently smashed up, the gas and electricity cut off, and the sinks unscrewed. No need to add that the grand hotels, ministries, and the Parliament (the Chamber of Deputies and the Senate) were occupied by the German administration.

Sheltering British soldiers was punishable by death, but the population was concerned about the fate of British civilians interned by the Germans. English-speaking French people and teachers at Parisian *lycées* took special care of them, creating an office of assistance, depriving themselves of delicacies in order to send them cakes and tea, knitting socks and pullovers for them, and temporarily adopting their children. It was said that the graves of British fliers who had died in France were covered with flowers and that their funerals were attended by large crowds. Paris took on an unusual appearance. In addition to having road signs written in German, the streets were almost deserted. Most of the vehicles on the streets were German. The only French vehicles to be seen were those authorized to carry food, and their number decreased every day.

Gasoline was a scarce commodity. What one saw was mostly German trucks, either military or touristic, giving soldiers the classic tour of Paris: the Invalides, the Place de la Concorde, the Louvre, the Eiffel Tower, Notre-Dame, the Panthéon. The Germans requisitioned from all over the place seats to make the military trucks more comfortable, and it was a curious sight to see these trucks carrying soldiers seated on Renaissance chairs or Louis XVI sofas. When they entered the basement of the Panthéon, which contains the tombs of several famous Frenchmen, the German soldiers were requested to stand at attention before the tomb of Jean Jaurès, "victim of his pacifism in 1914."[15]

As for the Parisians, their mode of transportation was the métro, second class, while the Germans were entitled to a free pass, first class. One no longer saw French cars but, on the other hand, swarms of bicycles, generally pulling behind them a trailer fitted out to carry merchandise. The appearance of Paris totally changed. Bicycle garages had to be set up, and the rules of the road were modified. Even taxicycles that reminded one of sedan chairs or Chinese rickshaws, were created.

Daily life was hard. The German hold over the economy made itself felt. The Germans put a general commissariat at the Banque de France and commissioners at all the other banks; banks could not pay any check without authorization. Safe deposit boxes could be opened, but only in the presence of a German, who appropriated all the foreign currency, valuables, and unmounted jewels.

The Germans were said to have contacted all the important companies (machine construction, armament, electricity, chemical) and offered them their economic cooperation, the first condition being the elimination of Jews. They searched the archives of commercial records and required that all registered invention patents be surrendered to them.

At the beginning of the Occupation, the Germans had been paid in Occupation marks, whose exchange rate had been arbitrarily set at twenty French francs. All soldiers received two marks a day to spend in occupied territory, and they proceeded to empty the stores of chocolate, liquor, champagne, wine, silk underwear, furs, shoes, silk stockings, and leather goods. German civilians came in large number to make purchases.

Price controls were imposed, and no increase was possible. After the Banque de France began paying four hundred million francs daily in occupation costs, the mark disappeared from circulation; nonetheless, the Germans, their pockets full of francs, continued to make their purchases.

The German women also went shopping. They were easily recognizable in the street. Here is the wife of an officer or a high official, dressed in new clothes, leaving the best Parisian stores; there is the woman soldier in simple uniform who has been unable to swap her cotton stockings for silk stockings. She is making purchases for after the war. Nurses wear long loden coats and gray aprons. But little by little the coats are shortened, some even begin putting lipstick on their lips. Ah, the ambiance of Paris!

What especially preoccupied Parisians was how to feed themselves. Potatoes, of which Germans were especially fond, grew scarce, earning the Germans the appellation *"doryphores"* [Colorado beetles], parasites that eat potatoes.

Milk was sold, parsimoniously, only to children and the sick. But we were told that German nurses distributed it to German soldiers at the railroad stations. No more coffee but only an unpalatable mixture. Yet, in the cities where the German troops were stationed, real coffee was being roasted, and the merchants, worn out by the incessant demands of the people, were forced to display signs reading, "The coffee we are roasting cannot be sold; it is reserved for the German troops"; some people parked themselves nearby, just to smell the aroma of good coffee.

Nothing exasperated the "occupied" people as much as the sight of Germans who were served complete breakfasts with ham, eggs, butter, *café au lait,* and so on, while they themselves had to suffer food shortages. Although it was true enough that the Germans too had ration cards, the Parisians were convinced, rightly or wrongly, that the Germans could have as many coupons as they wished. They smoked good English cigarettes issued out of the enormous supplies left behind by the British commissaries, cigarettes that the average French civilian could not obtain. During the three days of the week when cakes could be obtained, the Germans filled up with pastries and feasted on them, while in front of the store windows silent people who no longer had enough to eat stared at them.

People were apprehensive about the coming of winter, for destitution was widespread in Paris, which had counted seven hundred thousand unemployed—a number that kept increasing. There was no coal, and the unemployed were forced to sell a few of their coupons in order to obtain some money. They had to accept any kind of work offered to them; it was in this way that specialized workers were recruited by the Germans, who sent them to Germany. The first convoys, as well as the machines of certain factories, had already left for Germany.

Stories and rumors were passed around by word of mouth among the four million Parisians. One day all of Paris was talking about a German officer who, having been well taken care of by a French nurse, said to her as he was leaving, "If ever we should have to leave Paris, find a good hiding place and store provisions for forty-eight hours, for we have received the order to massacre everybody and loot everything."

The populace believed that numerous Englishmen, disguised as Germans, had dropped into Paris by parachute and were still there. A woman claimed to have met a German soldier with a pleasant personality and added, "He must have been a disguised English soldier."

Parisians tried to guess secret military events from external signs displayed by the Germans: "They are sad today; that means that things are not going so well in the war with England" or "The barges of the Seine that they requisitioned have come back; that means that the invasion of England has failed or that they have given up the idea." With irrepressible optimism I wrote in a letter dated November 1940: "The Occupied Zone seems to say to the Unoccupied Zone: 'You who do not have to obey the occupying authorities, you who consequently are freer than we are, why don't we see you take action?' But the truth is that it is now only a question of attitude and not a genuine reaction. There is the feeling that France will pull itself out of this, without knowing exactly how. One waits and hopes."

3

To Be Committed at the Age of Twenty

A WINTER IN TOULOUSE

Following this stay in Paris, I rejoined my parents in Vichy, where they had resided since May, thanks to an *Ausweis* (pass) obtained in Orléans. My father, who was able to get an appointment as correspondent for the New York *Morning Journal,* wrote articles that had to be approved by the censor. He tried to send the maximum amount of information on the politics of the Vichy government and questioned me at length on the events taking place in Paris.

I didn't expect to stay in Vichy. I was, above all, busy looking for something to attach myself to. I answered an advertisement published by the mutual aid society of the *Figaro* seeking an instructor of *philosophie* in Lons-le-Saunier.[1] My parents could not decide whether to live in Vichy or to pass the winter in Lyon, where my sister was a student in the senior class. There was also talk about the government returning to Paris, in which case my father was thinking of doing the same thing, so as to be able to continue his job as journalist. Professor Meyerson advised me to come to Toulouse, where I would be able to find work and pursue my studies.

I therefore left at the end of November 1940 for Toulouse, where I boarded with a landlady near the railroad station. Professor Meyerson put me in touch with a young academic who was preparing a thesis on forgiveness. I was assigned the task of researching the necessary documentation and of preparing reading lists for her. It was exciting work that forced me to spend entire days at the university library, and I was paid well enough to be able to resume my studies.

When my sister came to join me, we took up residence in a *pension* in which resided many students who had fled Paris. Many of them were Communists who had been uneasy ever since the German–Soviet nonaggression pact. The first members of the Toulouse Resistance were to be recruited from their ranks.

Students and penniless escaped prisoners from German camps joined the *chantiers de jeunesse*.[2] I met some of them parading in the streets of Toulouse and singing "Une fleur au chapeau, à la bouche une chanson. . . ."[3] At our *pension* we met Clara Malraux,[4] who had taken refuge there with her little girl, who was eight or nine years old. Small talk prevailed. We waited. Jean-Pierre Vernant urged us to eat radish leaves: "They're full of vitamins." He was an instructor in *philosophie* at the Toulouse *lycée* and left on weekends to join his wife and baby in Narbonne. Every person in this group, which included several Jews and children of mixed marriages, had good reasons for not returning to Paris.

The census of Jews was taken in the Southern Zone in June 1941. Either I did not know about it, or I pretended not to. We were all silently against Vichy but kept quiet about it. I worked; I passed the exam for the certificate in English with distinction. The school year was coming to a close. My father was unable to stay in Vichy after the census. He traveled a great deal in the Southern Zone. I left for Cannes, where my mother had taken up residence, while my sister stayed in Toulouse. The thesis on forgiveness was never written. The young woman who was preparing it had been arrested and would die in a camp.

For me this stay in Toulouse was a period of transition: I wanted to lead a more active life.

JULY–OCTOBER, 1941: DECISIVE MEETINGS

Summer came, my work was interrupted, and time seemed to have stopped. My mother rented a small apartment in Cannes. Did it feel like a vacation in Cannes in July 1941? The luxury hotels facing the [Mediterranean] Sea were full of rich refugees, the shop windows displayed luxury clothing, and the weather was beautiful. Food products were rationed, but there was enough food for everybody. Not much was known on how the war was coming along except that Great Britain was holding out in spite of the bombings. I found it difficult to endure this idleness. My dentist, Raymond May, to whom I confided my moods, pointed out that I should be able to find work in Marseille. Hence I left for that city, where I made contact with one of my father's friends, Dika Jefroykin, who, I later learned, was the representative of the Joint in France.[5] Undoubtedly because he knew about my work on behalf of Spanish children, he recommended me to the Unitarian Service Committee, where I met Herta Field, the American person in charge. She informed me that the Unitarians had set up kindergartens in the camp of Rivesaltes, near Perpignan, and that the OSE [Œuvre de secours aux enfants], another international organization, was looking for a resident social worker. I was crushed by this piece of news: "Children in camps? That's impossible! Pétain would not allow it."

Perplexed, I went to the OSE branch at 25, rue d'Italie in Marseille. Adrien Benveniste, a young *agrégé* in literature, looked into my situation and urged me to contemplate a future that I refused with all my might to consider: "Schooling for Jews? That's finished. We must think of manual labor" (the famous return to the soil and to manual labor advocated by Pétain).[6] He suggested that I undergo a probationary period of reorientation, which would be repeated in the near future. Baffled, I told him that I would think about it, but I left with him a schedule of my comings and goings. Several days later, I received a telephone call about a meeting with Andrée Salomon at the OSE. Once again I found myself at the rue d'Italie. When I got there, I passed on the stairway a lady wearing a blue turban, accompanied by a young man whom I barely noticed. The lady was Andrée Salomon, who took the two of us to the synagogue, without making it clear whether it was for a meeting or a religious service.

There, seated on a low wall in the courtyard, she questioned me about my studies, my family circle. She seemed to know my father, at least by name. She spoke very rapidly to me—in German—of the camp of Rivesaltes, to test my ability to converse with the internees, many of whom were natives of the provinces of Baden and the Palatinate. Still incredulous, I learned that there were at Rivesaltes entire families that had been rounded up one night in October 1940 in these *Länder* and sent to France.

Andrée Salomon drew up for me a historical summary of the activities of the OSE in the camp: a resident physician, Dr. Malkin, who had followed the internees from Agde to Rivesaltes,[7] had been at his post there for about a year. He dealt with the medicosocial problems of the internees, especially those of the children. Another OSE delegate, Charles Lederman, was being forced to leave the camp; I found out later that he had been accused of encouraging people to escape. They were thinking of replacing him with a young woman.

Andrée Salomon also talked to me about the activities of the international organizations that worked together in the camps to improve the lot of the people inside. Working in cooperation with the Quakers, or Society of Friends, the Cimade,[8] Swiss Aid, and the Unitarians, I would have as my assignment to arrange the liberation of Jewish children. I would be required to live inside the camp.

From the very first meeting, Andrée Salomon, with her royal bearing, made a great impression on me. Yet she was only thirty-three years old. She seemed self-assured, and this assurance acted as a tonic on me. She didn't seem to have any doubts that I would take the job, and she even set certain conditions: if the camps were transferred to Africa, as the rumors had it, I would have to follow the internees. Faced with her determination, I was ready to go to the ends of the earth.

Upon my return to Cannes, I consulted my father. Just as he had encouraged me to join the delegation to Spain, so he encouraged me to accept and expressed his confidence in my ability to handle the job.

Several days later, I telephoned Julien Samuel (the young man I had passed on the stairway) to confirm my acceptance of the position, and I was astonished to hear him say to me: "I'm very happy about it."

THE OSE AND ITS HISTORY

I made my way to Montpellier, where I was welcomed by what was called the administration of the OSE. There I found Lazare and Olga Gurvic, who spoke French with a charming Russian accent. Touched by my young age, they welcomed me warmly. There were also Germaine Masour and Jacques Rather, also Russian, whose immense generosity I would later discover. I made the acquaintance of Dr. Joseph Weill, a famous physician from Strasbourg, who had taken refuge in the Dordogne. He had joined up with the OSE, bringing with him a whole group of Alsatians, Julien Samuel among them. I also met René Borel, the devoted and conscientious head accountant, of whom I very quickly learned that he was not even Jewish. They explained to me the nature of the OSE.

This organization, founded in Russia in 1912 by a group of young physicians, had been intended to bring medical aid in a "nonsectarian, apolitical spirit" to the Jewish victimized by pogroms. It deployed teams in Jewish communities, organizing aid to the refugees and the victims.

The revolution of 1917 led the founders of the OSE to emigrate and to transfer their activities to the countries that bordered Soviet Russia, into which thousands of Jewish refugees were beginning to flock. Toward the end of 1922, local networks were set up in Bessarabia, Poland, and the Baltic countries. At the OSE Congress held in 1922, its leaders decided to create an international federation of national organizations in Berlin. This federation assumed the name of Union-OSE, and its first president was no less a personage than Albert Einstein. But, with the advent of Nazism in 1933, the Berlin office, subjected to persecution and prohibitions, was forced to move to Paris under the presidency of Professor Besredka [professor of biology at the Institut Pasteur in Paris]. In 1935, Lazare Gurvic, secretary-general of the Union-OSE, founded OSE-France. He set up communication with the OSE branches in Great Britain and in the United States and sought a new financial source to fund OSE's activities. While retaining its Russian initials, OSE-France changed its name [from the original Russian name[9]] to Œuvre de secours aux enfants [Society for Assistance to Children].

From 1936 on, the OSE was forced once more to refocus its activities when it began to receive, first from Germany and then from Austria, Jewish children whose parents hoped they would be safe in France (the France of the Popular Front). It was in this circumstance that the first children's homes were opened, in Eaubonne and Montmorency, and that the medicosocial society added a section to provide aid to children.

With the beginning of the war in 1939, the children in the charge of the OSE became "enemies of the nation" overnight. Starting in June 1940, in a France split in two, the organization had both to shelter these children in the Unoccupied Zone and, at the same time, to welcome the waves of refugees fleeing the German invasion of Belgium and the Netherlands. It was at this time that the headquarters of the OSE was transferred, first to Vichy and then to Montpellier, while part of the administrative staff remained in Paris under the direction of Dr. Eugène Minkowski.

Strengthened by its long experience, the OSE was quickly able to put in place centers to provide medical and social aid to the refugees in the Southern Zone.

I visited the Marseille center, which was run by Julien Samuel and Dr. Zimmer. From what was explained to me, I clearly understood that we had always to keep one objective in mind: to strengthen the ability of adults and children to cope with hardships. In addition to providing this medicosocial aid, however, we also had to offer special assistance to the foreign or stateless refugees who had been interned in camps by the law of October 1940. I knew nothing of these camps. Charles

Lederman, whom I was to replace in Rivesaltes, explained to me that they had been created to concentrate in one place foreigners who were "on the margins of the economy" as a result of the curtailment of their rights and their forced idleness. In February–March 1939, the first camps were hastily set up to shelter—temporarily, it was said—Spanish Republicans and members of the International Brigade who were seeking asylum in France. Later, after the beginning of the war against Germany, "enemies of the nation" were interned: German and Austrian nationals, also stateless, considered by the decree of 18 November 1939 to be "individuals dangerous to the national defense and the public safety." Either Jewish or anti-Nazi, many of them had taken refuge in France since 1933 but had been unable, for various reasons, to emigrate across the Atlantic as they had hoped. In addition, there were refugees from Belgium and the Netherlands who, after the collapse [of their nations' fight against the German invaders] and exodus, fled as far south in France as possible, only to be stopped by the Mediterranean and the Spanish frontier. But as they too were considered to be "on the margins of the economy," they also ran the risk of being interned after the promulgation of the October 1940 decrees.

If all these people took refuge in France "of their own free will," this was not the case with the Jews rounded up by the Nazis in the night of 22–23 October 1940, in the provinces of Baden and the Palatinate and in part of Württemberg. They were convoyed westward despite the reaction of the Vichy government, which, not having been forewarned, at first refused to accept them but in the end conceded. It was then that nearly seven thousand men, women, and children were first interned in Gurs and then transferred to Rivesaltes.

THE PHILANTHROPIC SOCIETIES

The first people to visit the camps in the Southern Zone were military chaplains in uniform. Two of them, Rabbis René Samuel Kapel and Henri Schilli, had from July 1940 on alerted the Jewish philanthropic societies such as OSE, ORT (Organisation-Reconstruction-Travail [Organization-Restoration-Work]), HICEM (Association d'aide à l'émigration juive [Mutual Aid Society on Jewish Emigration]), and the Joint. Friction among the different organizations delayed any concerted action, which finally came about with the material and financial aid of the Joint, whose European center was located in Lisbon.

To improve their efficiency, nine Jewish organizations, meeting in Marseille in October 1940, merged to form the Commission centrale des organisations juives d'assistance [Central Committee of Jewish Aid Societies], or CCOJA. Rabbi Schilli, who visited the camps on a regular basis, took an especially active part in this coordination. Thanks to his initiative, the OSE assigned Dr. Malkin to the camp of Agde and later asked him to follow the internees to Rivesaltes. Some camp administrators, like the one at Gurs, immediately took an active role in the work of these societies.

Responsibility was divided among the different societies as follows: OSE was to set up day nurseries for young children, CAR (Comité d'aide aux réfugiés [Committee for Assistance to Refugees]) was to take care of the elderly, ORT was to set up workshops to train adolescents in such fields as carpentry and hairdressing, and HICEM was in charge of emigration procedures.

These Jewish societies rapidly became integrated within a larger grouping that included organizations of diverse allegiance, including the Quakers, the Cimade, Swiss Aid, and the SSAE (Service social d'aide aux émigrants [Social Service for Aid to Emigrants]). It was Donald Lowrie, of the YMCA who, in the autumn of 1940, suggested to the different philanthropic societies that they work together. Vichy's Ministry of the Interior,[10] to which he proposed this plan, welcomed it, it seems, enthusiastically. With twenty-five humanitarian societies, national and international, religious and secular, under its direction, this so-called Nîmes Coordinating Committee thus received the endorsement of Vichy. This working side by side proved to be of immense value. In 1945, Joseph Weill wrote on this subject as follows:

> The large societies frequently provided the last link to the outside world for the internees and the only proof of human solidarity still available. Intimately mingled with the unfortunate people, fighting their struggle, running serious risks as they brought them aid, the societies acquired a growing moral authority. . . . Very early, they understood the necessity of joining together and coordinating their efforts and their intercession. . . . In an atmosphere of equality and mutual trust, organizations of the utmost diversity and of differing goals formed side by side a single front of moral and material resistance. From October 1940 to March 1943, . . . the Coordinating Committee held its meetings in Nîmes without fail at least once a month, (whence its name), first under the presidency of David Lowrie of the YMCA, then of the Protestant minister [Pierre-Charles] Toureille. Thanks to testimonies submitted by teams operating in the field, this committee studied the life led in the camps, frequently interceded with state officials, kept international opinion informed of the disgrace of concentration camps. . . . It was in the areas of hygiene, the protection of children and the elderly,

the improvement of the camps' sanitation, general education, and occupational training that genuine, often significant, results were obtained.[11]

From November 1940 on, Dr. Weill, the OSE's representative at Nîmes, stressed the necessity of doing social work in depth and championed the priority of the [children's] liberations to the committee.

Such a priority was not self-evident: if the OSE and Swiss Aid designated the liberation of children as an absolute priority, other organizations that also belonged to the Nîmes Committee were unsure, holding that it was more efficient to use the available money to improve the living conditions inside the camp. The amount needed to take out a single child could be used to help at least four inside. As for the American committee of the OSE, it supported the plan to liberate the children interned in French camps.[12]

In fact, the alternatives were not as clear-cut as all that; one had to work equally on the liberation of children and on the improvement of the internees' living conditions, particularly the struggle against cachexia (general physical wasting and malnutrition). The OSE worked at Rivesaltes in three areas: medical aid, which consisted of bringing supplementary food to the frailest people; the liberation of children and the finding of places to shelter them, which also meant taking complete charge of their education and health; and, as much as possible, their emigration.

Several hundred emigrant dossiers were being prepared. The rules were specific: the only persons who could emigrate were children under fifteen years of age, in good health, with someone in the United States who would assume responsibility for them. They had to be provided with entry visas, of course, and especially with exit visas from French territory, which were difficult to obtain. It seems that Pétain was worried that the arrival of these children in the United States would turn the American authorities against his government, which was still considered by Roosevelt as the legitimate government of France. The first two convoys left Marseille for the United States.[13] As a result of numerous intercessions by the Coordinating Committee, permission to liberate children under fifteen years of age was granted. But the OSE had to assume responsibility for finding shelters for them and, especially, for obtaining the authorization of the *préfet* of the *département* that would take them in. Dr. Weill thought that the parents, reassured about the fate of their children, would be able to organize themselves better . . . perhaps even to escape?

I was delegated to Rivesaltes to put into effect the liberation of children when-

34

ever places were fitted out to receive them in institutions run by the OSE, the Quakers, or Swiss Aid. Another OSE team did the same kind of work at Gurs under the supervision of Ruth Lambert. One of my assignments was to obtain the parents' approval, to prepare the children for the separation, and to take the necessary administrative steps.

Homes had been fitted out to receive and shelter the children liberated from the camps: Montintin, Le Masgelier, Chaumont, Chabanes, the boarding school and nursery of Limoges, and the Château des Morelles at Brout-Vernet.[14] Homes that became too small were closed and their children transferred to larger ones; in all cases the children's origins and religious beliefs were taken into account (certain homes were designated "of strict observance"). The one that would be of special interest to me, I was specifically told, was the sanitarium at Palavas-les-Flots, near Montpellier. Since March 1941 it had welcomed children liberated from the camps for a "recuperation" before they were taken to the homes installed in Creuse and Haute-Vienne.

On the way from Montpellier to Perpignan,[15] I suddenly became conscious of having joined a large organization. I felt secure with such warm-hearted Russians, with the very strong Andrée Salomon, and with Dr. Joseph Weill, who had given me valuable advice and clear instructions. They all seemed to have confidence in me.

Andrée Salomon introduced me to the *préfecture* at Perpignan as the resident OSE social worker at the camp of Rivesaltes.

Finally, on 3 November 1941, we "went up" to the camp in a taxicab.

35

4

Rivesaltes
Behind the Barbed Wire

NOVEMBER 1941: MY ARRIVAL AT RIVESALTES

The gates went up as we showed our passes. A French flag waved at the entrance of the vast camp. Rectangular barracks, whitewashed, apparently in good condition, were aligned every ten meters [about every ten yards]. The paths between the blocks were deserted, when suddenly some children came to meet us. Dirty and in rags, they painfully advanced on the stony soil, wrapped in gray blankets. They carried rusty cans—they were going over to Swiss Aid to get a warm drink. This was the reality of the camp. Two worlds faced each other: I, well dressed, wearing a red, close-fitting garment I had knitted during the summer by using the wool of an old pullover, a skirt, a cape of blue loden, and good shoes with crepe soles, bought at Saint-Jean-de-Luz after the armistice, at a time when merchants, fearful of a German confiscation, were selling off their stocks; the children all bent over and shivering in their dirty blankets. What a contrast, from the very beginning, between the places I came from and the destitution of the camp!

The barracks were built with textured cement; the floors were made of rough cement. Two-level compartments were demarcated by blankets hanging from the ceiling every two meters [six feet]. There entire families swarmed in every direction, sticking together to keep warm in an indescribable promiscuity. It was dark, cold, and humid: there was no heating system. An acrid smell of human sweat floated in this never-ventilated lair. Outside, the tramontane[1] blew, and several sanitary tubs toppled over. In this sinister place, the thin partitions allowed the wind to seep through and to spread fecal matter throughout the entire camp.[2]

36

The supply of water was inadequate, and there was no central sewer for drainage. The smell of human decay pervaded everything. Clothing was shredding into rags. Rodents lived in the camp, and malaria had become endemic.

Efforts were being made, I was told, but amenities improved slowly, despite the intercession of philanthropic societies.

At the end of each of the barracks could be found a tiny room, that of the leader, which he shared with his family. Four walls, a window, a door, a camp bed made up a minuscule but genuine palace in which one could have some privacy.

While crossing the Spanish block where I was to live, I thought of the weeks that I had spent in 1939 in a Spain torn apart by civil war. It was here, then, that these soldiers, battered in body and soul, had come to grief,[3] as had these women and children so marked by years of deprivation that they seemed immured in their misery. All these foreigners spoke French badly and knew no one on the outside capable of sheltering them. Hence, escapes were infrequent.

Andrée Salomon helped me settle down in the barrack assigned to the philanthropic societies; I was to occupy a small room that was sparsely furnished but that had electricity and could be heated by a small Calor. A second bed was set aside for Andrée, who came to the camp about every ten days in the course of her systematic rounds of the camps in the Southern Zone. Ten rooms were fitted out in the Block J barrack (the Spanish barrack) to be occupied by the [philanthropic] societies' officials, while the same amount of space elsewhere was occupied by sixty internees. There certainly was no comfort in that place. There was but a single source of water, most often frozen, a washbasin, and a pitcher. But we were given the opportunity of taking care of our needs in a bucket, while the internees were obliged, day and night, to go to the sanitary tubs rattling in the wind. Very quickly, I thought of myself as privileged. Moreover, I was never to hear any of my companions, who were "voluntary internees," complain of their living conditions.

HISTORY OF THE CAMP

At a distance of several kilometers from the village and railway station, the camp of Rivesaltes extended as far as the eye could see on a stony plateau; its six hundred hectares [1,482 acres or 2.3 square miles] were largely devoid of vegetation. This military camp had been transformed in January 1941 under the jurisdiction of

Vichy's Ministry of the Interior to accommodate the surplus of internees from the overpopulated camps of the Southern Zone, particularly the camp of Gurs. Rivesaltes was to serve a variety of functions until November 1942.

When I arrived there in November 1941, there already was a population of about twenty thousand persons (of whom five thousand were children from four to fifteen years of age), made up of soldiers, manual laborers, poets, painters, businessmen, expectant mothers, old people, and children. They had been brought together by chance, spoke different languages, came from different cultures, and had nothing in common. As Dr. Joseph Weill noted, "Each center can be compared to a *sous-préfecture* [administrative division] that has endured a long siege and whose disparate and idle communities have reached the depths of poverty, thus decreasing the general resistance and severely undermining its moral resistance, which has already been reduced by various administrative and political measures."[4]

Among the internees could also be found some who had been arrested for illegally crossing the demarcation line [the border between northern, German-occupied France and southern, Vichy-ruled France] or for black marketeering. Gypsy families, too, could be found there.

What struck me from the very beginning, in addition to the improvisatory nature of the population transfer, was the lack of communication among the groups that had been thrown together by a historical accident on an out-of-the-way plateau.

I was not trying to find out who was responsible for this and why. I attempted above all to find my place—I who had interned myself of my own free will—without letting myself be overwhelmed by a feeling of powerlessness that was overtaking me as I confronted the immensity of the task I had to accomplish. The shame that gripped me was salutary; it forced me to take action.

I overcame my fears because I felt myself supported by clear instructions. To conform to the administrative directives, I adopted an attitude of strict legality, having as its sole objective Andrée Salomon's "save the children" and as its sole counsel to "look into misery the way a physician looks into illness," given by Joseph Weill, who then advised "not to feel pity but to look after and, if possible, to heal." And Charles Lederman reminded me: "Your role above all is to be on the scene."

On 8 November 1941, I wrote to my parents:

By the way people follow us with their eyes, I understand the usefulness of our presence. The internees trust us because we share their hard life. A woman said to me in amazement: "You're French? Does the real France still exist?"

I'm afraid to hear bitter words spoken against France. Yet they keep quiet, they—like me—want to continue to believe in her. I try to delude myself into saying to myself that, no, this is not the real France. . . . I was hurt when a nurse, otherwise a good girl, said to me this morning: "After all, all these foreigners had to do was to stay home, they all speak German. They're Krauts; what are they doing among us?" She forgets that the Germans are in Paris.

Upon my arrival, I decided to do my work by myself and not to ask for help, even for household chores; very quickly, however, I got an orderly, a housemaid, an assistant for block meetings, and a young secretary. I understood that it was essential to tear the largest possible number of internees away from idleness. And the supplementary ration of bread I was able to give them was not negligible, either. I accustomed myself to this life of isolation. I forgot that not far from here life went on as usual, that children went to school and still gathered around the family table in warm rooms.

THE ORGANIZATION OF THE CAMP

To me, the camp was first of all a community of different groups compelled to live together. But it was also a system governed by an implicit regulation that no one understood.

The purpose of the camps was to apply the prefectoral directives on a local level. The camp commander's office had to transmit to the prefectoral office all applications for visas, transfers, and liberation. It coordinated the camp's services, organized the office staff and postal censorship, supervised the proper functioning of the camp's management, decided the manner in which the internees were to spend their time, and imposed penalties for minor disciplinary infractions. Its power was even greater to the degree that its limits were unknown and left to individual interpretation.

The camp commander, a Reserve captain and graduate of the École centrale [university-level engineering school] of Lyon, had been transferred to Rivesaltes from the camp of Argelès, where he had been administrator. His qualities as a human being could not be denied. He was very friendly to me, and his relations with the philanthropic societies were always correct. Yet he appeared to be indifferent to the drama taking place around him. Undoubtedly, one has to harden oneself to "manage" such a system. Later on, because he was considered too "soft," the manner in which he exercised his functions was closely watched. He was held responsible for the loose discipline that prevailed at Rivesaltes: the failure to call the roll in the barracks and the regrettable moral slackness brought about by the free movement of people between the blocks, which the administration more or less tolerated, and which was further aggravated by the black market that never stopped growing.

The purpose of the people called "the functionaries" (clerks, nurses, cooks) was in fact that of keeping the camp functioning. The "guards" had a special place in this large system: they had to prevent people from going beyond the assigned limits and to compel them to respect the rules they all flouted. They had not chosen this line of work. Most of them were Alsatians or Lorrainers who had been expelled from their province by the German advance and had taken refuge in this region and were temporarily out of work.

The distinction between guards and internees became clearer every day. Contempt seemed to have transformed the guards into jailers. To them, the internee was no longer a human being. The slogans of Nazi propaganda, the xenophobic watchwords of the Vichy press, all contributed to remove the last scruples they might have felt toward those outcasts whom no legislation protected, and abuses of power multiplied: a guard slapped a woman who didn't comply fast enough with an order; Mme. Z., who took the greatest pains to cook a few meager bits of food along a fence, had her pot and its contents confiscated; Paula S., a pretty young twenty-two-year-old woman, was jailed, the pretext an attempted theft at the camp store, the real motive her refusal of the advances of M. X., an administrative employee.

As for the neighboring French population, they seemed to be very disoriented. Thousands of refugees were looking, as best as they could, for a place to live. As for the prisoners held in Germany—nearly two million of them—all hope of their imminent return had been abandoned. Once the armistice was signed, Pétain devoted himself to the task of persuading the French that it was they who were responsible for the defeat: "Our defeat was caused by our immorality." He offered collaboration as the only way for France to become, all on its own, a political partner of the Reich.

A search for scapegoats ensued when finding food became an obsession. The forced idleness of Jews, thrown out of their economic livelihood, was interpreted as a sign of their taste for luxury and the easy life. They were held responsible for the black market and for the rocketing inflation. The Vichy press inflamed these rumors. People were afraid of foreigners and everything was done to limit the settlement of interned families solely to *départements* where camps were located.

The problem of food was more striking in the camp than anywhere else: about one hundred grams [about three and a half ounces] of bread at noon and in the evening, and a soup with artichokes, turnips, or rutabagas. Twice a week officials passed out a small slice of meat, once or twice some jam, and, for children, the legal quantity of milk.

Theoretically, the food rations were the same as those for all French people, but the real conditions were quite different. Outside the camp it was possible to procure nonrationed food, to engage in barter, to resort to the black market. One could also prepare inventive combinations out of rationed nutriments: carrot cake, chestnut puddings, artichoke purée. Many people cultivated a plot of land or were acquainted with some farmers. Certainly, there was a shortage of bread, coffee, sugar, and meat everywhere; people found it difficult to feed themselves, but no one died of hunger. All these amenities were absent inside the camps, and many children were ill and anemic. It was therefore necessary to improve the overall provisioning of food.

A department for the purchase of nonrationed merchandise from wholesalers of the Marseille and Toulouse regions had been set up under the supervision of Julien Samuel, of the OSE. This department had been charged with the task of contacting the prefectoral offices in order to obtain gift vouchers for other goods. At Rivesaltes, Swiss Aid, to which the commission allocated a monthly credit, served rice and milk to children in the morning and milk for the *goûter* [afternoon snack] five times a week.

The medical situation was as disastrous for the adults as for the children. At the end of the summer of 1941, Dr. Malkin, a representative of the OSE, was named medical inspector of the schools in the camp. He had to report his activities to the head physician responsible for the sanitary services, whom he managed to convince of the need to have children systematically vaccinated, with the highest priority given to diphtheria and tetanus inoculations.

For the adults, given the lack of resources, one could not deal with prevention but only care for those most seriously afflicted. When "the illness of hunger" struck down an increasing number of adults, Dr. Malkin devoted himself, as a first priority, to taking all possible actions to ensure their survival. To the food provided by the camp, he added the appropriate nutritional and medicinal requirements. When the number of persons who had fallen ill surpassed the number of available places in the infirmary, Swiss Aid took over the distribution [of these supplements] in the blocks themselves. Once alerted, the Joint obtained the necessary funds.

Plunged into this Ubuesque[5] world, I felt myself to be part of an immense chain of solidarity. Through Andrée Salomon, I remained linked to the directorate of the Montpellier OSE, whose pragmatism and efficiency I very quickly came to appreciate. I passed on the maximum amount of information possible on the daily life of the internees and their needs to Dr. Joseph Weill, who was in charge of the Commission on Hygiene and Aid to Children and the Elderly. He could make use of that information and pass it on to the Nîmes Coordinating Committee. These raw data were then transformed into concrete proposals that could be applied in the field.

I felt myself to be the recipient of decisions to the degree that I was kept up to date on the discussions held about the choices to be made. Yet I never asked myself where the money was coming from. It was only after the war that I learned of the role played by the Joint in creating a policy that established its priorities in accordance with the available funds.

When I arrived at the camp, I made it my responsibility to carry out my instructions to improve the living conditions inside the camp and to liberate the children. Dr. Weill was inflexible, his position on the matter clear: "the camps must disappear." As a body the Nîmes Coordinating Committee took his side, but, in order to achieve the greatest efficiency, it was necessary to reconcile the collaboration between the different philanthropic societies and the agreement reached with the Vichy authorities.

I felt very strongly that the simple human presence and attitudes of the philanthropic societies' representatives toward the internees did not fail to have some influence upon the guards. This discovery comforted and guided us.

I jotted down in my logbook:

> Peter came to get me, because the guards carry off everything at the distribution of packages. I run over to the mailroom. Outside, a long line is waiting in the cold. Children especially, for the parents have found out that the children managed better than they themselves in these circumstances. The packages that came in during the week form a large pile behind the table that the guards have placed at the entrance of the

building. The floor is littered with paper and empty cartons. Confiscated goods are stacked against the wall—loaves of bread, milk cans, dry sausage, and chocolate.

I get closer. Here is Hans, whose mother, severely ill, has not left her bed for two weeks. Anxiously, his eyes follow the thick fingers that are cutting the string—bread, sausage, a box of pasta, a can of milk. The child holds his breath. I try to sound jocular: "Come on, you're not going to take this away from this kid. Don't be more unkind than you really are!" I've won; Hans carries off his package, untouched. He turns around at the door and gives me a look of gratitude and happiness.

I stay there during the distribution. I offer a few cigarettes to the guards. The censorship becomes gentler.

MY FIRST VISITING HOURS

I had a desk and everything needed to set up a file. An internee suggested that I buy his typewriter. I accepted.

On 6 November 1941, I held my first office hours. On the door of Office 43 of Block K was posted the notice: "Placement Center-OSE. Visits every day except Saturdays and Sundays, from 11 A.M. to noon and from 4 to 6 P.M." The waiting room was very quickly filled up. They knew I was here "for the children," to arrange their liberation. The camp's administration asked us to establish a priority scale for children, in accordance with the doctor's decisions, the civil status of the parents, and whether their placement outside the camp had been authorized. Seeing the eagerness of the mothers who rushed over to my office and implored "Nehmen Sie mein Kind weg" (take my child), I thought that it should not be difficult to obtain their permission.

The placement certificate, once granted, was transmitted by the prefectoral chain of command to Perpignan, which made the final decision and notified the camp. Because each liberation was unique, the process took a long time. The beds in the children's homes were reserved months in advance, and when the certificate finally arrived, the child for whom it had been intended might have fallen ill, perhaps could not be moved, or perhaps had already been transferred to some other place. Everything then had to start all over again for someone else. I thus jotted down in my journal of 22 December: "We've finally obtained the order to free ten little girls for whom the home at Crocq had reserved ten places. But when the list of names reached the camp, six of them could not physically leave for reasons of health and risk of contagion (lice, scabies)."

My job was to ensure the simplification of these administrative procedures so as to liberate a maximum number of children in a minimum amount of time. It would take me seven months to bring about the liberation of four hundred qualified children.

In November 1941 I mentioned some office visits: "The waiting room is filled long before opening time. We should add curtains on the windows, photos on the walls, and also some flowers, so that the visitors can feel at ease with and have confidence in us. Women follow one another. . . ."

Mme. Zomper was the first one to tell me her history. Her hair was gray, and the fingers of one of her hands were paralyzed. With tears in her eyes, she told me of her marriage in Poland and of the birth of her two sons: Jacques in 1926 and Alex in 1928. She talked to me about her happy family, ruined by the economic crisis of 1929 that struck her husband's business and forced him to emigrate. He took up residence in Liège [Belgium], where his family soon joined him. The oldest of the children was three years old and the youngest barely one. Once again the family settled down to normality. The father again picked up his job as metallurgical worker; the children went to school and received a good education. Then the war broke out. At first, Belgium was spared the conflict, but in May 1940 the Zompers fled toward France to escape the German occupation. M. Zomper enlisted in the Polish army. Events now followed one another in rapid succession: demobilized by the armistice, he was assigned to a company of foreign workers. His wife and their two sons were interned at Brens [a camp near Albi-Gaillac] and then transferred to Rivesaltes. Mme. Zomper's voice caught. She came to talk to me about her oldest son. Jacques had completely changed since his arrival in the camp. He used to be a quiet, polite, affectionate boy. Now he was wild, withdrawn, peremptory, and brusque with her. "One would have thought he holds it against me, as if it were my fault. He speaks to me in a tone almost of hatred. He cannot bear this idleness. If this continues, mademoiselle, he'll turn out badly, I feel it."

Then she hesitated, looked at me out of the corner of her eye, as if to gauge whether she could confide in me, and added: "He tried to escape, but they caught him and brought him back to the camp in handcuffs. He is only sixteen years old. Imagine, five policemen for one sixteen-year-old kid. My son, handcuffed, like a common criminal! . . . Ever since he's returned, he has been like that; he's mad against the whole world, mademoiselle. If he remains here, he'll turn out badly. . . ."

44

Mme. Zomper was weeping. After his escape, Jacques showed up at the OSE, saying that he had come from Belgium. He was then placed at [the children's home of] Montintin, where he worked in the carpentry shop. But at the end of several months, the *gendarmes* [the national police] picked up his trail and brought him back to the camp.

Knowing all the while that Jacques could not be liberated as a child, since he was older than fifteen, and almost certain that I could not legally make a single exception on his behalf, I promised Mme. Zomper to intervene, and she left comforted. The very fact of having been able to talk, I believe, was of some relief to her.

(Jacques, as well as his brother, were able to join up with a convoy of children leaving for the United States. But the parents, who remained in France, were deported.)

As for Mme. Kaufman, she was still undecided about whether to separate herself from her son, whom she brought with her to introduce. Walter was a handsome boy of thirteen, with intelligent and shy eyes. M. and Mme. Kaufman, from an old German family, had led a comfortable life in Mannheim and would not have thought of emigrating had it not been for the events of Kristallnacht.[6] M. Kaufman, forewarned, was able to avoid being arrested, but the grandfather, seventy-two years old, was sent to a camp in spite of his old age.

M. Kaufman's import business was about to collapse; the family's existence became precarious. Walter's older sister left Germany in 1939 for London, where, like so many other young girls, she found a position as a nanny. The declaration of war in September 1939 put an end to the Kaufmans' attempts to emigrate. In October 1940, they were expelled.

"After several hours in prison," Mme. Kaufman told me, "we had to sign a paper stating that we left all our possessions in Germany to the Union of German Jews."[7]

> We then left by truck for the railroad station. We had no idea what they were going to do with us. We were afraid of being sent to Poland, and we were relieved to learn that we were going in the direction of France. When we arrived at Gurs in the middle of the night, we had to wade in the mud for hours before we were able to stretch out to sleep on the ground. All our baggage had been left outside. When we collected it, a part of it had disappeared, while the remainder was soaked. Then we were transferred to Rivesaltes.

She then opened her handbag and held out a picture of herself. "Here, look, that was only two years ago." I was flabbergasted by the change. She continued:

If you only knew how I suffered the first time Walter whispered timidly, "Ma, I'm hungry," and I was unable to give him anything! If you only knew how unhappy I became when I saw the dirty shirt worn by my husband, who since our marriage has worn only impeccable white shirts. You're smiling, mademoiselle, but you should know that life is made up of little moments of happiness and little moments of suffering. We are at the moment too brutalized to be able to feel the horror of our hopeless situation. The only things that matter to us now are hunger, cold, and the absence of any family life. Here we've become like animals.

Walter listened, all ears, but he still did not understand French well. I asked myself what he himself had felt at the beginning of his stay in the camp. But time was pressing; many women were still waiting for me. I promised to visit the Kaufmans in the barracks.

After hearing Mme. Kaufman's story, I wrote in my journal: "I am tired and slightly discouraged this evening. I've tried to enter three of this afternoon's visits here, yet each of those I held today deserves for the same reason a more extended development than the few sketchy lines I jotted down on the lists, where I briefly record the history of the families. These are but sketchy outlines, yet how striking they are!"

IN THE BARRACKS

I very quickly realized the necessity of moving around the barracks. I went through the Spanish block where I was staying. The Spanish refugees had been out of their country for more than two years, had been hunted down by the supporters of Franco, and were not accustomed to living without the freedom for which they had fought in vain. With a few exceptions, there were only women and children. Ever since their arrival in France, they had lived secluded in the camp. One would have thought that they had settled into their misery. Many children were born here. I asked myself what would become of all these children, whose mothers, already shaken by their painful earlier experiences, did not wish to be separated from them. In fact, not everyone took the same approach. The Spanish mothers obstinately refused to be separated from their children. The Jewish mothers, feeling the threat of a different type of danger, were more disposed to listen to reason and to rely on us.[8] I was struck by the fact that all these human beings, though horribly abused, listened to us, the "resident social workers," and placed their confidence in us. We were the link between them and the camp's administration, and also between them and the outside. Our function as intermediaries reassured them. Moreover, they saw us live with them and share their hard existence to some extent. This solidarity brought us closer.

The welcome they extended to us was as surprising as it was touching. As soon as we arrived, a group was formed in each barrack that accompanied us.

Dr. Malkin was especially popular. Children ran over to him from every which way, calling him "Doctor Injection, Doctor Injection!" It was he, in fact, who had vaccinated them all. I was envious of the ease with which he moved about, while I still was continually self-conscious, fearing to appear distant toward these uncared-for men, women, and children to whom I was slowly getting accustomed. Wasn't it a sign of arrogance to move around freely among human beings who had been deprived of their freedom?

Women, mothers, came to see us, imploring our help. My sensibility as a newcomer led me to feel deeply every person's wound. I had difficulty holding back the tears that welled in my eyes and the immense pity that overtook me. I incessantly repeated to myself Dr. Joseph Weill's admonition: "Look into misery the way a doctor looks into a patient's illness."

Mme. Gniewesch, strong and desperate, held out her child and said: "Take this one first; he's three years old and can't stand on his legs. He's just had measles, and I can neither feed him decently nor take care of him as I would like to. I'm exhausted. Please. Let him live, if it's our fate to die."

And, as if it were necessary to convince me, she added: "Don't think it's that easy for me to separate myself from my children. Never at home in Antwerp did I ever leave them, even for a day. But I feel that if they stay here, they'll be lost. You're young, mademoiselle, you, too, will be a mother one day. Try to understand me."

Léon Gniewesch was born on 3 March 1938 in Antwerp. He came to France in May 1940 with his mother, his father (who was of Polish origin and who had been a diamond worker in Antwerp), his two brothers, Henri and Jacques, and his sister, Frieda. After having followed the route of exodus—Chateauroux, Montélimar, the Belgian Red Cross shelter—he was finally interned in Rivesaltes with his entire family. When the first teams of foreign workers were formed,[9] the father, liberated from the camp, left with the hope that he would be quickly joined by his wife, as they had been promised. Mme. Gniewesch remained alone with her four children. An energetic woman, she fought to have them released from the camp. Frieda was the first one to leave for a home of Swiss Aid in Haute-Savoie [a *département* in the French Alps, near the Swiss border]. By pleading Léon's poor health, we succeeded in liberating him for our nursery at Limoges. Henri and Jacques left the camp in February–March 1942 and departed for the United States with the May 1942 convoy. Their mother, for whom an exception was made—a three-day pass enabled her to go to the embarkation port of Marseille—said to us upon her return: "I am at peace at least about these children."

Léon was transferred to [the OSE children's home of] Masgelier as soon as his health improved. It was there that he found himself in August 1942 at the time of the first roundup of foreigners [for deportation to the concentration and extermination camps]. Mme. Gniewesch, still at Rivesaltes, was at first exempted from the deportation as the mother of a child under five. But when the age limit was lowered to two years, her departure could no longer be prevented. M. Gniewisch was deported from the team of workers he had joined. They left, in their separate ways, toward the same fate.

On the day of his deportation, M. Gniewisch received, through us, a letter and photos of his two sons in America. He left with a smile on his face.

As she got into the deportation train, Mme. Gniewisch, passing in front of the camp commander of Rivesaltes, said to him: "You're letting a mother of four children be deported, and you knew these four children."

In September 1942, Léon was transferred to Chambéry and placed with his sister in a home run by Swiss Aid. Knowing that the parents' wishes had been for the children to stay together, we managed, during the liberation of France, to place Léon and Frieda in our home at St. Paul. On 30 November 1945, an aunt in Belgium wrote to us, expressing her wish to take the children into her own home. In turn, on 6 February 1946, an uncle in Palestine also claimed them. In order to bring the family together, before we could make any decision, we needed to determine the plans of the brothers who had left for America. On 29 April 1946, we received their answer: it had not been their intention to stay in the United States, and they hoped to emigrate to Palestine. It was there that the four children were finally reunited.

JANUARY 1942: OUR LIFE IN THE CAMP

Reinette (alias Simone Weill)[10] rejoined me in the ranks of the OSE. She occupied a room in the same barrack I was in, and we succeeded in obtaining two additional rooms to set up a cloakroom and a pantry. Her job, like that of Dora Wertzberg, was to help Dr. Malkin in his struggle against "the illness of hunger." But with her special kind of radiance, she tried to have Jewish and Spanish adolescents, who had up to then ignored one another, meet; in this way, she tried to create groups of boy scouts and girl scouts.

However difficult our daily life might have been, I felt free because I could leave the camp. The OSE rented a room from a resident of the city of Rivesaltes where we could once in a while wash ourselves more comfortably or sleep in a real bed. In addition, Andrée Salomon compelled us to take a rest every five weeks. I went for several days to Cannes, where I participated with André Weil in a fund drive in the grand hotels of the [boulevard de la] Croisette. I explained, with all the firmness I was capable of mustering, that five thousand francs were needed to ensure the three months' room and board that would enable us to liberate one child.

We were a small, coherent team, bound together by friendship: Reinette and Dora, my colleagues at the OSE, and Jacqueline Lévy, the kindergarten teacher from the Unitarian agency. We often met in the evening, and the discussion became very animated. Through the force of circumstances, we had acquired an incontestable authority over men and women who had once occupied an enviable place in society and who were often twice our age. They accepted our advice, also our criticisms. By what right were we allowed to intervene in matters that should have been considered private? Why did they seem to believe us when we spoke of a better tomorrow? During our nocturnal conversations, we also talked about the feeling of satisfaction we all felt in our lives, however austere, because we felt ourselves useful.

Our first objective was to alleviate the hardships endured by the internees. Andrée Salomon made me understand the importance of recreating a semblance of communal life in the camp. Not all of them were devout, and, being of diverse origins, they did not all speak the same language; but, when in December 1941, we celebrated Hanukkah, the Festival of Lights,[11] a feeling of communion never before felt took hold of us. Thus I noted in my journal:

The entire Jewish block celebrates the first day of Hanukkah. I asked my father to explain to me the source and meaning of this festival. With a shaky hand, one of the veterans lights the first small flame of the gigantic *menorah*[12] that had been made by the internees. And the traditional canticle, sung by hundreds of voices, rises as the night descends upon the camp. For the moment, suffering has given way, and I too am seized by this immense hope.

The YMCA office was located in the middle of Block B, where Mlle. Pertrizet and the young minister André Dumas were organizing "leisure activities" in the camp. It was a barrack like any other, in which the team had been able to fit out a theater, a recreation room, and a library. A young internee whitewashed the walls, another one painted the decorative panels, and a third one made up a book catalogue. The incredible transformation in their bearing and morale confirmed my intuition: helping the internees escape their idleness was as important as increasing their food rations.

For its part, ORT installed workshops for carpentry, shoemaking, commercial art, and the manufacture of objects in raffia, intended for adolescents who wished to begin or to continue their apprenticeship.

There was also Elsa Ruth, in her blue and white uniform, a soothing and maternal symbol of the Swiss Aid barrack, a haven of peace in this tormented life. For me, she represented the Switzerland that had escaped war and put its neutrality at our disposal. I was intimidated by her incredible patience in untiringly polishing little red apples before handing them out. The apples then suddenly became the symbols of some place elsewhere where a good life must exist. It was to this barrack that I most often went to draw the strength necessary to endure the enveloping shadows.

THE CHILDREN IN THE CAMP

Children were changed rapidly by life in the camp. Their energy was monopolized by the search for food and the struggle for existence. As social and familial conventions lost their efficaciousness, children became aware that they had to take charge of their own survival. Set in motion by primitive instincts, in a jungle where paternal authority had vanished, where arbitrariness had taken the place of justice and "system D" [*système de débrouillardise,* or "street smarts"] that of discipline, the brightest child, the most skillful in securing his daily subsistence, took over from his parents; but his sudden superiority was a heavy burden to assume. Some children, dirty and slovenly, brazen and rebellious, formed little gangs that acknowledged no authority over them. Others remained for some time the same well-groomed, polite, well-behaved children, until one day, their own brakes suddenly no longer held. For them all, it was the same road to the disintegration of moral values.

It was essential that we protect the children against themselves and against their environment, permit them to renew their links with the past, open up future prospects for them, preserve their physical and moral health, and watch over their education.

We understood how precarious our actions would become if we did not manage to tear these children away from the camp. We needed urgently to offer them a context in which they could preserve their identity. That is why our adherence to Dr. Weill's imperative to "get the children out of the camp" was absolute.[13]

At that time children were being placed in the homes run by the OSE (after a short stay at Palavas-les-Flots, near Montpellier), by Swiss Aid, and by the Quakers—but also by the EIF[14] at Moissac. Very few children were placed with outside families, though, possibly, some were placed with Jewish families known to the OSE.

These departures confronted us with a very worrisome question. Deeming it essential that the children and parents continue to see one another, we arranged meetings between the families inside the camp and the liberated children. Very soon we had to give in to the evidence that these meetings were satisfactory to neither group.

Thus, when we brought Anna and her sister Martha to their father, who had sunk into a profound melancholy since their departure, we thought we had brought him some comfort. But the meeting had no salutary effect on him and only saddened the children. The sight of their father's decline led them to refuse to leave the camp again, as if they had suddenly become all too clear-headed in confronting the horror of the situation. As the memory of their new life receded, they discovered the degree to which life in the camp was intolerable, and they convinced themselves that they had no right to leave again. We then had the utmost difficulty in getting them to return to the children's home.

And when we brought over Sabine, sheltered in a neighboring Jewish family, to see her mother for several hours, she barricaded herself behind a wall of indifference. Unrecognizable, prettily dressed, her hair looking beautiful, she didn't at all resemble the child we had known. With me, she was extremely distant. And in front of her mother who had aged and turned shabby, who was badly dressed and trembling from emotion, she displayed a revulsion that no one could miss. Turning her back to her mother, she ran toward Mme. D., with whom she had found shelter and whom she called *"maman."* She categorically refused to kiss her mother and to speak to her, asserting that she did not speak German. Her departure was a relief to me. To her mother, her brief stay was but a new source of sorrow.

It is for this reason that Reinette and I were opposed to a plan that would have set aside a barrack to receive in rotation children whose parents were still in the camp. The plan was well intentioned—preservation of family bonds—but each day we were better able to understand that it was not possible to have healthy family communication in the camp.

On the other hand, we always sought to encourage meetings on the outside. Each time an occasion presented itself, we tried to obtain exit passes of several days' duration so that parents could see their children, if possible in their new surroundings.

The experience we had just undergone with Sabine also confirmed another idea: placement in families was not ideal for the child who was brutally cut off from his surroundings, the more so because these placements were not final and because the sheltering family could separate itself from the child at any moment. That, by the way, was to be the case with Mme. D., who in 1944 decided to "give us back" Sabine, who, for the second time, so to speak, lost her family. (Her mother having been deported, she went to live with close relatives in the United States.)

Everything led us to believe that children's homes offered the best kind of transition toward freedom. There children lived communally with others who shared the same experiences and at the same time remained bound to those who were still in the camp. They could adapt to their new environment, without giving the impression of betraying their relatives for a substitute family. The rupture was less definite and the relations between the youngsters allowed each one to accept the situation better. In the long run, it became clear that this communal placement was particularly beneficial to older children, who were less capable of blending into a new environment.

THE CHILDREN'S HOMES

In February 1942, I took advantage of a convoy of children that we—Dr. Malkin and I—were accompanying as far as Limoges to visit the children's homes in that region.

Beginning in the fall of 1939, three chateaux in the vicinity of Limoges had been rented in anticipation of an evacuation of children from the Paris region—orphans, children in need, and refugees from Germany. Obviously, permanent homes had to be created. A topnotch staff was recruited from those who had been barred from their profession by the 1940 Statute of the Jews. Each home also was to offer the services of a full-time physician, who supervised the children's medical condition at close range. Starting in 1941 with the arrival of children released from the camps, the physicians developed a sustained policy of good nutrition and intensive care. A systematic policy of vaccination was put into effect. The problems were also psychological: the children were unquestionably happy but were unable to forget the camps. It was only in the homes that they came to realize fully what their previous existence had been like, and they therefore developed genuine phobias about hunger. They had to be stopped from stuffing themselves with inordinate amounts of food. Very worried about the fate of the relatives left behind in the camp, they entrusted me with packages of tidbits they had set aside from their desserts.

The activities set up in the homes were both educational and recreational. Practical experience had to take the place of diplomas, since the staff personnel in the great majority of cases had grown up in youth movements before the war. In addition to numerous manual activities and the professional and artisanal activities (carpentry, dressmaking, tanning) that were offered, an academic curriculum was provided by teachers who had been excluded from public teaching. Classes in English and Spanish were also set up for children destined for emigration.

From November 1939 to February 1944, the OSE managed and funded eighteen secular and religious homes, located mainly in the center of France. These homes received about eight hundred children. The preferred sites were located away from urban centers; the aim was to organize a semiself-sufficient life to which the children lent their support. They were located in [the *départements* of] Creuse, Haute-Vienne, Savoie, and Haute-Savoie and also in the south. Rest centers, rural centers, and professional schools took in primarily adolescents. These centers were created for those children whom the authorities had agreed to liberate on condition that they would be officially and fully taken care of by the philanthropic societies. In fact, according to French law, one is considered an adult at fifteen, with all the resultant administrative consequences, in particular the obligation of carrying an identity card.

The reception centers[15]—like that of Vic-sur-Cère in the Cantal, opened in

June 1942 and designed for young women—offered professional training. The rural centers offered farm training to young men and women who had left the camp. Thus, the property of Charry, in the Tarn, turned over to them about forty hectares [about eighty-nine acres] for reclamation and cultivation. Some young people were placed on farms, and everyone expected, given the known success of this kind of enterprise, that they would develop a rural orientation. Professional schools also enabled them to acquire training in the hotel trade, crafts, dressmaking, and other trades.

In the homes, the children, too, were put to work. The pedagogical system was based on training in communal work. It was essential that the children share with one another their secret scars—depression, fear, humiliation, separation from parents—for this helped them regain confidence in certain virtues: perseverance, loyalty, dignity, courage, and self-mastery.

The home of Palavas-les-Flots, on the Mediterranean coast, welcomed children severely weakened by their internment in the camps. It owned a solarium and provided intensive care. It had the advantage of benefiting from *Préfet* Benedetti's support: he was generous with the issuance of certificates of shelter that made the liberation of children possible. The home of Palavas held only thirty-three beds (in 1942), and the residents quickly found that they had to give way to newcomers. Hence, this home functioned as a revolving door, receiving the children as they left the camps before dispersing them to different OSE centers: Le Masgelier, Montintin, and Chabannes.

The chateau of Masgelier, one of the largest OSE homes, was opened in 1939 to receive the children evacuated from Paris at the beginning of the war, when fear of bombings was widespread. This old chateau, with a large park and outbuildings, was established solely for the purpose of providing a refuge for children; it contained dormitories, refectories, showers, and study halls. A state school was installed there, with lodgings for the teachers. A report drafted in 1942 read:

> The education and supervision of the 122 children of the home are ensured by an experienced personnel. The children pursue academic courses and work very hard in the two-hectare herb garden and in an orchard comprising about a hundred fruit trees. The herb garden and orchard have become priceless additions to the provisioning of the home: except for potatoes, all the vegetables come out of the herb garden. . . . The girls are learning dressmaking. A group of boys have been received by the local craftsmen for training. In the spring of 1942, the management of the home finished fitting out on its grounds a pavilion built to receive fifty older boys. It will house a special

school that will train master masons, thus preparing adolescents for a working career and ensuring their future. All the children are intensely involved in physical activities. They have a sports and athletic field and play games outdoors. The arts too are taught, notably drawing and singing. . . .[16]

The task of Georges Loinger, who had been recruited by Dr. Joseph Weill, was to train teachers at the children's homes who would manage the physical education and the technical leisure and activities of the children; he likewise created a sports and leisure department. Born in Strasbourg in 1910, Georges Loinger, a prisoner of war, escaped during the winter of 1940–1941 to join up with his wife, Flore, at La Bourboule [a noted French spa]. She had been staying there ever since the chateau de la Guette, where she had been director, had been evacuated after the departure of the Baronness Rothschild for the United States.[17]

TO LIBERATE THE CHILDREN

I returned stimulated by my visit to the [children's] homes, profoundly convinced that regrouping them in a collective setting was the best solution.

I continued to work on the liberation of children. Thanks to a salutary mistake, I let out two children over fifteen years of age. Without noticing it, I had made them younger by a year on the lists drawn up on the applications for liberation. The OSE at first took me to task for this error, but since the camp administration did not notice it (I sometimes wonder whether the employees working on the exit papers knowingly closed their eyes), we went on with our work, enabling us to liberate several other adolescents.[18]

Unfortunately, several children remained at Rivesaltes because their parents could not bear the idea of separation. I remember a little girl of twelve swearing to her dying mother that she would take care of her father. Both of them were deported soon thereafter.

It was at this time that the OSE decided to give priority to the systematic emigration of foreign children and orphans without any family in France. This plan required the cooperation of all the philanthropic societies, whether Jewish or not. In order to accelerate a process already set in motion, everything was done to call the attention of American public opinion to the fate of the children.[19]

Beginning in May 1941 (date of the departure of the first convoy to the United

States), the OSE created a permanent branch office to organize a group emigration and to find new homes across the Atlantic. An increasing number of requests were made to the Canadian, Mexican, Argentine, Cuban, and even Chinese governments (Venezuela and China each agreed to take in one child).

Those intending to depart for Argentina found themselves faced with numerous obstacles. First of all, a valid national passport was required, which was not officially available to stateless people. Then, after February 1941, German passports were no longer renewed, while Argentina refused certificates issued by Polish offices. This dashed the hopes of thousands of Germans and Poles whose plans for emigrating to Argentina were already under way.

The second convoy left France in August–September 1941. The children were cleaned up and their hair brushed, Andrée Salomon explained, "so as to give them the appearance of good health."

In my journal, I noted that, in May 1942, I had requested a special three-day pass for parents who wanted to watch their children embark at Marseille and depart with the third convoy. I assumed the responsibility returning them to the camp, in front of the person in charge of the department of liberation, who laughed at my naiveté. Yet I turned out to be right. On 15 May I wrote: "The children left happy, and all the mothers returned to the camp. Several of them told me how painful this return had been to them at the end of three days of freedom. They also asked themselves when they would be able to see their children again." A marginal note composed after the war stated: "Of these ten women, nine were deported and none returned."

On the occasion of the last convoy of liberated children, a big party, which was attended by Germaine Masour, a member of the OSE directorate, was organized in the camp on 21 May, my birthday.

There remained only five Jewish children, whose parents could not bear to be separated from them. My mission accomplished, I left Rivesaltes.

Vivette Samuel's mother, Rachel Hermann, in Russia before the First World War (From author's personal collection)

Vivettte and José Hermann in June 1928 (From
author's personal collection)

Nahum Hermann during
the Second World War (From
author's personal collection)

Left, Vivette Samuel's father, Nahum
Hermann, in Russia before the First World
War (From author's personal collection)

COLLÈGE D'ANNEL
CHATEAU DE LA SOURCE
PRÈS LA CHAPELLE ST-MESMIN
(LOIRET)

Gare Orléans { Service d'Autocars
Station à l'Allée du Château

☒
☎ } LA CHAPELLE ST-MESMIN
Tél. 51 (LOIRET)

Mit diesem Schreiben unterzeichnet Mme S.Préaut-Cassel,directrice
au Collège d'Annel dass Mademoiselle Vivette Hermann als Sprachlehrerin in
meinem College während des Krieges gearbeitet hat.Nun ist es mir leider un-
möglich Sie auf weiteres zu engagieren da mein mobilisiertes Lehrerpersonal
wieder zurück is t .

Nun möchte ich die deutschen Autoritäten bitten Ihr den Übergang
in das Unbesetzte Gebiet zu erleichtern,da ihre Eltern dort wohnhaft sind.

Unterzeichnet Hochachtungsvoll.

M.S.Préaut-Cassel

Vu par nous, Maire de LA CHAPEL
ST-MESMIN, légalisation de la signa-
c. Mme Préaut Cassel
sus apposée.

Le 12 OCT. 1940

The officially validated document giving Vivette Hermann permission to pass from the Occupied to the
Unoccupied Zone in October 1940 (From author's personal collection)

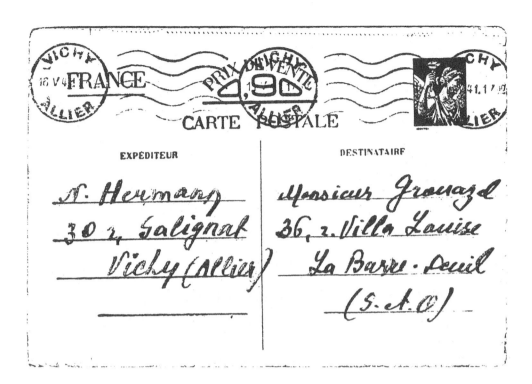

Carte interzone, seule correspondance officielle possible entre les deux zones.

Vichy le 15.5 1941

Sommes en bonne santé — fatigué

légèrement, gravement malade, blessé

tué — prisonnier

décédé — sans nouvelles

de Vaus — La famille — va bien

besoin de provisions — d'argent

nouvelles, bagages — est de retour

travaille à — va entrer

à l'école de —

allons — le

a été reçu

Donnez de vos nouvelles, santé, travail, école. Nous nous maintenons.

Affectueuses pensées. Baisers

Signature.
N. Hermann

Interzonal card, the only official correspondence permitted between the two zones (From author's personal collection)

UNION O.S.E.
ŒUVRE DE SECOURS AUX ENFANTS

DIRECTION CENTRALE
PARIS, 92, Champs-Elysées

Repliée à MONTPELLIER
12 bis, Rue Jules-Ferry, 12 bis
TÉL.: 24.43

ORGANISATION PHILANTHROPIQUE
FONDÉE EN 1912 ET DÉCLARÉE A PARIS
SOUS LE N° 170.699

MAISONS D'ENFANTS :

Villa HELVÉTIA
6, Rue de Valmy, MONTMORENCY (S.-&-0.)
Tél. : Montmorency 20-78

Villa des TOURELLES
113, Rue de Paris, SOISY-s/Mcy (S.-8-0.)
Tél.: Soisy 28-60

CHATEAU DU MASGELIER
par LE GRAND BOURG (Creuse)
Tél. : 19 à Grand Bourg

CHATEAU de CHABANNES
par St-PIERRE-de-FURSAC (Creuse)
Tél.: 3 à St-Pierre-de-Fursac

CHATEAU DE CHAUMONT
MAINSAT (Creuse)
Tél.: 17 à Mainsat

CHATEAU DES MORELLES
à BROUT-VERNET (Allier)
Tél. : 13 à Brout-Vernet

Villa MARIANA
Boul. des Tasses, St-RAPHAËL (Var)
Tél.: St-Raphaël 199

CHATEAU MONTINTIN
Commune de C.-Chervix (Haute-Vienne)
Tél. : 7 Château Chervix

INTERNAT
8, Cours Jean Pénicaud
LIMOGES (Haute-Vienne)
Tél., 26-51
Annexe : INTERNAT
Château du Mas-Jambost
LIMOGES (Haute-Vienne)
Tél. 38.70

INSTITUTIONS :

Œuvre de Protection Sanitaire
des Populations Repliées
TERRASSON (Dordogne)

Centre Médico-Social
25, rue d'Italie, MARSEILLE
tél. Garibaldi 01 45

Montpellier, le 3 novembre 1941.

Mademoiselle Vivette HERRMANN
Assistante-Résidente
Centre d'Hébergement de RIVESALTES.

Mademoiselle,

Nous avons l'honneur de vous confirmer votre engagement comme assistante-résidente au Centre de RIVESALTES, comme déléguée de notre Oeuvre de Secours aux Enfants.

Veuillez agréer, Mademoiselle, l'assu-rance de nos sentiments très distingués.

Pour le Comité-Directeur :

Mme A.Salomon   Docteur J.Weill

Letter confirming the hiring of Vivette Hermann by the Œuvre de secours aux enfants (OSE) in November 1941 (From author's personal collection)

A group of children, bowls in hand, at Rivesaltes in 1941 (From author's personal collection)

The inside of a barrack at Rivesaltes (From author's personal collection)

Left, a group of children at Rivesaltes in
1941 (From author's personal collection)

MARSEILLE, LE 13 OCTOBRE 194 2

CERTIFICAT DE LIBERATION

Le Jeune BRENIG Théodore
dont les parents ont été dirigés en ZONE
OCCUPEE, a été libéré du CENTRE DE
BOMPARD et confié à l'UNION GENERALE DES
ISRAELITES DE FRANCE, le Lundi 5 Octobre
1942. Cet enfant a été laissé en FRANCE
avec le consentement des Parents.

L'INTENDANT DE POLICE:

A group of "liberated" children at Rivesaltes in 1942 (From author's personal collection)

Left, a certificate for the liberation of children
drawn up by the prefecture of Marseille
(From author's personal collection)

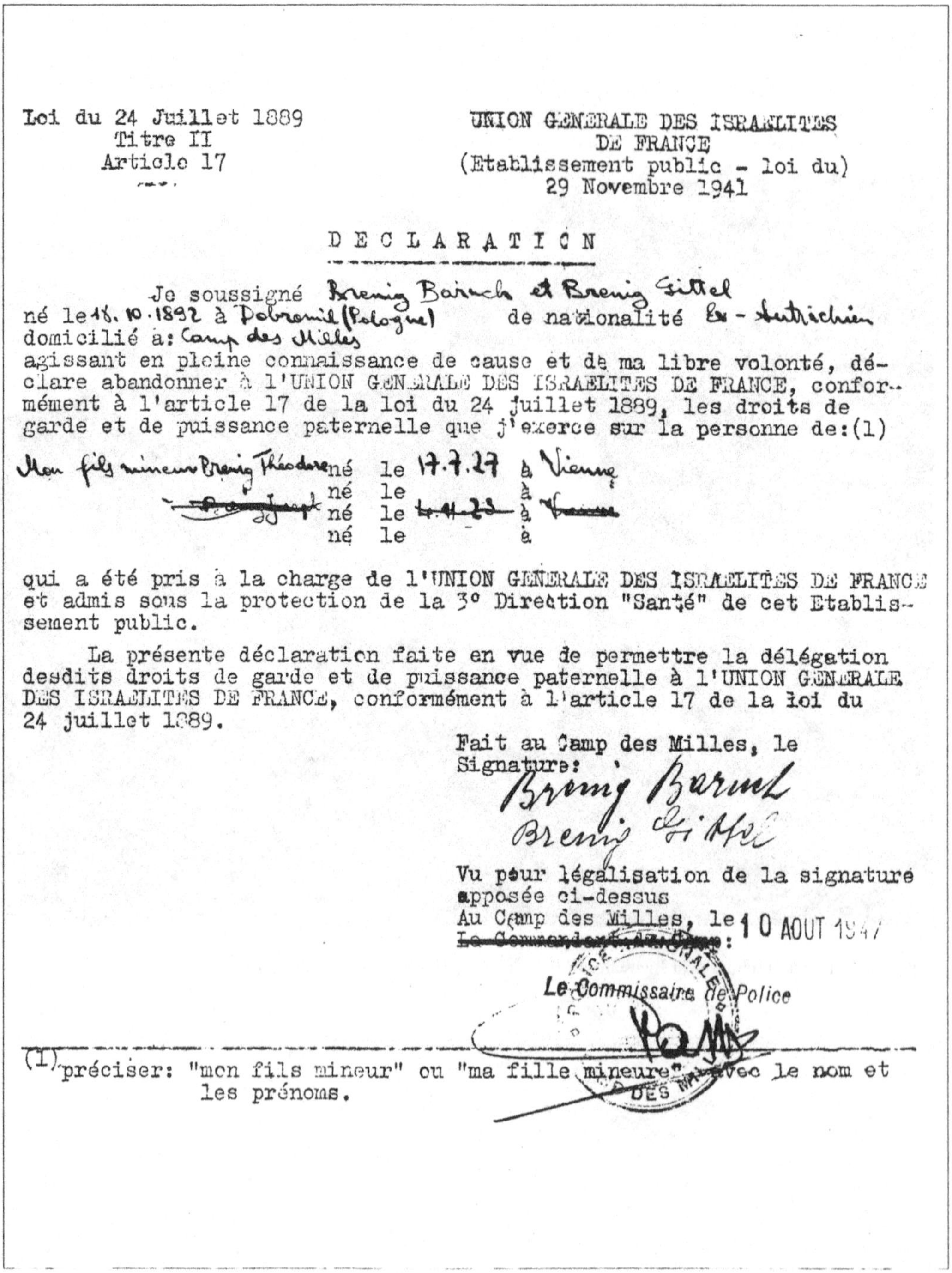

Loi du 24 Juillet 1889
          Titre II
        Article 17

UNION GENERALE DES ISRAELITES
           DE FRANCE
(Etablissement public – loi du)
       29 Novembre 1941

D E C L A R A T I O N

    Je soussigné *Brenig Baruch et Brenig Gittel*
né le *18.10.1892* à *Dobromil (Pologne)*   de nationalité *Ex - Autrichien*
domicilié à: *Camp des Milles*
agissant en pleine connaissance de cause et de ma libre volonté, déclare abandonner à l'UNION GENERALE DES ISRAELITES DE FRANCE, conformément à l'article 17 de la loi du 24 juillet 1889, les droits de
garde et de puissance paternelle que j'exerce sur la personne de:(1)

Mon fils mineur Brenig Théodore né   le *17.7.27*   à *Vienne*
                né   le   à
                né   le *1.4.23*   à *Vienne*
                né   le   à

qui a été pris à la charge de l'UNION GENERALE DES ISRAELITES DE FRANCE
et admis sous la protection de la 3° Direction "Santé" de cet Etablissement public.

    La présente déclaration faite en vue de permettre la délégation
desdits droits de garde et de puissance paternelle à l'UNION GENERALE
DES ISRAELITES DE FRANCE, conformément à l'article 17 de la loi du
24 juillet 1889.

                    Fait au Camp des Milles, le
                    Signature:
                    Brenig Baruch
                    Brenig Gittel

                    Vu pour légalisation de la signature
                    apposée ci-dessus
                    Au Camp des Milles, le **1 0 AOUT 1947**
                    ~~Le Commandant du Groupe~~:

                    Le Commissaire de Police

(1) préciser: "mon fils mineur" ou "ma fille mineure" avec le nom et
        les prénoms.

The Union générale des israélites de France (UGIF) surrender form that parents had to sign in order for their children to be entrusted to a philanthropic society (From author's personal collection)

The children and teachers of the Couret home in October 1942 (From author's personal collection)

The Couret, one of the children's homes of the OSE (From author's personal collection)

Two children's homes of the OSE: *above,* Montintin; *below,* Le Masgelier (Both photographs from author's personal collection)

A children's home of the OSE: Chabannes (From author's personal collection)

Andrée Salomon and a group of children forming part of the first convoy to the United States, in Marseille in 1941 (From author's personal collection)

SECRÉTARIAT D'ÉTAT AU TRAVAIL

**COMMISSARIAT A LA LUTTE
CONTRE LE CHOMAGE**

Hôtel International
— VICHY —
Tél. 43 - 71 - 72

Réf. N° ___ C.G/MOE
à rappeler dans la réponse

ÉTAT FRANÇAIS

Vichy, *le* 10 Juillet 1942

ORDRE DE MISSION

     A la demande de Monsieur DONALD A. LOWRIE, Président
du Comité de Coordination pour l'Assistance dans les Camps
et sur proposition du Chef du Service Central de la M.O.E.,
     Mademoiselle HERMANN Vivette
     12 Rue Constantine à LYON,
est autorisée à visiter les Groupes de Travailleurs Etrangers.
     Le rôle de l'intéressée devra se limiter strictement
à un travail d'aide et de secours.
     Les Chefs de Groupements et leurs agents voudront
bien faciliter la mission de Mademoiselle HERMANN dans toute
la mesure de leurs moyens.

          Le Commissaire Adjoint
          à la lutte contre le chômage

The commission allowing Vivette Hermann to visit the Foreign Labor Battalions (From author's personal collection)

5

At the Time of the Deportations

JUNE–JULY 1942: TO BECOME ENGAGED AT THE HEIGHT OF THE WAR

I left for Lyon, without answering a summons from the Lyon police that had been sent to my parents' address. For me, this period of June–July 1942 was a time of readjustment. I missed the clear instructions of Dr. Weill and the support and example of Andrée Salomon in my new job as the OSE delegate to the Amitié chrétienne [Christian Friendship] of Lyon. On the other hand, I had the opportunity to become better acquainted with this organization, especially the disconcerting and admirable personality of *abbé* Glasberg. He was at that time priest of the small parish of Saint-Alban in Lyon. He was said to be of Jewish origin and born in the Ukraine. In 1941, he had succeeded in getting a large number of people out of the camp of Gurs by providing them with lodging and false papers. From November 1941 on, he had organized self-administered centers that gave refuge to internees "on vacation" from internment camps. The moral strength represented by the Amitié chrétienne and his support were extremely valuable to the Resistance movements, which were then in the process of developing. I knew that *abbé* Glasberg and Joseph Weill waged the same battle. When the threat of deportations began to loom, neither one of them hesitated to use any and all means: false identity cards, transfers from one center to another, switching of dossiers, and so on. In the very heart of the city, at 12, rue de Constantine, an important center was created for the forging of false papers. Sought by the Gestapo, *abbé* Glasberg was forced to leave Lyon in 1943 and, under the name of Covin, became priest of a small rural parish.

Under the direction of Jean-Marie Soutou, my work consisted of visiting the Groupements de travailleurs étrangers [Foreign Labor Battalions] of Savoie and

Haute-Savoie. I was commissioned by Gilbert Lesage[1] of the Social Services at Vichy to "inspect" sanitary conditions. The OSE asked me to verify the fact that the children were not interned there with their fathers. The living conditions in the GTEs seemed to me very much more humane than those at Rivesaltes. The men worked outdoors and were relatively well nourished. The administrators of the camp who welcomed me seemed to have nothing to hide.

I brought back with me a boy about twelve years old whom I entrusted to a social worker of the OSE. Several weeks later, while I, along with a Red Cross team, was provisioning a train of foreign workers at the Lyon railway station, I recognized his father. I could therefore reassure him about the fate of his son. Later on, I learned that the father had been deported and that the entrances and exits of the railway station were not being guarded. It would have been easy to help the man escape, but we still had so little information that the idea did not occur to me. We had naively passed out fruit.

I circulated among the different OSE centers of Montpellier, Marseille, and Lyon. The last was directed by Charles Lederman, whom I had replaced at Rivesaltes. The director of the Marseille center was Julien Samuel, the young man I had met in October 1941 in the company of Andrée Salomon during my first visit to the OSE.

Julien and I had corresponded during the preceding months, I from Rivesaltes, he from Marseille, both of us very deeply absorbed in our work and already very attached to each other. His great kindness, his natural elegance, the attention he paid to other people made an impression on me; but I had no inkling, during our first meetings, what the young man would mean to me. He was later to confide to me that he had immediately fallen under the spell of a young woman who had left an altogether comfortable life to take up residence in a camp. Julien hoped to found a "Jewish home," while I remained fiercely secular. We still hesitated to merge our destinies.

Julien was born in Mulhouse [Alsace] in 1912, into an orthodox Jewish family, whose four children were raised to respect religion and traditional customs. Julien's mother died in childbirth when he was two years old, so he transferred all his affection to his father. He completed his schooling at the *lycée* Fustel-Coulanges in Strasbourg but, despite his good school grades, did not pursue higher education, since his father urged him to take a job. After performing his military service in Dijon, Julien worked in the insurance company Trieste-et-Venise (coincidentally, my father had managed a branch of this company in Paris). As soon as Hitler took power in 1933,

Julien became a militant member of a Jewish movement in Strasbourg. At the beginning of the war, in June 1940, his regiment retreated into the Vosges, where he was taken prisoner. After a short period of captivity, he escaped and crossed the mountains on foot. Recaptured at Raon-l'Étape,[2] transferred to Germany, and escaping again in October 1940 with Fastré, a fellow prisoner, he walked across the annexed Alsace and the Vosges and crossed the demarcation line in November near Bordeaux, where he was demobilized.

Recruited by Joseph Weill, Julien had as his first task at the OSE to organize a supply system for the camps of Gurs and Rivesaltes. To cope with the new economic conditions, he put into place a network of supplies and obtained the necessary permits to send (nonrationed) fruit and vegetables to the internees in the two camps. He had also brought about the creation of social committees in the camps that were charged with the task of distributing these products equitably.

In June 1941, he accepted the mission of installing at Marseille a medicosocial center to be run by the Unitarian agency and the OSE. He became regional director of the OSE, while Dr. René Zimmer occupied the post of chief physician.

We became officially engaged in August 1942 and set the date for our marriage.

When I was introduced to Julien's family, which had taken refuge at Gannat in the vicinity of Vichy, I found an orthodox environment, suspicious of the young and modern stranger that I was to them (my Russian background). A four-year-old nephew summed up their confusion in these words: "Why does Aunt Vivette put lipstick on her nails?"

As for my father, who had already met Julien at work, he was captivated by his gentleness.

To be united in such circumstances was perhaps a way for us to face adversity. Compelled to live in a somber present, we put our trust in the future. The final victory, however, seemed very far to us. Our marriage was to take place in the month of October in the children's home at Couret, near Limoges, in Haute-Vienne.

AUGUST–SEPTEMBER 1942: ROUNDUPS AND DEPORTATIONS IN THE UNOCCUPIED ZONE

During the three months of our engagement, we witnessed the first roundups of foreign Jews in the Unoccupied Zone and their internment at Rivesaltes, Les Milles, and Vénissieux. The great roundup of Vel' d'hiv' had already taken place on 16 July. Thousands of persons, including women and children, had been arrested.

We were at a turning point in history.[3] For the first time, children were being arrested in Paris and in the Unoccupied Zone. The OSE was certain that they would face the risk of death from that moment on. Everyone capable of taking action was mobilized to help them escape death.

For a time we had thought that the Southern Zone (so-called free and under the sole jurisdiction of Vichy) would be spared. This was not the case at all. The roundups and deportations began in August 1942.[4] The first people affected by these were the internees in the camps.[5] Then, foreign Jewish families who had sought refuge in the Southern Zone were in turn massed by the thousands in the sorting centers.[6] At first, [only] refugees who had entered France in 1939, after the declaration of war, were involved. A few days later, exemptions [from the roundups] became rare. Hour by hour, new criteria were put into effect for putting people under arrest. The operation extended to unmarried people from sixteen to forty years of age who had entered France after 1933 and to the spouses of old men who could not be deported (because they could not be transported). Exemptions applied only to parents of children under two years of age (no longer up to five years) and no longer covered military volunteers unless they had received a field commendation. Men who had been freed a day earlier from sorting centers were brought back. Officials searched for children so that they could be deported with their parents in the name of the family reunion [policy] decreed by Laval, although the Germans were as yet not claiming children [for deportation].

The number of children in the homes increased considerably. The numerous arrests and the pervasive reign of terror led parents to entrust their children more spontaneously to the OSE or some other philanthropic organization. The capacity of the homes to shelter children, [however,] was soon exceeded; extra beds had to be added everywhere. But, by the end of August, the homes had become truly unsafe. Children were being arrested individually, always in the name of family reunion. These arrests affected only those children whose parents had given their address and who were found on the lists. But it was too risky to leave the eighteen hundred children who had just been liberated from the internment camps in the homes where they were staying. Adolescents camped out deep in the forests to avoid being caught.

An article in the newspaper *Aujourd'hui*, published in Paris on 15 August 1942, tried to give a humanitarian twist to these arrests:

> Since yesterday four thousand Jews[7] arrested in the Unoccupied Zone have been deported into regions where they will be able—under careful watch—to do work useful to the European community. They will rejoin an approximately equal number of their co-religionists originally from the Occupied Zone. Henceforth, the stateless sons of Israel will learn that there no longer is a safe asylum for them on the other side of the demarcation line. . . . Let us say at once that, contrary to certain rumors, these undesirable people left our territory in the company of their relatives. There never was any question of separating wives from their husbands and children from their parents. And if they wish to pursue their business, they will be driven to do it in family.

It was no longer idleness, crowding, and illness that the philanthropic organizations had to struggle against but clearly death itself. It was necessary to set oneself against family reunion and to hold fast to the priority objective of the liberation and emigration of children. Such was the course of action to which we had to adhere unswervingly. We alerted the American and the Swiss charitable organizations through indirect channels. The vital necessity of having Jewish children leave France had already been emphasized since January 1942 in an American publication of the OSE.

It was imperative that all approaches to this issue be intensified. Hence, from September 1942 on, Joseph Weill established a link between the French authorities and Admiral Leahy, the U.S. ambassador to Vichy. In October, the United States granted five thousand visas assigned to the American [Eleanor Roosevelt's] Committee for the Care of European Children. Laval, afraid that Vichy's politics would be criticized by the U.S. government and people when the children arrived, agreed to authenticate only five hundred of these emigration visas. The American landing in North Africa in November 1942 cut off the ongoing process. The United States's entry into the war marked the end of diplomatic relations between Vichy and Washington, and several days later, the invasion of the Unoccupied Zone by German troops put a stop to any chance of the children's departing. Stopped in Marseille, the group of prospective emigrants that had been granted visas was placed under house arrest. The French authorities had to be approached several times before the OSE finally recovered these children and put them back again—for a time—into the homes that had sheltered them.

At the camp of Rivesaltes, at the camp of Les Milles, at Vénissieux, the rescue of children had again become an absolute priority.

RIVESALTES AGAIN

When I left Rivesaltes in June 1942, there remained only five [Jewish] children in the camp, from whom their parents were unable to separate themselves. But other families had been newly interned. Learning that they risked being deported, Andrée Salomon settled into the camp with a team of social workers. Here is the invaluable report she drew up of the events of that period:[8]

> The morning of 3 August witnessed the first callup. All those who could not prove their membership in an exempt category were concentrated in Block K, surrounded for the occasion by a new barbed wire fence. These first deportees did not include any children. On 7 August the delegates from all the philanthropic organizations were called together by the camp administration for a private meeting with the members of the Perpignan prefecture in charge of the screening of the internees. It was thus that we learned the terrible news: henceforth, children would be included in the measures taken for deportation.
>
> The children had to be taken out of the camp at all costs. Miss Elms, the Quaker delegate, immediately took a first group with her in her own car and came back the same day in search of others. The camp administration agreed to validate this departure as a regular liberation. Hence, not a single Jewish child remained in the camp. However, entire families were being brought in every day that had been arrested at the demarcation line, at the Swiss frontier, or picked up in the vicinity. For a fortnight, all the children in the camp under sixteen years of age were able to leave immediately and were provided with a regular certificate of liberation. They were sheltered in the children's homes of various groups (Swiss Aid, OSE, Jewish Scouts). . . .
>
> However, the rumor spread that the liberated children would be called back to the camp for the purpose of being "reunited" with their families. Messages were immediately sent out by couriers to the different children's homes so that the children in danger could be dispersed as quickly as possible. It was too late, however. The next day, the first [group of] children was seen arriving in handcuffs.
>
> The camp administration requested the societies to decide on the procedures to be used for recalling the children. It seemed therefore possible for the societies to continue to act. The delegates of the OSE refused to discuss this procedure. This so-called

reunion, which meant deportation and undoubtedly death, had to be prevented at all costs. This inflexible position led the camp administration to stop cooperating with us. At the same time, however, it also stopped consulting the records of the societies and of the prefectures that listed the destinations of the children who had previously been liberated.[9] Thus, the evil had been limited in scope.

A note had been addressed to all the blocks asking the parents to indicate their children's residence, regardless of age. The social workers then rushed into the blocks to inform the parents what was awaiting them if they cooperated with the census—a painful task that allowed the adults to guess the fate that likely awaited them, as well. How could we have induced them to leave their children without conjuring up the danger all of them were going to face?

We, who already knew, did not know how to act toward them or what to say to them. Our convoy escorts, who had accompanied the first trains up to the demarcation line, returned totally disillusioned: the men had been separated without pity from their wives. What sense, therefore, was there in this entire farce of reunion? The wagons had been stripped of the sanitary containers with which we had supplied them. What good were all these desperate efforts to obtain buckets and pitchers in an already impoverished Southern Zone? Baggage, too, had been snatched from its owners.

It was common knowledge that four thousand children separated from their parents had been deported from Paris in similar conditions. If we could still delude ourselves about the fate of able-bodied men and women fit for work, we continued to wonder about the fate of the others—the ill, the disabled, the children. . . .

The social workers threaded their way among those who had just registered their children. Carefully so, since they could not give away their identity; they indefatigably went from one person to another, repeating, "It's not necessary for you to be here; leave, return to your barracks." The old-timers, the ones we knew, understood; the others, alas, delivered up their children without knowing it. But we had to act prudently to be able to remain there, to stay informed, to anticipate the worsening of measures, to exert an influence upon the administration and our colleagues. Once again, the role of witness assumed by the social worker proved to be of the utmost importance.

To wear down the officials, we tried to have them accept the most complicated procedure for the recall of children. Our aim was to get them to answer to the *gendarmes* who would be waiting for instructions on the subject of the children they had searched for but had been unable to find: "Well, you've done your duty; you may go home now."

But, suddenly, without even knowing how it had happened, about a hundred children found themselves one morning concentrated in Block K, destined for the next deportation. Included among these children were some who had just arrived with their parents, who had been arrested in the vicinity or transferred from another camp. There were also some who, despite our efforts, had been recalled to the camp for a reunion.

The convoy was ready to leave. Our efforts until then had been preventive above all.

We had tried to prevent the children from entering Block K. Now they were there. It was up to the screening commission to get them out.[10] Hence, we had to intercede with it.

All our intercessions with the commission led nowhere, the order was precise: the children had to leave. Yet, a few days earlier, it had been possible to liberate a group from the camp of Les Milles and another one from Vénissieux. But here the children were too numerous to make it possible for us to make an isolated effort name by name. The OSE then requested permission to assume responsibility for the installation of a children's barrack outside Block K. The arguments put forward were valid: the children should be spared the crowding, malnutrition, illness, and rats that abounded in Block K. But we said nothing about the real motive for our proposal, which was to prepare both groups for a separation that neither wished. It was necessary for us to make the adults see that their children could be saved, even if they themselves could not.

But another idea occurred to us. While all hope seemed lost, we played our last card and sought to obtain by pity and remorse what we had been unable to obtain by persuasion. Face to face with these children of all ages collected here—dirty, tired, frightened, even destitute—the French officials were bound to be moved. We did not like to play this way with feelings, but it was our last resort. Hence, when, on Sunday, the next day, on a nice, sunny afternoon, two high officials of the *préfecture* arrived with their wives in the camp, we took them to the barracks that housed children of the same age as their own. We showed them these children so that they would become aware of them, so that they at least would know the nature of the crime in the offing. But they— the representatives of Vichy—did not know what to do.

It was then that our secretary-general joined us from Montpellier and went with us to Perpignan to try out on the *préfet* our last approach for liberating that group of children (those under the age of sixteen; as for the others, they unfortunately had no chance at all). We argued that the children at Les Milles had not been taken away. "Yes," answered the *préfet*, "but it's only temporary."

"Nor are they leaving from Vénissieux."

"Yes, but for this reason important people have been placed under house arrest."[11] And, as we showed him what a monstrous idea it was for a hundred children from the Unoccupied Zone to be given over for extermination: "What can you do?" he answered. "France lost the war, and we no longer have an army."

All that we were able to extract from him were ten so-called deficient children, and it was really a gift that he conceded to us, either out of generosity or out of lassitude. It was appalling, for we had to make a choice. We had to choose those ten children (who in reality became twenty in number) that we would thus restore to life, deliberately letting others go to their death. . . . It was in fact an action taken wholly arbitrarily, for our choice involuntarily went to the children we knew—the ones whom we had liberated months before—the wards of the philanthropic societies, those whose parents had held them out to us with the greatest eagerness. This deep injustice obsessed us for months and still weighs on our conscience today. It is not humanly possible to commit a greater act of injustice. . . . Twenty children were thus saved while eighty-two were deported from Rivesaltes.

But we continued to do our best to try to liberate other children. Thus, when a young nurse from the Swiss Red Cross came to the camp to arrange for the liberation of two families who held exit visas [to emigrate] overseas, the OSE profited from her presence to demand the liberation of a group of children for Switzerland. And such was the state of confusion at that time that two families were liberated while hundreds of others were deported with visas in their pockets and twenty children were temporarily entrusted to the OSE, even though it was clear that they would never be able to leave for Switzerland, at least not legally. . . .

We never succeeded in finding out what made it possible for some to be spared, while others were not. Little eleven-year-old Hans, all by himself, asked to see us and the president of the screening commission and pleaded in favor of his parents and aunt. And this family man, to whom had fallen the horrendous lot of deciding other men's fate, was touched and gave them their freedom. Two girls who were of the same age as the daughters of an important official were liberated, while two others, whom a guard found one night on the point of escaping from a children's barrack, got to know the inside of the camp prison.

For some people did escape. From Block K at first. There were young women disguised as nurses who were provided with false passes. One day, a young boy who had just arrived with his parents was walking with them toward the terrible Block K. Someone in a low voice told him to break off from the rest of the convoy just as he was passing in front of Barrack II and to wait for us. The little fellow obeyed us. He left his parents and walked toward Swiss Aid, where our scout, who was threading his way among the people, lent him his big hat, his khaki shirt, and his pass, with which he was able to leave Block K. There were also escapes from the camp, but, in spite of the risks involved, they mattered little to us compared with the efforts that the liberation of children entailed.

Once again, everything changed—suddenly. Hearing no response from Vichy, the *préfecture* of Perpignan assumed the responsibility to liberate children under sixteen years of age in the [*département* of] Pyrénées-Orientales, as long as we submitted their files to the officials. Then, every evening, at the time when the convoys were arriving, social workers were on the lookout for newly arrived children and, while giving them milk, explained to the parents the possibility of liberation, advised separation, and urged them to readjust the children's age if they were sixteen years or older. The next day, these social workers, with lists in hand, introduced themselves to the camp's administration, asking to be admitted into the children's barrack and, file after file, beseeched and tried to obtain the great liberator "L."[12] Soon thereafter, the children left the camp for Perpignan, where the reception and placement [in the children's homes or with individual families] had been organized.

And it went on like this until the [German] occupation of the Southern Zone and the transfer of the last internees out of [the camp of] Gurs.

Four hundred and twenty-seven children had been saved from deportation.

LES MILLES

The liberation of children was also the first order of priority at the camp of Les Milles. The camp was known as a place of internment for foreigners on the point of emigrating to the United States. From Les Milles one was able to take the last administrative steps before departure. Women and children were given refuge—precariously—in requisitioned hotels in Marseille. In one of my short stays in Marseille at the beginning of 1942, I visited the "assigned residence centers," where the women and children transferred from Les Milles stayed. The Hôtel Bompart and the Hôtel du Levant, guarded by *gendarmes*, were administered by the camp at Les Milles and by Vichy's Ministry of the Interior. Accustomed to the isolation of the camp of Rivesaltes and its rigorous climate, I found the living conditions at the Bompart and the Levant precarious but tolerable.

The social service team of the OSE, led by Julien Samuel, was authorized to step in to improve the living conditions in the camp itself, which was an abandoned tile factory situated on the road to Marseille five kilometers from Aix-en-Provence. Ever since the declaration of war, German and Austrian refugees in France—Jews or opponents of Hitler's regime who were determined to leave Europe—had been interned there, often after having passed through other camps. As I have already indicated, they were considered from their arrival on, and in spite of their deliberate choice of France, "enemies of the nation" and interned for that reason. Also at Les Milles were survivors of the International Brigade, who had fought on the side of the Spanish Republicans and had taken refuge in France in February and March 1939.

In the spring of 1940, numerous departures for the United States led the government to close the camp of Les Milles. It was opened again in August 1942, and the deportations began on 4 August. They affected the victims of recent roundups in the region.

Julien was very involved in the efforts to rescue the maximum number of internees from deportation. At that period, while we made our way to Gannat to meet his parents, he was still distressed and shocked by the events and mentioned them as little as possible—so little that I didn't know very much about the efforts made by the OSE.

AUGUST 1942: THE NIGHT OF VÉNISSIEUX

As a result of the roundups carried out in the region of Lyon, more than a thousand persons were interned in the military camp of Vénissieux. On 28 August the best-qualified representatives of the philanthropic organizations spent a stormy night presenting, with irresistible eloquence, cases to the screening commission in an effort to exclude them from deportation. Appearing before the commission were Dr. Weill, Charles Lederman, and the newcomer Georges Garel, of the OSE, Claude Gutman, of the Jewish Boy Scouts, *abbé* Glasberg, of Amitié chrétienne, and Gilbert Lesage, of the Service social des étrangers. The convoys were due to leave at three in the morning. Taking a chance on a legal exception that Vichy had revoked the day before—without notifying the *préfecture* officials—the team succeeded in securing the liberation of children up to the age of fourteen.

This is what Joseph Weill wrote of the night at Vénissieux:

> We feverishly notified the parents and obtained, after much persuasion, the authorization to take over the care of the children. By the use of certain stratagems, we were able to exclude from the deportation convoy all the children and adolescents, about a hundred of them. At the moment of separation, the parents proved to be of admirable dignity and calm. Almost all of them informed us of their last wishes, handed their jewels and clothes over to their children, and often expressed their wishes as to their education and future. Many of them blessed their children with a biblical phrase. They asked them to be courageous, worthy of their Jewishness, and not to forget them. And with an abrupt gesture, they turned around to hide their emotion. Not one of these mothers went back to their children.
>
> We then collected the children in the dining hall to feed them and to distract them while their parents were being sacrificed. We got the promise from the bus drivers to drive their vehicles past the illuminated windows of the dining hall so that the parents could leave feeling reassured. No one will ever forget those tearful looks, those silent glances straining for a last look at their children. Toward seven o'clock in the morning, we had the children get into the bus, while we hid the bigger ones underneath the seats. . . .

The separation of children from their parents gave rise to heartrending scenes. The camp physician, Doctor Adam, witnessed twenty-eight attempts at suicide during the night. We tried, as best we could, to falsify the civil status of the adolescents; finally, 108 children and 60 adults (pregnant women and those who had a French spouse or child) were successfully snatched from deportation.

The children were brought to the headquarters of the Jewish Scouts of Lyon and entrusted to the care of the OSE. Several hours later, the regional *préfet*—who had just been informed of the latest telegrams from Vichy ordering the cancellation of all exceptions—furiously demanded that we return the children. A woman official at the prefecture forewarned the OSE of the danger. When the police buses showed up at the center to pick up the children, they had all been dispersed. [Pierre] Cardinal Gerlier [archbishop of Lyon] covered up this dispersion and the sheltering of the children among host families. When summoned by the *préfet* Angeli, upon orders from [René] Bousquet,[13] Cardinal Gerlier, attended by Father [Pierre] Chaillet, refused to turn the children over and declared, "There is a limit beyond which Christian conscience cannot pass. The children were entrusted to us, they will remain in our care, and you will be informed of their places of residence only if we have the express promise of the government that they will not be handed over to Germany." The children were thus saved by the skin of their teeth, but Father Chaillet was arrested and placed for three months under house arrest in a psychiatric hospital in the [*département* of] Ardèche. As for the OSE persons in charge who were directly involved in this incident, they finally made the decision to swing over to clandestine activity.

A turning point took place in the organization of the OSE, which was fully aware of the limits on its official work and legal activities. The lesson of the night of Vénissieux was clear: all Jewish children were at risk. It was absolutely necessary to give them a non-Jewish French identity and to disperse them in non-Jewish surroundings. The children's homes themselves had to be dissolved: they were in danger of being ambushed.

Dr. Weill gave Georges Garel the responsibility of organizing that dispersal. At the end of 1942, he introduced him to a small group he had gathered at Lyon and presented the plan to form clandestine networks for concealing children in non-Jewish families and institutions. Georges Loinger, an expert in crossing frontiers, was to be responsible for working on ways to cross into Switzerland.

OCTOBER 1942: AN OSE MARRIAGE

Our civil marriage took place on 6 October 1942, in the intimacy of the Marseille city hall. Julien and I then left for Limoges. As we changed trains, we escaped an identification check by the skin of our teeth; Julien proudly announced, "We have just been married," and they let us pass without verifying our papers.

The religious ceremony was celebrated at Couret, near Limoges, in an OSE religious home for young girls, in the presence of our respective parents and our mutual friends. I had made a tailored suit with black and white square patterns, and I had made my own veil. It was therefore an "OSE marriage," experienced by all as an act of hope, at which were present about fifty little girls and adolescents liberated from the camps.[14] I discovered the Canticle of the Seven Blessings there. Mrs. Meyerson[15] sent me a beautiful letter; to be united at this moment, she said, had something of the spirit of resistance in it: "Like the birds that build their nests in the trees, twig by twig, secure from the storm."

We spent our honeymoon resting for several days in a *département* where food was plentiful. I then settled down with Julien in an apartment he rented on the rue de la Corderie in Marseille.

We spent five months there; as a young married woman I was idle for the first time in my life. I got to know Julien's friends. For a while I learned to be "solely" my husband's wife. The problem of feeding ourselves didn't worry us too much. I prepared all kinds of recipes out of the chestnuts found in abundance there. Every Friday night, Julien observed the Sabbath with a little gift or flower. We were happy.

I found myself in a paradoxical situation with respect to the law: I was married, but, since I had not had my papers corrected, they were still under the name of Vivette Hermann, and I was still not registered with the census, whereas Julien was. The manager of a hotel where we stopped one night gave me a dirty look ("A young woman and a Jew").

OCTOBER 1942–1943: MARSEILLE

Because I had passed various times through Marseille, where a team of the OSE had already been functioning, I already knew the work of the philanthropic organization. To familiarize myself with its services, I underwent a period of training in a hospital-like environment.

True to its vocation, the OSE had developed activities indispensable to maintaining the physical and moral health of adults and children, whether they were refugees or internees. It was still Dr. Weill who planned the work and ensured its coordination.

The same spirit of cooperation among the charitable societies prevailed in Marseille that had developed at Rivesaltes. The Unitarian–OSE collaboration had made possible the development of a multipurpose dispensary at 25, rue d'Italie that offered consultations in general and specialized medicine, radiology laboratories, dental care and prosthesis, and two social work offices. René Zimmer, the head physician, had surrounded himself with a small but efficient team. A library had been put at the disposal of about sixty Jewish physicians who were forbidden to practice their profession. They met there regularly and organized a series of lectures. The proposal for a school to train social workers, however, had to be dropped in April 1942.

The social service team was also responsible for the distribution of meals to the refugees and applied itself to the education of children of foreign origin and to the specialized apprenticeship of adolescents in ORT centers and the Jewish Scouts.

Under the direction of Andrée Salomon, the young licensed nurse Fanny Loinger watched particularly closely the children at the Hôtel du Levant. A kindergarten had been fitted out for about thirty youngsters, to whom the Quakers daily distributed bowls of rice. Also under the supervision of Andrée Salomon, Margot Stein, at the Hôtel Bompart, without any special training, took over the job of kindergarten teacher and, with the help of some internees, established educational activities and the distribution of a daily snack. Permission was obtained to enroll the French-speaking children from the Hôtel Bompart in the district primary school. The other internees were given lessons by a woman internee in the afternoons. Likewise, English lessons were offered to those who intended to leave for the United States.

The existence of a kindergarten freed the mothers for handling certain administrative matters and for meeting their husbands whenever the latter were able to obtain an exit pass.

As at Rivesaltes, we tried to break the compulsory idleness of the adults. The internal organization of these two hotels made it possible to create workshops for manual labor and courses in dressmaking (operated by the ORT), which gave the internees an opportunity of making small objects (such as raffia sandals) to sell on the outside. Their morale was sustained by regular visits by the OSE social workers, by Herta Field and Fanny Zimmer, and especially by the hope of their forthcoming emigration.

INCORPORATION OF THE OSE INTO THE UGIF

It was only in Marseille that I learned of the change in the legal status of the OSE. Since 29 November 1941 (a few weeks after my appointment as resident social worker at Rivesaltes), a law, valid in both zones, had regrouped all the "Jewish philanthropic organizations" into the UGIF (Union générale des israélites de France [General Union of the Jews of France]).[16] Most of these social service organizations, as well as the UGIF, settled in Marseille. The headquarters of the OSE remained in Montpellier.

The decision to accept its incorporation into the UGIF was difficult to make: the OSE waited until March 1942. It then chose to take this legal route—even if it was directly under Vichy's control—in order to be able to proceed with its work, even while already planning to begin to operate clandestinely. Joseph Milner assumed the leadership of the Third Directorate (Health) of the UGIF in order to be its OSE representative. In this manner, he hoped to guarantee the organization a legal and official framework that would provide a much-needed cover for its clandestine activity. The OSE would not have been able to scuttle itself completely in order to become unofficial (as did other organizations that refused this subordination to the government) without losing at the same time all of its children's homes and institutions. After its incorporation, these were left to the care of the Third Directorate (Health) of the UGIF.

In September 1942, Dr. Weill announced, at a meeting of the [OSE] management in Lyon in which Julien participated, that the moment had come to plan the closing of the children's homes and to gradually put an end to the very existence of the official organization.

Until November 1942, the OSE, benefiting from its privileged position as an international philanthropic organization, had seemed to pursue its medicosocial activities in complete freedom and had continued to maintain links with the other organizations of the Nîmes Coordinating Committee. That remained the case until the entry of the United States into the war [against Vichy on 8 November 1942].

One must remember that the yellow star, which had been imposed in the Northern Zone in June 1942, was not worn in the Southern Zone, which certainly facilitated the work of all OSE members, whether official or clandestine. The personnel of the UGIF believed themselves safe from roundups—at least this was the widespread belief—because they carried the UGIF card.[17]

NOVEMBER 1942: THE GERMANS INVADE THE SOUTHERN ZONE

We were still in Marseille on 11 November 1942, when, following the American landing in North Africa, the Germans and Italians invaded the Southern Zone. Italian troops settled in eight *départements* of the southeast (including Cannes, where my parents still lived). Marseille was occupied by the Germans.

After the Allied landing, the opening of a new front and the rout that was suffered by Rommel's armies [in North Africa] no doubt abated our anxiety. We hoped that the Vichy government would protest [against the German and Italian occupations of the Southern Zone, which was still, according to the 1940 armistice, officially ruled by the Vichy government]. We still believed in the possibility of a collusion between de Gaulle and Pétain, a myth that collapsed shortly afterward.[18] We began to fear, then, that our status as French citizens would no longer protect us, even if the fact of not having to wear the yellow star as in the Northern Zone cheered us a little. Nevertheless, a decree of December 1942, passed by Laval, required that henceforth the word "Jew" be stamped on Jews' identity cards. The destruction of the old harbor in January 1943 led to the roundups of foreign Jews in Marseille.

The Italians protected the Jews who flocked en masse into the areas surrounding Nice, Grenoble, and Megève. Undoubtedly because of the intervention of Angelo Donati, cofounder of the Franco-Italian Bank in Nice, and because he meant to assert the Italian prerogatives in the region, Alberto Calisso, the Italian consul in Nice, insisted that the fate of Jews in the region occupied by Italy was the responsibility of the Italian, not the German, authorities. Angelo Donati tried to evacuate the Jews to North Africa. He failed to do so, but many of them succeeded in crossing into Switzerland or in going into hiding before the Germans arrived in the zone. For his part, Moussa Abadie, of the Garel network, saved children by placing them in foster families and in the convents of the region, thanks to his cooperation with Monsignor [Paul] Rémond, bishop of Nice. Odette Rosenstock, the physician who worked with Abadie as an OSE assistant, was arrested and deported. When she returned from Auschwitz, she married Abadie.

Everything in Marseille was in a state of flux. The OSE there had just moved out of its quarters when the Gestapo tried to set a trap there, but, since the space had been taken over by another organization, the trap failed. When alerted, the directorate of the OSE opted to close the center and to disperse all its members.

We therefore left Marseille and our friends. I was expecting a child and lived from day to day.

6

The Hunt for the Children

MARCH 1943–MARCH 1944: LIMOGES

Six months after my wedding, I was back in Limoges. We lived first at the Hôtel du Faisan, opposite the railway station, and then in a small flat that Dr. Weill helped find for us. Our landlords proved to be very warm people. I subsequently found out that they had just lost a daughter the same age as I.

I was still not registered with the census, my identity card was still in the name of Hermann, and I didn't appear on the list of the employees of Limoges. In December 1942, however, I received a UGIF card with my married name on it, stating that I resided in Lyon. This was one of the methods used to throw pursuers off the track.

Although pregnant, I decided to start working again: Julien and I were going to work together. During the hiatus in Marseille, I had witnessed the gradual shift [in the OSE] from legal to clandestine activity. From now on, knowing the truth about the deportations, we could only lend our support to the new direction the OSE was taking. We had promised ourselves that our marriage would not jeopardize our outside work, and we agreed to run any risk to keep the children away from a programmed death. If 108 children had escaped deportation in the night of Vénissieux, it was thanks to the determination of a small group of men and women who were able to convince parents to "abandon" their children.[1] It was now up to us to take over, to help the children survive. All possible means were implemented, above all the hiding of children in non-Jewish families and institutions. The placement network could not be put into operation in one day; therefore, the official organization would have to coexist with the clandestine channels.

Julien and I opened an official UGIF office—Third Department (Health) in Limoges. Since November 1942, the Germans had been occupying the region, which appeared relatively sheltered. Food supplies were ample and the *préfets* of Haute-Vienne and Creuse[2] appeared to be kindly disposed toward our activities. We installed the OSE office at 29, rue Louis-Blanc, on the second floor[3] in a two-room flat, each room of which had an exit directly to the landing.

Our work consisted of coming to the aid of refugees and of discreetly breaking up children's homes. This action extended to the area that included Brive, Dun-le-Paleteau, Guéret, and Chateauroux, as well as the *département* of Indre. My job was to ensure the coordination between the official and the clandestine teams. I also handled secretarial duties and maintained the center's account books. I had no intention of taking too many risks by personally seeking out and placing the children, but working did not seem to invite any more danger than not doing anything at all.

Julien directed the center, but he also supervised the illegal activities of the OSE (e.g., forged identity cards, food coupons, financial aid, and the closing of the children's homes). This dual activity proved decisive when it came to disguising or evacuating the children sheltered in the numerous homes of the region. We rigorously abided by the golden rule concerning the security of the organization and of persons, namely silence. I was unfamiliar with many of the things Julien did. Moreover, he said, "One can always be put under arrest. There is no risk in talking if one does not know anything."

The teams carried out the process of hiding children in foster families as well as of distributing food ration cards—obtained through the good will of the prefectoral headquarters—to the refugees hiding in these regions. Of course, these clandestine networks were not in direct touch with the Third Department (Health). Their members never came to the rue Louis-Blanc, and they did not communicate among themselves.

A GIVEN NAME, BEARER OF HOPE

The events were so dramatic that we felt ourselves privileged to be together, to expect a child, to work. We did not need much, didn't pay much rent, and lived from day to day. I benefited from a ration coupon book that included supplements, first as a pregnant woman, and later for the baby I nursed. (With "the return to the soil and the family" [slogan] extolled by Pétain,[4] women were once again nursing their babies. Even the politics of food supplies encouraged them to do so.) Always sur-

91

rounded by our OSE friends, we lived in a convivial atmosphere that I would not find again after the war. With few means and "coupon points for textiles," I managed to be elegant, and, as a supreme luxury, it sometimes happened that we were able to dine at a "black market" restaurant, despite the presence of many Germans.

I was to give birth in August and stopped working a month earlier. The administrators at Chambéry sent to Limoges one of their associates, Pierre Dreyfus, who had just replaced me, and I took advantage of this transfer to change my identity. Pierre Dutertre and I were working together on the "transfer of power" on 14 July [the French national holiday], when I felt the first contractions about eight o'clock in the evening. Watched over during my pregnancy by Dr. Nerson, a friend from Strasbourg who had taken refuge in Périgueux, I was to give birth in a small clinic, with a midwife present. I went there on foot. Julien joined me and stayed with me during the delivery—a very uncommon thing in those days. I could not stop thinking of Julien's mother, who had died during confinement, and of the horrible stories about my mother's confinement in the Port-Royal hospital, but everything came out all right in the end. In order to emphasize the hope that we still placed in France on this 14 July 1943, we gave our daughter the first name of Françoise.[5] We also gave her the name of Julien's mother, Sara (without the "h" in the French style) to indicate our joint contribution [to her birth].

Our OSE friends crowded around me and lent me a cradle, a baby carriage, and some clothing. Thanks to the presence of Régine, a sixteen-year-old girl from the Couret home who had come to help me, I was able to resume my work pretty quickly. Régine, who was born in Germany, seemingly saw in me the mother she had just lost to deportation. At that time, I was too young to play this role, but she herself acted as a mother to my daughter, to whom she transferred all her affection. Her presence by my baby's side subsequently proved to be of crucial importance.

With my return to work, I dedicated myself particularly to my role as liaison; I didn't stay at the office all the time but went often to the children's homes.

THE BREAKING UP OF THE CHILDREN'S HOMES

During the roundups of the summer of 1942, *gendarmes* came searching for children whose parents had given them their address, still believing—before the social service teams did their work in the triage centers—[the official line] of family reunions. The OSE decided to shelter the adolescents who ran the greatest risk; while they were being transferred, the decision was made to change their identity. Thus began the business of forging false papers and of concealing children in homes in the Italian zone (e.g., Saint-Paul, Moutiers), which seemed to be free of danger. Two new children's homes were opened there, but the sudden capitulation of Italy in September 1943 opened this border region to the risk of reprisals. The danger increased because at that very moment it became more difficult to cross the Swiss border and the manhunts in the regions of Nice and Savoie had become more ruthless. It was necessary to return the children to the children's homes in central France that they had just left while they waited for us to find them safer shelters. In the meantime, the network of counterfeiters had been consolidated and the children's homes had become relay stations, thus allowing the children as well as the employees to disappear from one center and to reappear the next day in another center under a new identity. The OSE created a department of evacuation based in Limoges and organized the dispersal of the children. This dispersal was gradual in order not to arouse the attention of the Occupation authorities and the French police. A too rapid closure of the homes would have aroused their suspicion.

Life went on as the children's homes were being dismantled. Religious holidays were still celebrated in the hope of providing a few moments of serenity to the children, and of allowing them to preserve their family traditions. They pursued their schooling and, once a week, were brought up-to-date on the state of the world.

THE UNDERGROUND; THE GAREL NETWORK

With Georges Garel, whom he met at Vénissieux on 29 August 1942,[6] Joseph Weill set up a new form of organization for the OSE. Georges Garel, who until then had worked in the Resistance under a false, "Aryanized" identity, had the advantage of being a newcomer to the OSE. He agreed to organize a network in the former Southern Zone on the partitioned model of the Resistance networks.

An electrical engineer, he gave up the position of leader of Resistance armaments in the Southern Zone to devote himself to the rescue of Jewish children. He set two conditions: that his organization have no association whatever with the UGIF-Third Department (Health) or with any other Jewish organization and that the members of his team work under an "Aryanized" identity—whether genuine or not—and be professionally integrated into a non-Jewish organization. The necessary resources were to be secured via Switzerland or Portugal by the American [Jewish] Joint [Distribution Committee], which supported this clandestine activity.[7]

Georges Garel, who camouflaged his identity behind forged papers and a fictional professional cover, was endowed with extraordinary *sang-froid:* "The job indicated on the papers was that of porcelain salesman. When his suitcase was opened, one could see inside plates and cups with a universally known trademark. What was neither seen nor suspected was what was hidden underneath: blank identity cards collected from understanding mayors and thousands of bank notes to distribute to all the regional leaders."[8]

A TURNING POINT

We sensed a change in people's attitudes around us. The French began to find that time was dragging. The prisoners of war had still not come back (they had been gone more than two years), and tension increased throughout the country. Since September 1942, the STO (Service du travail obligatoire [Service of Obligatory Labor]) had forcibly recruited 350,000 workers to meet the Germans' unreasonable demands. The news from the BBC of London, picked up clandestinely[9]—the invasion of the Soviet Union by the German army and the opening of the second front,[10] the fall of Mussolini, the Italian capitulation—all gave rise to the belief that German victory was not irreversible. Perhaps it no longer paid to be an anonymous informer. A larger number of people were now ready to contribute, to resist in their own way. The deportations of children, arousing popular indignation, led the people to take action. The moment seemed favorable to mobilize non-Jews in favor of the rescue of children.

The OSE found its first and most valuable support among important Catholic and Protestant individuals and among leaders of secular charitable organizations sensitized to the plight of Jewish children since the deportations in the summer of 1942. Monsignor [Jules-Gérard] Saliège, archbishop of Toulouse, immediately offered to place twenty-four children under false identities in Catholic institutions and families. He provided Georges Garel with a certificate carrying his signature and an assurance that the bearer was "of good and certain faith," conferring upon the latter the confidence and support of numerous Catholic organizations. As a result of his first efforts, Georges Garel found that he had three hundred places in the area around Toulouse at his disposal for the children. Monsignor [Pierre-Marie] Théas of Montauban was likewise won over to this cause.

The Protestant church,[11] notably because of the bonds that the Cimade had renewed with the OSE, also brought considerable aid to the clandestine organization then in operation. Pastor Boegner, head of the Protestant church in France, invited families to help the Jews. The help offered by the people of Chambon-sur-Lignon, a Protestant village, was particularly valuable, since the commune is surrounded by forests at an altitude of a thousand meters [five-eighths of a mile].[12] The children hidden there by the peasants could therefore take shelter in the vicinity whenever there was a police raid. André Chouraqui and Madeleine Dreyfus kept contact with the children placed in Chambon-sur-Lignon. She later told this story:

> I remember one day when there remained for me to "find a place" for two fourteen-year-old boys—a very difficult business. I went from place to place throughout the area around Chambon, places more or less near it and carrying such pretty names as La Rionde, La Suchère, Le Pont-du-Chollet. . . . Nobody wanted the two boys. I came up to a rather old couple, the Courtials, and told them my "fable": "city children who are hungry. Of course, they have their food coupons and the air of Chambon." The Courtials' answer was friendly but firm: it was not possible for them to take them in. They themselves were too old, and these boys were too big. Having thrown out a feeler, I decided to disclose the secret: "The truth is that these are two young Jewish boys whose parents have been arrested and whom the Germans are looking for everywhere to imprison with their parents." No more hesitation. "But you should have said that before. Of course, bring them, your two boys."

Other Protestant villages, especially in the Cévennes,[13] also sheltered children. In this way, hundreds of children could be concealed all across France in families that had been recommended by prominent people who were willing to protect the OSE activities in a given area.

The foster families were often contacted through the intermediary of an important religious person in the region or of a woman teacher, who was generally the only one in the village to know that the child was not only a "refugee" but also a Jew. Among the foster families were many large families for whom the care of an additional child was not too burdensome. They often lived in the countryside and also benefited from being able to meet their own needs for food. For the most part, they were women whose husbands were prisoners in Germany and who found moral support in the presence of a child. In some cases, the family received modest financial aid, but sometimes it was simply a matter of performing a generous deed.

THE ORGANIZATION OF THE GAREL NETWORK

The Garel network managed to place nearly nineteen hundred children in less than a year, and by the summer of 1943 it covered almost the entire Southern Zone.

Given the extent of this activity, it became necessary to restructure the network. It was reorganized into a two-tier system: by *département* and by region. Four large regions were demarcated, with the center of decision-making remaining in Lyon under the responsibility of Georges Garel. Each region was run by a leader who was responsible to Georges Garel and whose mission was to search out and keep track of the placements of children in families. As for the adolescents, they were registered under non-Jewish identities in *collèges* [institutions that provide secondary schooling outside the state system] or in secular or religious institutions.

Three sections were subsumed within the network. The first put together the forged papers and forged ration cards intended for children and the clandestine personnel; the second was assigned the job of dressing up the children to look their best upon their arrival; and the third—the transportation section—had to step in as quickly as possible when a large number of children had to be transported in an emergency (in case of accident or unexpected and massive crowding). The Sixth Division of the Jewish Scouts of France[14] once more lent us a strong hand.

The OSE was always preoccupied with what would happen to the children after the war. It was for this reason that it finalized, with the help of the International Red Cross, a practical system of coded lists that contained all the information on the origins of the children and their hiding place. These lists, stored in safe places, made it possible once the war was over to find the children again and to identify them.[15]

Three types of solutions were contemplated with regard to the dispersal of the children: placement in a secular or Christian institution or family under a false identity; a clandestine crossing of the Swiss border, intended first for those at the greatest risk, notably the boys, and entrusted to Georges Loinger; and emigration to Palestine, via Spain, taken over by Elizabeth Hirsch (known as Boëgie).

All the children were not suited for a clandestine placement, because of their ignorance of the French language, their young age (which made it difficult for them to obey instructions), or their typically "Semitic" physical features. The latter put the entire clandestine network at risk. Others, such as slow or incontinent children, were difficult to place: after many intercessions by Charlotte Rosenbaum, a great many of them (about seventy) were sent to school centers in Lourdes for children evacuated from bombed areas.

It was essential that we be fully acquainted with the children before directing them to new lay or Christian centers or foster families. Robert Job, who was in charge of the evacuation plans, remained in constant contact with the directors of children's homes. and Germaine Masour ensured their liaison with all levels of the Garel network.

Germaine Masour's activities were at the heart of the Garel network: she was active both in breaking up the last children's homes of the OSE and in organizing the groups that she often led to the Swiss border. She was put at the disposal of the Garel network of Limoges, where her job became wholly clandestine. She relates:

> I was assigned the job of acting as liaison between the children's homes located in Creuse and Haute-Vienne and the leaders of the clandestine groups. The first task consisted of finding or fabricating forged papers for each child and teaching him not only his alias but also the way to act in his new surroundings. Thanks to the help of Catholic, Protestant, and lay societies, a great many children found shelter in religious boarding schools and *collèges*. The youngest ones were put out to wet-nurses in return for a fee.[16]

The clandestine system involved certain constraints, in addition to the codification of information on the children and their families. "But," she added, "many Resistance members in the Limoges region helped us in our work."

THE CHILD IN HIDING

After many risks and errors, the forged papers were now faultless. [Hiding] places were less difficult to find, and the staff was rather large. There were few hitches.

Nevertheless, difficulties still remained when one had to have little Gérard Lévy, who was only six years old, accept that his name would be Gérard Leroy from that moment on, and the little Tuchhändlers—two brothers and one sister—understand that henceforth they would be called Drapier.

What kind of treasure was it that provided the wiles and imagination needed to accustom each child to answer to a given name other than his own? How happy we were when the child began to join in the game and no longer wanted to give up the prescribed fiction!

Of course, little snags did happen—for example, Annette Bernay, who told her nurse, with all the mischief of her seven years, "You know, I'm also called Annette Bernheim, but Mademoiselle Martha said I should not say that."

The preparations for departure had other surprises in store—looking over the luggage, first of all, and hunting for family souvenirs, books, and class notebooks, because someone had forgotten to erase names and compromising dedications that had to disappear, and removing Hebrew prayer books and Bibles that children from devout families had so much difficulty parting from. "That's all that remains from the house, mama gave it to me before I left," said the children, tears in their eyes. "I'll be very sure to keep it for you," said the social worker, moved but unrelenting. And the trip began. The child did not know where he was going, nor did the social worker at the departure point generally know. Her mission was to lead him from Marseille to Valence, to Limoges, or to Chateauroux and to place him in the care of her colleague at a given address. It was the new person's job to extend the chain. Thus, there were two, three, or four transporters who relayed the valuable cargo from hand to hand. All they knew of the child was his alias, and he knew nothing of them, for checkpoints were common in trains and railroad stations; thus, it was better not to know anything and to invent everything, rather than take the risk of betraying oneself. But the children often had difficulty tolerating these essential security measures. Out of nostalgia or rebelliousness, they sometimes tried to run away.

Gabriel was eight years old when his mother entrusted him to a Parisian agency. She had long hesitated to separate herself from him, but her husband had been arrested, and she could no longer bear being hunted down with her small child. Information was taken on his civil status, the address of friends in France and abroad and that of his only other relative—a cousin in Palestine. Gabriel was attached to a convoy to [the *département* of] Isère: he was sheltered for several months by a family near Grenoble, and then one day in May 1944, a young woman he did not know came to get him and took him to Valence. The city was being bombed.[17] Gabriel was handed over to a new woman in charge of a convoy who brought him to Lyon. Again a bombardment; then a third convoy leader and continuation of the journey by an unlikely itinerary to Toulouse, where a fourth young woman took over the delivery of the child. Again bombing, and descent into an air-raid shelter.

At the end of the alert, officials noticed that Gabriel had disappeared. They looked for him for two days and finally found him in a Catholic center attached to an underground network, to which he had been handed over by the police, who had picked him up in the street. Gabriel did not reveal anything about his identity. But the trip was not over yet, and when the child had to climb up into the train with a fifth convoy leader, he turned toward her and asked, "Madame, can you finally tell me where I'm going this time?" They had to lie to him, for he was leaving with several other children for Spain.[18]

From one end of this invisible underground chain to the other, people waited in anguish until they received news of each child's safe arrival. The parents, if still alive, waited anxiously for the promised letter [announcing their child's safe arrival]; the social worker was eager to appease the pangs of her conscience after the terrible responsibilities she had assumed and to inform those who had entrusted the child to her [that the child was safe].

A child in hiding could not disclose his identity to anyone, not even to other children who could prove their Jewishness. For him, this was the most difficult and painful aspect of his clandestine life. Dissimulation was no longer a game but a genuine torment that left him alone with his lie. With the loss of his name, which he sometimes tried to forget so as to stay alive, he lost everything that made up his being and his memory. His alias had become the only sign he could transmit when being passed from hand to hand, without his understanding the reasons for the constraints to which he was forced to submit.

In a situation of such absolute solitude, lived by children so young and so ill prepared, was it possible to retain one's own identity for long? Could a child who had thus lost his points of reference ever hope to be found one day by his relatives? Can one imagine the bewilderment (in all senses of the word[19]) that such a child must have experienced?

To put the matter in a better light, only one person in the foster family—the mother—knew the true identity of the child she had taken in. To no one else could the child speak. He thus lived in perpetual tension. The most sociable child withdrew into himself. A thousand memories haunted him. He would have liked to forget so that he could respond to the kindness of the people around him. Rumors reached him about events in which relatives, whose fate he was unaware of, were immersed. He also heard antisemitic talk: "Those Jews, there are too many of them. We should kill them all." By a superhuman effort, he kept silent, and was ashamed of his silence. He was compelled to avoid the only Jewish boy in his school, to whom the other children were so nice. One day, this boy's eyes were red from weeping: his grandfather had been deported. In his turn, he clumsily tried to say a few words to him. He heard the answer: "Oh, you, you won't be able to understand." To reveal the slightest confidence would be foolhardy and would oblige him to leave the town, for it would put his foster family in danger.

The most difficult thing of all was that he didn't have the slightest information that would enable him to understand his situation. He repeated to himself over and over again, "Why?" Roger was very lucky compared to the other children: he was able to speak of it with his "foster mother" when his pain became too great. Yet he could not accept his false identity. He could lie to enemies who were capable of harming him, but could he answer with a lie or with silence those who tried to bring him out of his loneliness? Whence, as soon as the liberation was announced, he began to run through the village, shouting: "I'm Jewish, my name is Roger Waksman."[20]

Within the OSE, the story is told between tears and laughter of the little girl in the children's home at Couret who had been taught to speak of the rabbi who regularly visited them as "Monsieur the Priest." Seated in a train compartment with other travelers, she turned to her neighbor who had asked her, "Haven't you forgotten to say goodbye to Monsieur the Priest?" and answered, "No, but I forgot to say goodbye to his wife."

AT A TIME OF DANGER

We tried to act as best as we could in this kind of confusion. Problems sometimes arose in foster families, obliging us to transfer the children. But how could a child decide whether to obey his parents who forbade him to leave his shelter or the social worker whom he didn't know and who tried to shelter him in a different place?

Mme. Courbet, at that time a welfare worker in a Parisian agency, told the poignant story of an attempted rescue:

> Mlle. Berthe asked me this morning to leave for Ozoir [seventeen miles east of Paris], in Seine-et-Marne, from which I had to bring back two children placed with a foster mother. I didn't ask any questions; all that mattered was for me to know the place where I had to take them. It was agreed that I would bring them back to my residence.

I knew the name of the foster mother, those of the children, the destination of my trip, and that was all.

I went down to the small railway station of Ozoir. It was still summertime; the air was balmy, the morning was pleasant, but my heart was heavy. I was sorry I didn't know the motive that necessitated my bringing the children back to Paris. I simply had the order to go get them. I tried to set my mind at ease and to tell myself that the lookouts at the clinic must have foreseen everything about the children. But I didn't feel at ease inside me. I crossed a large forest; I was in a hurry to get there.

There I was before number 4, avenue des Acacias. I rang the bell, and from the end of the garden came a housewife, whom I must have been disturbing in her morning chores. Behind her came first a beautiful young woman fifteen or sixteen years old, then a sturdy and placid boy, who seemed to be around fourteen years old. I introduced myself as a social worker assigned to visit all the children placed in the *départe-ment* and asked Mme. Allain whether the children were still with her. "It's been a long time since they left my house," she answered me. I told her I was surprised at that. No noise from the house reached my ears; Mme. Allain had nothing more to tell me, she was waiting for me to leave. Instinctively, I looked the children in the eye. Mme. Allain told me they had been taken back by their mother and that she was very sorry that she could not give me their address.

As I walked away from the avenue des Acacias, I tried to stay calm. Perhaps it was better that way; the children had to have gone into hiding with their mother. But I was more distressed at that moment than I was when I had arrived there. I said to myself over and over, "Taken back by their mother, but why?" I walked alone on a road that seemed endless. I had a whole hour to wait before the next train to Paris. Suddenly I heard someone call me: "Madame, madame!" I turned around and saw the tall young woman running to catch up with me. "Madame," she said, "come back, Mme. Allain would like to speak to you." The foster mother waited for me near the garden fence. The tall boy was crying at her side. "Let's go back into the house," Mme. Allain said.

"Madame," she said in pointing to the young woman and the boy, who were weeping, "here are the children." I looked at these three human beings who, for reasons I could not yet fathom, had to be suffering horribly. Touched, I said to Mme. Allain that she had done the right thing to call me back, that together we would be stronger in protecting the children from danger, if there was any danger. I asked her to tell me about the life of the children since their arrival; by whom and how had they been entrusted to her? The boy no longer wept; his face seemed closed off, and he became hard, aggressive. He forbade his foster mother to speak to me, he kept close to her, and he obviously distrusted me.

The foster mother, not wishing to add to the child's distress, kept quiet and wept, her face buried in her hands. My job was thankless and cruel. These children had already been the victims of men's lies. They could no longer put their trust in anybody's word.

I was not supposed to say that I had been sent by the clinic, but I saw no other way of breaking through the obstacle of distrust the boy had erected between us. I suggested to the young woman that she come as far as the village post office, from which I would telephone the head social worker so that I could tell her the reason I had come to get them. I didn't want to resort to any subterfuge; the suffering and the courage of these children were great enough for them to hear the truth.

I told them of my job, the assignment I had selected, which made me a simple soldier who carried out unquestioningly the orders of her leaders. I gained a bit of their confidence. Then, simply and affectionately, I asked the boy to allow Mme. Allain to give me some facts about them. The foster mother was distressed. It was Rachel who told me their sad story.

The children were French, the father and mother Polish, simple journeymen tailors. The father had been arrested in 1941 and brought to Drancy [a detention camp to the northeast of Paris, from which Jews were deported to eastern Europe for extermination]. The mother had been in hiding since her husband's arrest. She first placed the children with a foster mother who mistreated them, then with a second foster mother, where they were subjected to the ill will of their neighbors. Aware of the danger each time, she was [nonetheless] able to change foster mothers. The third time, the children were placed with Mme. Allain, where they found a bit of peace, with the warmth, the love of a home.

The mother sometimes came to see them at Ozoir, laying herself open to all risks in order to embrace them. She could barely speak French. Her identity papers were not in order, and she no longer wore the yellow star. She took all kinds of risks to visit the only beloved beings still left to her. She had come a few days earlier, and at each visit she had repeated the same injunctions: follow no one, listen to no one, do not leave Ozoir at any cost.

I was distressed and no longer dared ask the children to follow me to Paris. Their mother's wishes were sacred. If something unfortunate were to happen to the children, how would I ever be able to show my face to her? My decision was made. I would ask Rachel to come to Paris—alone with me, since her brother did not wish to come. The boy stood up like a lion, yelled to his sister to stay, said that her mother had forbidden them to go to Paris and that they were safe at Ozoir.

I then took out my family record book[21] and asked Rachel to read in a loud voice: "Françoise Courbet, born in Paris on 22 December 1929." The boy did not understand, but Rachel did: she was of the same age as my daughter. Hence, she would be able to come undisturbed with me to Paris, see her mother, and know the reason for this transfer. I asked the foster mother to convince the young man, who reluctantly accepted this solution and wanted to extract from his sister the promise that she would come back that very same evening. The train often ran between Paris and Ozoir. Yet I asked him to be reasonable: his sister would sleep in my daughter's bed at my house, and I would bring her back myself the next day. Obstinately, he refused; he insisted that she return that same evening. Rachel begged me to listen to her brother's request. I then said to him that it would be their mother who would decide whether Rachel were to return the same evening or the next day.

It was lunch time, but nobody was eating. We had just gone through some painful moments. We would have liked to hold one another; we already felt the strength of the bonds that united us. Rachel was seated next to me; she looked at me affectionately. I talked to her of my daughter; she talked to me of her mother. If she had not had the responsibility of taking care of her brother, she would have stayed by her mother's side and worked with her, this unfortunate, hunted mother, who had no right to live yet had to work in order not to die of hunger!

Rachel spoke French without an accent. Nothing distinguished her from other young women. I asked her whether she would have liked to work in Paris. By using her photo, I would have been able to have an identity card made for her in the name of my daughter. She would have been able to work to help her mother, whom we would have sent to Ozoir for a rest with her brother: "You will live at my place; Françoise is safe among friends in Normandy, and you will be able to take her place if that's what you want."

Rachel put her arms around my neck and, weeping, said to me, "Why would you do this for me? I cannot believe it, you don't even know me." I simply told her, "I do it so as to deserve the right of embracing my daughter one day, to be able to say to Françoise one day that in her name her mother has saved a young woman like her, who had the same right to live as all young women." Rachel embraced me and remained huddled against me, and thus intertwined we spent a moment of deep emotion.

We all together went back to the railway station. I walked by the side of Mme. Allain, Rachel gave me her arm, the boy was on a bicycle. On the road we resumed our small talk, like peaceful people going for a walk.

The train arrived. Rachel and I separated from the other two. The trip was short, about an hour from the gare de l'Est [railway station in northeastern Paris]. We took advantage of being alone in our compartment by going through a general rehearsal: "I would accompany Rachel up to the rue des Armandiers where her mother was hiding; while waiting for her, I would go shopping and make a few purchases. If she was stopped, she would know what to answer: that her mother was waiting for her nearby. She would give the address of my residence.

Everything went off smoothly; Rachel saw her mother, who was unaware of the reason the clinic wanted to take her children back. She urged Rachel to ask for an explanation and, if necessary, to follow me with her brother. Mlle. Berthe at the clinic told us that there had been several denunciations in Seine-et-Marne, that the children were no longer safe in the *département,* and that they were afraid of a Gestapo raid. Rachel asked whether she could return to Ozoir that evening to warn her brother and come back with him to my home the next day. Mlle. Berthe said that it went without saying that the children would remain with me until Rachel got her identity card and that a shelter could be found for Jacques and his mother. I accompanied Rachel, who was completely reassured, to the gare de l'Est.

It was a Thursday. I stayed home all Friday long, waiting for the children to arrive. As soon as the clinic opened on Saturday morning, but before it got crowded, I asked for news. Nobody had heard anything about the children from Ozoir. They probably meant to spend a last good day with Mme. Allain. My mind set at ease, I stayed at the office preparing for my next trip: in a few days I would be leaving for Annecy to accompany fifteen children on their way to Switzerland. I was planning the railroad itinerary, gave some verbal orders, and got ready to leave. A secretary called me, "Madame, a woman asks to see you." My heart immediately sank; I could hardly walk. I entered the reception room. A mother, the mother of Rachel and Jacques, stood straight up, petrified with grief, and screamed: "Drancy, Drancy!"

The children had not been saved; they had been picked up at Mme. Allain's home on Friday morning.

THE SWISS SOLUTION

Switzerland took in many children. From 1940 on, the OSE even undertook to find sponsors for children who came from France in order to finance their schooling and their daily needs. Bonds of friendship were thus formed after the war between the children and Swiss families.

When the screw tightened around the Jews, the OSE had to submit to the antisemitic laws of Vichy and to separate itself from associates who were either foreign or at risk. Wanted by the police and risking deportation, the latter for the most part chose to cross the Swiss border illegally. Their presence in Switzerland helped maintain the bonds that had already been formed.

In turn, Dr. Weill, wanted by the Gestapo, himself settled in Switzerland in May 1943. From there he organized the reception of children and pursued contacts with Portugal, site of the European office of the Joint. He and Marc Jarblum obtained assurances that convoys of children under sixteen that entered Switzerland clandestinely would not be sent back. The office of the Union-OSE in Geneva, made up of Dr. Joseph Weill, Olga and Lazare Gurvic, and Hélène and Jacques Bloch, secured the reception and placement of children in Switzerland, as well as establishing the connections and the necessary steps to be taken with the international organizations.

From early 1943, the first wards of the OSE, under the responsibility of Georges

Loinger, were able to cross the frontier illegally and take refuge in Switzerland. After the Italian capitulation in September 1943, [however,] crossing the frontier became extremely dangerous when the Swiss authorities stiffened their position for fear of German reprisals. Nevertheless, the safety of the people in the children's homes had to be secured while the use of underground networks for crossing into Switzerland was intensified. This is what Georges Loinger had to say [on this matter]:

> Most of the time the trip took place in the following manner: once we arrived at Annemasse [French town in Haute-Savoie, only five miles from Geneva, Switzerland], where, thanks to the connivance of the railroad employees, we always managed to leave quietly by exits reserved for us, we went with the children to the reception center in the city that, with the support of the mayor [Jean Deffaugt], had agreed to feed and shelter the children. Around five in the afternoon, I picked up the children, who left the center as if they made up a little group of students. I had a basketball under my arm, and we walked, singing, along the Arve River to a small playing field hidden in the woods. That playing field was a kilometer away from the border, and we happily played until nightfall. The children, caught up in the game, totally forgot the danger that was lurking around us. Once night had fallen, we walked over to the border, far from any road or path. One of my comrades who belonged to the *maquis* of this region had been detached especially to be on the alert for the comings and goings of the Germans. He went ahead of us, and I followed with the group, which nervously stuck closely to me. Once we arrived at the barbed wire, which my comrade and I spread apart, the children quickly passed one behind the other into Swiss territory. They were almost immediately picked up by a customs man and led to a police station, from which they were directed to a reception center. For a time I went to pick up a convoy at Aix-les-Bains [about sixty miles from Annemasse] every two days, and, protected by fate, we always managed to cross the frontier. Sometimes it was in broad daylight while playing ball that we got near and the children crossed over.[22]

In other instances, the crossing was taken over by frontier runners who knew the region well and who had been selected by OSE members in Marseille and Grenoble. For a rather large sum of money, the runner led a group of children from a spot near the border, and when the [German] patrols were far from the selected spot—generally at night—he cut the barbed wire. Before the departure for Switzerland, a password had been arranged with the child designated as the group leader; he had to write down this word on a piece of paper and give it to the runner once the frontier had been crossed. This word testified to the fact that everything had gone well and that the runner could collect the agreed-upon sum of money. As for the children, they had documents with their real names sewn into their clothing underneath the armpit, which was to prove useful once they arrived in Switzerland.

Of course, clandestine border crossings were not always that easy, and the parents who had entrusted their children to others were apprehensive as they waited for the letter that would reassure them.

The children found safety on the other side. After a compulsory stay in a reception camp, they were taken in charge by the Union-OSE of Geneva and placed, under its responsibility, in Swiss children's homes.

BOUND FOR PALESTINE

Another road to safety that opened up to the young was that of Palestine. With the help of American Jewish organizations—including the Joint and HICEM—boats were chartered to leave from Spain. Hence, it was the crossing of the Pyrénées [which constitute the entire Franco-Spanish border] that proved to be the main obstacle. Here, too, it was the frontier runners who took charge of the convoys and led them to safe harbor. Efforts then began to obtain visas for everyone. The first chartered boat set sail in February 1944. Others followed.

Children who had a relative in Palestine received priority. One of the organizations stated: "From the moment they reached the shelters, we were held in suspense for many weeks by the steps to be taken in preparation for departure, their provisioning, and their movement to a secret place of assembly. Our emissaries and those of the Zionist organizations specializing in the crossing of frontiers competed with one another in their eagerness to succeed."

The children came from the four corners of France, and our social workers sometimes took as many as eight days to convoy a single child.

In a session held in Lyon in April 1944, the executive committee of the OSE decided to entrust Elizabeth Hirsch, a social worker and a former OSE leader in the Lyon region, with the task of escorting to Spain the majority of the children and of supervising them until their embarkation for Palestine. The committee intended to dispatch the children's social and medical documents to the Jewish Agency of Jerusalem via the Union-OSE of Geneva.

It was thus that six of them left together at eight o'clock in the morning of 8 August, with the others to join them several days later.

We changed in Perpignan [about twenty miles from the Spanish border], from where the railcar took us in the evening to the little village of Quillan. One of the frontier runners was waiting for us. There were already ten of us, for four adults had joined us in Perpignan. During the night we stayed at the runner's place, and the next evening we went up by truck to Rouse, the last [French] village in the Pyrénées, where we were welcomed at an inn. The rest of the convoy arrived the next day. We packed our luggage. We were twelve children and five adults, plus six runners. The caravan was ready the next morning at six o'clock. The only baggage we were carrying held food supplies and a few belongings for the children. The sun rose as we were leaving; the day promised to be beautiful. The runners walked ahead of the children. An old Spanish peasant, who was the leader of the runners, distributed a walking stick to every child; it amused them at the beginning to walk like real mountaineers, but they soon left them behind, for they would have liked to run, to walk faster. They were tired out by ten o'clock. Luckily, we were approaching the *maquis* who were going to grant us permission to pass. While the runners settled the formalities of passing with the head of the *maquis,* we chatted with the *maquisards.* They had already seen several convoys of children pass through, and they assured us that there was no reason to be anxious.

After having consumed warm drinks offered by the *maquisards,* we resumed our march and sang, "Ce n'est qu'un au revoir, mes frères . . ." ["Auld Lang Syne"]. At noon we lunched on the bank of a lake. An hour of obligatory siesta was announced. Then the march resumed until the evening, with a stop for the four o'clock *goûter* [snack] and from time to time a short halt to pass out a piece of sugar soaked in cognac or lemon juice.

The night had fallen, and we had settled down; the runners had made a fire that they kept going until five in the morning. Our little group went to sleep early (lying next to one another to keep warm), for tomorrow was going to be an important day: we were going to cross the frontier. Our climbing continued the next day without any unusual problems. Several stragglers whose feet had been bruised by the march made up the rear. Some of the runners were helping them.

Around six o'clock in the afternoon, a group of runners left to inspect various possibilities for crossing. The fog persisted, and they were still not back. Finally, the agreed-upon sign was given; we left in silence one after the other. We saw the mountain in front of us and above us, the chalet guarded by the Germans and barking dogs. All this was not reassuring, and I admired the children's discipline. . . .

We crossed the valley and tackled the mountain; night had fallen, and we were in a thick fog. After walking in a straight line for two hours, the runners noticed that they had taken the wrong path. This was the most serious moment of our trip, for everyone was exhausted. But face to face with danger, everyone gathered his courage and strength, and we continued our march. We finally found the right road. Having arrived at the end of the journey, the runners were forced to carry the children as they crossed the river separating France from Spain. Once on the other side, we were not even able to rejoice, . . . for we were barely able to drag ourselves a few more meters to find a shelter where we spent the night. . . .

In Barcelona the children were welcomed by the Joint in a villa outside the city, where they remained until their departure for Palestine. That took place in Cadiz, at four o'clock in the morning of 26 October. Several convoys that had gathered there left together—seventy-four of our children and two hundred adults.[23]

All the children who had participated in this event survived.

7

Going Underground

SEPTEMBER 1943: FROM CANNES TO LIMOGES

On the advice of Angelo Donati, my parents in August 1943 moved from Cannes and the Italian zone, which had become dangerously unsafe, to Limoges.[1]

After spending several weeks in a room rented from our landlords, they settled in a furnished apartment. My father carried on his work managing the clandestine Zionist movement Harsharot and collecting money to finance philanthropic societies within the Joint. My parents forged their identity papers; they retained their family name Hermann but changed their birthplaces and first names.

Unlike us, they did not possess a UGIF card, which still constituted a guarantee of safety. When they changed residence, believing that we were better protected, they left us a money box that contained gold pieces and securities. I decided to hide the money in one of the cushions of Françoise's baby carriage.

The situation was rapidly deteriorating in Limoges. Although Rabbi Deutsch carried a UGIF card, he was arrested during a roundup in November 1943. Julien immediately went over to the Gestapo to protest against this arrest, at the risk of getting himself arrested. He succeeded in winning his case, but we interpreted the incident as a warning.

PARIS: THE JEWS HUNTED DOWN

My sister José was the contact between Toulouse and Paris in a Resistance network formed by a group of friends. She received a small allowance that enabled her to live, and she had been given a bicycle, which, for her, was a real working tool. In

Paris she lived at the home of a friend, Monique Régnier, who used the rooms of the family maid to conceal English parachutists. Thanks to her friend's file in the registry office, she was able to obtain an identity card under the same name. There were therefore two Monique Régniers living in the same place, and they had to be careful not to go out at the same time. M. Régnier was perpetual secretary of the Académie française. When he learned of the arrest and deportation of the Jewish father of one of Monique's friends, he made a handsome gesture, at once naive and ridiculous: he lodged a complaint with the Ligue des droits de l'homme.[2]

My father received alarming news from what had once been the Northern Zone. Wearers of the yellow star were subjected to greater or lesser acts of persecution; prohibitions against driving, limitations on shopping hours in food stores, a strict curfew, all made it impossible to lead a normal life. And little by little, with panic spreading, people carried out even the most basic acts feeling sick at heart.

Thousands of households went so far as to deprive themselves of their monthly food rations because of the growing danger presented by the act of renewing applications for food coupons. Entire families were hiding among compassionate neighbors, in dark attics, or in remote towns and villages. Ill prepared for such an existence, the entire Jewish community gradually buried itself deeper and deeper into an underground existence.

The danger was everywhere, in the streets as in one's home. It threatened everybody, those who scrupulously followed the law as well as those who broke it. It was impossible to escape from it.

Those who were cut off from the news of the day were irreparably condemned. Their ignorance and their lack of contact with people who were better informed than they often proved to be fatal.

Several persons who were unusual in being in the know followed the fluctuations of antisemitic policies each day, thanks to pipelines established almost everywhere in the country and to the news that, in a roundabout way, continued to reach them from the rest of the world. They knew everything, or almost everything, about the fate reserved for the appalling deportation convoys, and they drew from this monstrous cataclysm the faith and energy with which to sustain their counteroffensives.

A generalized preventive action was clearly necessary in order to save those men, women, and children who were doomed solely because of their Jewish identity. For some time, teams had been operated in Paris to assist adults, rescue adolescents, and protect the children. Now it was necessary to imbue the majority with the will to defend itself, to instill a bit of optimism in the resigned and disspirited mass of people, to give them the courage, and the means, to operate in an illegality that they had once dreaded.

Clandestine actions were taken, some of which required financial help. Hence, numerous underground dens were set up for the forging of documents. Social workers, themselves operating under false identities, combed the cities and the countryside in search of shelters where those most in peril could be hidden.

And that's how we too became the victims of our excessive trust.

JANUARY 1944: THE ARREST OF MY FATHER

On 19 January 1944, while Julien was away, I saw through the window of the OSE office rationed food products being passed out. It was six o'clock; my work was almost over. As I descended the stairway, I passed my father and asked him to wait for me, to give me enough time to go shopping. We were going together to my place for dinner, where my mother was already waiting with Régine and Françoise. During the few minutes that I was absent, Miliciens and, it seemed, a member of the Gestapo in civilian dress entered the office and checked the papers of several persons there. Everyone except my father had a UGIF card. Pierre Dreyfus was there, with his card under the name of Dutertre; when he was asked, "Why are you working here for Jews?" he brazenly replied, "Because they pay well!" The Miliciens were looking for a Resistance member who, in the meantime, had arrived and who, noticing them, was able to get away. My father suffered the repercussions of their fury.

When he saw me return, he said to nobody in particular, "These are the gentlemen of the Gestapo." In a daze, I slowly walked over to my office, asked one of the Miliciens posted in front of the door that separated the two apartments to let me pass—I don't know what miracle led him to step aside without asking me any questions—I crossed an empty apartment and found myself on the stairway landing. I felt as if I had been pulled by a higher power; I had been thinking of Françoise. It was only when I found myself in the street that I began to tremble. However, I returned to the house to warn the members of another organization, which was located on the ground floor. Then, frightened to the core, I went over to our apartment.

My first reflex was to leave with my mother, Françoise, and Régine to stay with friends. I went over to the railway station in the evening to meet Julien. My father

111

had been arrested and incarcerated in the prison at Limoges. Before being taken away, he had succeeded in giving to Denise Vormus the money from the Joint earmarked for children's clothing. After being arrested, he was able to gain time before giving his true address. The Gestapo had emptied and sealed my parents' apartment.

My sister arrived in Limoges the next day, hoping to find the entire family around Françoise, whom she did not yet know. She learned the terrible news.

Julien's efforts to have the Gestapo release my father failed, as did the organization of an escape attempt. Nevertheless, Julien decided that we should reopen the office. We safely put up Françoise and Régine with our friends the Loingers, who lived in the countryside. Georges Loinger, in addition to his work with the OSE, was part of the network of Résistance combat [the oldest and best organized of the Resistance groups in southern France], but I was to learn about that only later.

My mother, too, left to take refuge in the neighboring countryside. We remained in Limoges during the entire period during which we were receiving news about my father. I was able to write to him, and I sent him a photo of Françoise with José, which meant that my sister was certainly there, that nothing had happened to us. My father was able to answer me.

When we learned that he had been transferred to Drancy, we decided, in agreement with the OSE directorate, to close the Limoges office. The situation had become too dangerous. Henceforth, all activities had to be done clandestinely.

When she was back in Paris, my sister tried the impossible: she got in touch with a woman who claimed to be able to get my father out of the camp of Drancy for twenty-five hundred francs, a considerable sum of money at that time. José collected the money from people around her, especially from Maurice Brennet at the Joint. We were certain we would be able to reimburse him in a short time. In a squalid coffeehouse she met the woman and slipped the money to her under the table. By the way the woman looked at her, my sister understood that she had lied and that she would do nothing; but the attempt had to be made, even if not much faith could be placed in it. José knew that our father, who was close to Jewish organizations, was aware of what was happening in the camps.

Without mentioning it to me, my sister also contacted Henriette Lutz, a friend from the *lycée* Fénelon, and brought her up to date on the situation. The Lutzes were Communists. Since the birth of their little girl, who was somewhat younger than Françoise, they had ceased working in the Resistance. Very moved by the arrest of my father, they did not hesitate to offer their papers to us: their marriage certificate and Henriette's birth and baptismal certificates (Claude was Protestant and Henriette was Catholic). A go-between transmitted them to us in Limoges. All we needed was to buy identical blank certificates commercially, glue our photos on them, and, thanks to the authentic documents in our possession, have them rubber-stamped in the Limoges city hall. My name therefore was Henriette Lutz; she was very close to me, and I had no difficulty in being called by her name. Julien became Claude Lutz and Françoise, Christine Lutz. Julien and I tried to call each other "darling" so as to avoid committing a blunder.

THE TIGHTENING OF THE SCREWS

The roundup at the children's home of La Verdière at Marseille took place in October 1943, followed by the deportation of the children and their director, Alice Salomon. This was followed by the arrest of my father in Limoges. On 8 February 1944, the Gestapo arrested the members of the Chambéry [OSE] office; this led Alain Mossé, formerly a high French official and director of the OSE at Chambéry, to assert that this was the end of the immunity conferred by the UGIF card. This fact was confirmed by the arrest of the members of the UGIF in Lyon. Fizer, who led children to Switzerland, was also arrested. The woman director of a children's home in Limoges received a letter from Fizer, sent from the camp of Drancy. The message, full of hints, urged the immediate scuttling of all the children's homes. Finally, two letters from Alain Mossé that arrived several days later brought out the gravity of the situation: they implied that the work of the OSE was well known to the German police.

Henceforth, the process of breaking up the homes had to be accelerated. The children who were still there under false identities had to be evacuated at once. The task was onerous, since each one of them had to be provided with identity papers and clothing. Departures took place in a heavy atmosphere filled with anxiety, for the railway stations were under the surveillance of the forces of law and order—the Milice and the Gestapo.

In general, the French people displayed a great deal of sympathy for the children, and many offered to take them into their homes. The approximately five hundred children still in the children's homes in February 1944 could quickly be dispersed across the territory by the Garel network, sent to Switzerland thanks to the relay station installed in Lyon by Jacques Salon, or placed in the homes of the Secours national or in convents.

In order to confuse the children's pursuers and to preserve the facilities of the children's homes, it was necessary to entrust these empty institutions to official organizations: Le Masgelier was placed at the disposal of the *préfecture* of Creuse, which sheltered other children there; Poulouzat and La Pouponnière became homes of the Amitié chrétienne; the château at Brout-Vernet became the house of Secours Quaker [Quaker Assistance]. The centers of Montintin and Chabannes were once again taken over by the Ministry of Labor at the beginning of the liberation of France in June 1944. The last homes were quickly closed. The *préfets* frequently agreed to requisition them to avoid arousing the Germans' suspicions.

Convoys to Switzerland increased in number, despite the increasing surveillance of the border. It was then that the OSE had Julien and me install a clandestine unit in Chambéry, the crossroads between Lyon and Switzerland.

MARCH–JUNE 1944: CHAMBÉRY

As we were making our way to Chambéry, we passed through Paris, where we found the Lutzes again. Despite the folly of this act, we lunched with our friends in a restaurant. We had their official papers; they left theirs at home. But they appeared to be at ease, and happy to be able to resist in their own way.

Once we arrived at Chambéry, we first got rid of all compromising documents and then settled down in a furnished apartment near the police station. We were the only occupants of the house. What had happened to the others? We didn't ask any questions. Julien was supposed to be an insurance agent, a profession he had practiced in Strasbourg. He had a labor contract from a company in Limoges, which was a valuable cover. He took the precaution of paying a visit to the pastor of Chambéry for the purpose of obtaining a baptismal certificate. He explained to him that he had been circumcised in his childhood for medical reasons and that he was afraid he would not be able to give proof of his religion should the need for verification ever arise. The pastor agreed to get into contact with the Protestant authorities (where the real Claude Lutz had been baptized by his grandfather) in order to obtain the document. Thanks to the Lutzes' papers, we felt ourselves protected from danger.

We were on active duty. Our job was to guarantee communication among the different persons in Lyon who organized the crossings into Switzerland. It was a strategic location because it was situated near the frontier, through which funds were being transferred. Our apartment served as a dropoff point for members of the organization, who sometimes slept at our place. Julien regularly went over to René Borel's apartment in Lyon, where clandestine meetings took place. The news from the eastern front was good, but the rumor was circulating that the Germans possessed a secret weapon.[3] Departures for Drancy were intensifying. We learned that my father had left for an unknown destination.

MARCH 1944: NELLY

At the beginning of the month of March, Nelly, Julien's sister, who lived at Raon-l'Étape [in Lorraine] was incarcerated with her husband and her three children. Because her husband had been a prisoner [of war] in Germany until then, she had been safe from roundups and even received the allocations given to prisoners' wives. It was upon his return that the whole family found itself imperiled: from being a prisoner who had come home thanks to the exchange,[4] he became a Jew and thus endangered his entire family.

I decided to help them, or at least to release the children, and I left for Paris and Écrouves [a village near Raon-l'Étape].

The trains were crammed; the trip was very long, I left my little girl of eight months in Chambéry. Passing through Paris, I found the city somber and poverty stricken. I felt a shock at the food counter at the Austerlitz railway station when I saw young woman holding a child in her arms: my child? The resemblance was disturbing. Every kind of tragic scenario possible flashed through my mind: kidnapping, arrest.

As soon as I arrived at Écrouves, I made contact with a social worker. She informed me that Nelly was pregnant and that she had refused to leave her children with neighbors at the time of the roundup. The woman, too, had offered to keep them, but Nelly did not want to be separated from them. She had no premonition of what was likely to happen, as is revealed by the letters she sent to her father at Gannat.

On 27 March 1944 she wrote:

> Here everything is fine, thank God, we are still happy to be here, but always fear what tomorrow has in store for us. . . . The building looks like the other one but has only one exit, and all the windows are barred. We use them for hanging our laundry. . . . We were compelled to keep our straw and straw mattresses, dirt and dust are everywhere, but everyone does the best she can, we have a very energetic room forewoman. There is naturally no shortage of discussions and disputes; 560 women of all ages and from all kinds of social classes are not made to get along, and the noise is deafening. We have an almost military regime here, and now they're taking the roll call several times a day. . . . The children are rather enjoying themselves with all these people and with other children, but it takes me forever to get them to sleep and eat on the ground. . . . Annie's instructor has promised a package that she and the students have prepared in common, it will undoubtedly arrive tomorrow. . . .

Despite my efforts, it was not possible to liberate the children, and I couldn't really know whether it was Nelly who refused to be separated from them or whether it was the doing of the camp administration. Her last letters, trying to reassure us, gave us a glimpse of both a growing fear and a total ignorance of what was to come. The very last one was very short, scribbled quickly, with fear and hope intertwined: "For two hours now we have been in the midst of being loaded onto cattle trains, whose destination is undoubtedly Drancy. Everything is fine. . . . The camp has fed us before the departure. Don't send any more packages. Thanks for the last one. Good-bye. See you soon. . . . Our morale is holding up. May God protect you."

APRIL 1944: LISON AND PAUL

This catastrophic event convinced Suzanne, Julien's older sister, to send her children to Switzerland. Lison and Paul left in April 1944 in a convoy led by Georges Loinger. This departure enabled us to really comprehend the anguish felt by the families that had entrusted their children to us.

As soon as Georges Loinger signaled his return to Chambéry, my job was to confirm to Julien, who had spent the day at the clandestine headquarters, that everything had gone well—through a coded telegram dropped off at the Lyon general delivery station. Julien calculated that my telegram would arrive around noon. Starting at noon, therefore, he went over to the post office every half hour—no telegram. Filled with anguish, he by chance met a woman friend whose child was part of the same convoy. She too had received no news of the border crossing, but her news was to have come from another source. During the trip bringing him back to Chambéry, Julien could not help imagining the worst. He thought of his sister's grief, of the children's misfortune, of our possible arrest. Who knew whether the children had given out our address, and whether the Germans had already taken away his wife, daughter, sister?

Seeing him come back so deadly pale, my sister-in-law and I froze with fear. Yet we had certainly seen Georges Loinger, and we had sent the telegram as agreed. We got the explanation later: because of an error in sorting, the telegram was at the post office but in a neighboring box.

APRIL 1944: A VISIT FROM THE GESTAPO

I had a miscarriage upon my return from the trip to Écrouves. I didn't know I was at the beginning of a pregnancy. Had I known, would I have exposed myself to such risks?

I was barely recovered when the Gestapo showed up at our place around six o'clock in the morning.

We were in the midst of Passover, but in spite of the Jewish holiday I had refused to buy *matzos* on the black market. We were the Lutzes and could not afford such a blunder. I don't dare imagine what would have happened had the Gestapo found packages of unleavened bread in our place.

We were still in bed when they rang at the door, so it was Régine who opened it. They didn't give her time to warn us and immediately entered our room. Françoise was seated on the bed. We got up quietly.

They immediately proceeded to an anatomical examination of Julien, who fortunately had a medical certificate that explained his circumcision. They likewise "examined" Françoise. They remained very correct, but I was totally shattered. I later cried over it out of sheer humiliation.

They showed us a notebook that carried our address, luckily without our name. They had arrested someone at the Swiss frontier and were trying to trace back the network by following up the list in his address book. Julien explained that we had not

117

been living here for a long time and that [the listing] had to refer to other tenants who had previously lived here. They searched the apartment, our suitcases. We had no compromising documents in the house except for food ration coupons to be distributed to children hidden in the region. Under the pretext of heating up a bottle for the baby, I went to the kitchen and burned everything in a wood stove. In the meantime, they interrogated Régine to learn whether I went to church—they had seen my baptismal certificate. She spontaneously gave the most intelligent answer one can possibly give: "Oh, not every Sunday, only on major holidays." With their permission, I sent her out to get some milk, asking her in a whisper to warn our friends. I thought she would take advantage of this [opportunity] to get away, but she came back, saying, "They would have suspected something."

They finally left and took our papers for verification. I prepared breakfast as if nothing had happened. We were seated around the table when they came back, threw our papers down, and left without saying a word. We had not moved throughout the visit. To flee would have been a sign that we had lied. They might even have been waiting for us downstairs. We knew that in such cases, one should above all not try to escape.

MAY 1944: THE ARREST OF JULIEN

Julien left for a clandestine meeting in Lyon on 8 May 1944. I had asked him to bring me back some cherries. I received a telegram that very evening—at that time I didn't try to figure out how it had been brought to me during the curfew.

The telegram said, "Claude seriously ill; take all precautions to avoid contagion." Julien, under the identity of Claude Lutz, had been arrested.

I immediately left with Françoise, Régine, and the cushion containing our money to stay with friends. At the time Julien was expected to return, I nevertheless went over to the railway station. Germaine Masour, whom Georges Garel had sent to forewarn me, was getting off the train.

She explained to me that when their secret meeting was over, Julien had accompanied Maurice Brenner, the representative of the Joint in Lyon. Both were worried about Jacques Salon's absence from the meeting. While pacing up and down on the Bellecourt bridge, Julien noticed Jacques on the opposite sidewalk; he yelled his name and crossed the street to join him and was immediately surrounded by Miliciens. Figuring out that Jacques had been made to walk around the city as bait, he pretended to have made an error. Jacques exclaimed, "But, sir, we don't know each other" several times. Julien was immediately subjected to an anatomical examination and, despite his medical certificate, was arrested with Jacques, even though no connection between them had been established.

Maurice Brenner kept on walking. It was he who had sent me the telegram. He was carrying a small suitcase containing a large amount of money destined for the network. If he too had been arrested, the consequences, for him as for his companions, would have been catastrophic.

Jacques and Julien were incarcerated in the Montluc prison, in the Jews' barrack. Jacques was interrogated and tortured, but he didn't say a word. The effects on him were permanent. Julien was not interrogated. I decided to leave for Lyon in order to make some efforts [on his behalf]. I asked the pastor who had helped us obtain Julien's baptismal certificate whether he could suggest a family likely to take in my little girl for some time. Françoise, who was not yet ten months old, cast such a spell on him (perhaps she felt that her life was at stake) that he offered, with the assent of his old nanny, to keep her at his place, with Régine to take care of her during my absence. I handed over the priceless cushion to Régine, explaining to her its contents, as well as food stamps she could use whenever she needed them.

As I was preparing all day for my departure, I was once more cheered up by the support given by all the people around me, so much so that I could leave my little girl without too much apprehension.

Upon my arrival in Lyon on 10 May 1944, I made contact with friends who worked in the Resistance. They made it possible for me to meet a guard at Montluc, an Austrian soldier. I prepared a package containing a sleeping bag, food, money, and a toilet kit with nail clippers. Thanks to the soldier's complicity, this package was in fact handed over to Julien. It was enough to let him know that Françoise and I were doing fine. Again, thanks to the soldier, I also received some news from Julien.

My attempts became crazier and bolder each day. I ended up going directly to the Gestapo, always to protest that "Claude" was not Jewish. Masour waited for me at the corner of the street to make sure that I would come out of it all right. I got the impression that the German soldier who received me thought that I was throwing myself into the lions' den. I was quickly sent away.

Not knowing what else to do, I decided to meet the pastor of Lyon with a letter of recommendation from the pastor of Chambéry, asking him to plead in our favor at Montluc. That pastor somewhat coldly listened to my explanation that there was an error, that my husband was not Jewish.

When I returned for another visit several days later, he received me in a rage and immediately said to me, "Madame, you've lied, you're a liar!" I later learned that while he had been dining out, a young man had innocently told him the circumstances of Julien's arrest and that Julien had passed himself off as someone else.

I didn't know whether the cause of his anger was the fact that Julien was Jewish or that I had lied to him. I didn't have the strength to probe more deeply into the matter. I got up and left.

I learned on 21 May that a convoy was going to leave for Paris, Drancy, and Compiègne and that Julien was part of it. I went over to the railway station, hoping to see him, even from afar.

The next day, I left with Pierre Dreyfus for Limoges in order to try to contact the insurance firm for which Julien had nominally been working. We arrived in the middle of the night, and Pierre lodged me at his place. Andrée Salomon called to find out whether we had arrived safely. She called back several moments later and joyously said to me these few words: "Vivette, you can eat cherries now." During my entire stay in Lyon, I had refused to eat cherries, which are found in profusion [there]. The meaning of this enthusiastic message was entirely clear to me.

The convoy that had taken Julien away had left Paris in the afternoon. Julien, Jacques Salon, and others who were in the same car decided to jump off the train during the night. The car was guarded at the two ends by German soldiers, who, after having eaten and drunk, ended up falling asleep. Thanks to the nail clippers I had sent Julien, his comrades and he were able to cut the seals on the windows. The train slowed down at the approaches to railway stations—it was later learned that this was the railway men's mode of resistance, which gave passengers the chance to escape *in extremis*. Julien was the last one to jump. The first thing that crossed his mind was that it was 21 May, my birthday; he preferred that his wife be a widow rather than the wife of a deported man, and he decided to jump when the train was nearing the station at Maisons-Alfort [about six miles from Paris]. As he fell, he dislocated his shoulder and found himself face to face with a French rail watchman who had received the order to shoot anything that moved. When challenged, Julien told the truth, and the watchman—by an incredible piece of luck—showed him the way and ordered him to be on his way. With his dislocated shoulder and without eyeglasses (they had broken during the fall), he left, groping his way to Maisons-Alfort, and finally found a physician, who set his shoulder, let him telephone my sister, and gave him a métro [subway] ticket for Paris.

Julien arrived in Paris dirty and in torn clothes, but it was early in the morning, and nobody paid any attention to him.

None of those who jumped off the train was killed. We later learned that the Germans, at the time of the roll call, acted as if nothing had happened. Being unable to catch the escapees red-handed, they preferred not to say anything.

Jacques Salon, who was taken in by the railway workers, took refuge with Dr. Minkowski. The mistreatment he had endured [from the Gestapo] had weakened him. He was secretly hospitalized in a clinic and stayed there until the liberation.

My sister went to Lyon to cheer me up and, not finding me there (I was at Limoges), she contacted Andrée Salomon.

I immediately left to meet Julien in Paris.

We were hoping to get back to Chambéry as quickly as possible, to obtain finally some news about Françoise, but first we had to get eyeglasses made for Julien and new identity papers. We lived in an abandoned apartment, with closed shutters and the lights turned off, to avoid being spotted. We were unable to live in the apartment in the Latin Quarter, for which my parents had continued to pay rent until 1943, when they had been given notice that it was vacant and requisitioned. Blackouts were frequent. Paris seemed dirty and cheerless to me. This stay, which in reality lasted only a week, seemed interminable.

We finally left, only to learn when we arrived at the Chambéry railroad station that the city had been bombed. I was terribly distressed. I ran all the way to the pastor's home. The house was intact. During the air raid alert, they had all taken refuge in a shelter. Régine even had had the presence of mind to bring the famous cushion with her—that's what the pastor told me. Still shaking, I entered the room where Régine was taking a nap. Françoise was standing in her little bed; seeing me, she turned her head away and refused to recognize me.

From then on we felt ourselves to be in too much danger to continue our work as usual. In agreement with the OSE, we prepared to cross into Switzerland. Our departure was set for 6 June 1944. We were waiting at Valence [a town about 180 miles from the Swiss border] when, very early that morning, Robby Epstein, who belonged to the Garel network, broke the news of the landing in Normandy [the Allied D-Day invasion, which led to the liberation of France and, eventually, the rest of Nazi-occupied western Europe].

We then decided not to leave.

8

Coming Out of the War

The landing of the Allies in Normandy was followed by a long period of waiting—waiting for the liberation, waiting for news from the front, for the end of the war, for the return of prisoners and deportees.

We prudently kept our identity papers in the name of Lutz and remained on our guard with our neighbors; but everything had changed; we felt ourselves reintegrated into the French community and ready to share its destiny. We congratulated ourselves for not having left for Switzerland. It was in France that we wanted to live this last struggle for freedom.

We then found refuge among the peasants in Saint-Innocent, a little village on the banks of the lake [Bourget] above Aix-les-Bains. The house was located near a church, and the priest came over to welcome us. We declared ourselves refugees without being specific about it. I went to mass on Sundays. We felt ourselves secure and took advantage of this period of respite. We often went to the lake with Régine and Françoise; German soldiers swimming there didn't think of bothering us. The war was coming to an end. A German victory was no longer conceivable.

It wasn't easy for us to get news from the outside. During the month of August, we saw German tanks leaving the area on the highway lower down in the village. They were evacuating the region without offering any resistance, but the war was not over for all that. Battles continued to rage in the Vercors.[1]

Julien and I went over to Aix-les-Bains on 21 August. French flags were unfurled there. A jubilant crowd was singing, crying, embracing one another; it was an explosion of happiness. Had these people on the street been collaborators in the past, or had they been members of the Resistance? No matter, it was an extraordinary day; it was better not to ask too many questions. Several days later, Americans arrived in jeeps, vehicles we had never seen before.[2]

The press and the radio were free again. I could hardly stand the various settlings of scores, the denunciations that ominously recalled the opening days of the Occupation. Women suspected of having had [sexual] relations with Germans had their heads shaved in public and were exhibited in the street. I found this intolerable and was angry at myself for not having intervened.

Meanwhile, my sister, José, who was later decorated with the Military Cross, worked in a Resistance network in Paris. The news of the liberation of the capital reached us on 25 August. General de Gaulle was walking down the Champs-Elysées. We left Saint-Innocent for Aix-les-Bains.

It was at that time that we learned through Georges Loinger and Emmanuel Racine of the last drama of the underground network: the death of Marianne Cohen, a young member of the Jewish Scouts, who had been arrested with a group of children she was ready to lead secretly into Switzerland, and the arrest and deportation of Mila Racine, several days before the liberation of Annemasse. A group of very young children had left the Grenoble railway station under her escort. The trip itself had taken place without mishap. Having gotten off before reaching Annemasse, the children were amusing themselves singing on the road when a truck full of German soldiers stopped. The soldiers questioned the convoy leader about the children's destination and offered to take them there. Marianne had given as the address the nearest house of the Secours national [National Aid Society], all the while knowing that no group like hers had ever stopped at this house. Yet she hoped to find there a welcome at once cooperative and understanding. That was not to be the case. When the truck arrived there, the director, for unknown reasons (misunderstanding? cowardice?), declared that she was not expecting anyone. The result: interrogation and search. They found in the lining of the clothing the authentic documents needed by the children for residence in Switzerland. They were arrested and locked up. Marianne Cohen, afraid that the children would be subjected to reprisals, turned down the opportunity to escape offered her by Emmanuel Racine and by the mayor, Jean Deffaugt. Her body, horribly mutilated, was found in an open grave after the liberation of the city at the end of August. The children had been saved.

SEPTEMBER 1944: COMING OUT OF THE UNDERGROUND

Aix was liberated, but the war was still going on. Battles were raging on the Russian front and Germany, although bombed, was not surrendering; fighting went on in eastern France. Food shortages continued. We still needed food coupons, a situation that was not to end for some time. Women obtained on the black market parachute material out of which to make clothing. The Americans were passing out chocolate, cigarettes, chewing gum, cans of corned beef, and durable nylon stockings. New romances were blossoming.

When we went to collect our mail at the Chambéry post office, we were surprised to hear the postwoman, whom we didn't know, call us over. It was she who had received Maurice Brenner's telegram informing us of Julien's arrest and who, despite the curfew, had had it carried over at eight o'clock in the evening, wisely guessing the urgency of the message. She seemed happy to see Julien.

We paid a visit to the pastor who had sheltered Françoise and Régine, and we told him the truth. He confessed to having been distrustful of our statements until he received Claude's baptismal certificate.

The Jewish refugees were little by little leaving their hiding places. It was difficult to reestablish various means of communication. It was still necessary to have a special license in order to drive. The different members of the OSE renewed their mutual contacts. The city of Lyon became a rallying center; contact was also resumed with the Union-OSE in Geneva. Dr. Joseph Weill was not long in getting back to France. The OSE had to be able to function as quickly as possible.

The members of the OSE directorate met in Lyon on 25 September 1944. The first decision they agreed upon was the rapid opening of the main office in Paris. The presidency was returned to Dr. Eugène Minkoswki.[3] The structures of the association were laid out along two main axes: the medicosocial service, headed by Julien Samuel, who was to establish medicosocial branches throughout France; and the children's service, under the direction of Robert Job, whose main task was the reopening of the children's homes and the reception of dispersed children.

Andrée Salomon was given responsibility for renewing contact with the hidden children, and Germaine Masour that of creating a department for the reunion of families and emigration.

As for me, the OSE, and the Comité d'aide aux réfugiés [Committee for Aid to Refugees] from the beginning of September on, gave me the job of organizing at

Chambéry an emergency service for the Jewish refugees of the region. A local building with a telephone was quickly set up so that I could be on call. I was asked to act pragmatically, to respond to the most urgent needs: to help older persons and single women find homes.

Small centers were opening up all over the place. Adults found themselves in an extremely precarious situation in terms of material goods. In poor health, often penniless, and unable to return home, they were looking for the scattered members of their families, who had barely come out of their hiding places. At the Chambéry office, one had to be able to respond quickly, to improvise, without any directive other than that to "do the impossible." I was lucky to be backed up by Adeline Barsky, a school friend, who several years later was to marry Pierre Dreyfus, who had succeeded me in Limoges.

I worked long days; the task was immense. Before leaving in the morning, I took care of my little daughter, whom I then entrusted to Régine when I boarded the train to Chambéry. I came home late in the evening. I had no time to inform myself about events taking place elsewhere. I didn't read the newspapers. I didn't see the latest news in the movie houses.[4]

I was pregnant again. I was happy about it, we were living during the liberation of France, but I was afraid I would suffer another miscarriage because of my working conditions.

A team of social workers was set up to search for children hidden with foster families and in institutions throughout the region. The children's homes, which had been requisitioned in March 1944, were returned to the OSE. The first to be turned over were those at Montintin and Le Masgelier, then those in [the *département* of] Haute-Savoie. They were empty; the sanitary facilities had to be reinstalled. Furniture was provided by the Ministry of Prisoners, Deportees, and Refugees, clothing and bedding by the Joint. The children had to be taken back to school at the beginning of the academic year in October. Children who had remained on French territory were given priority in the distribution of placements in the homes, since the children who had moved to Switzerland were generally living in better conditions. The homes became overcrowded in no time at all.

The Joint gave considerable support on matters concerning the crucial problem of food supplies by providing us with basic products. The number of homes rapidly exceeded twenty. Robert Job hoped to substitute the notion of solidarity for that of philanthropy, which was current before the war, and the children's homes were no longer to be called orphanages. They no longer were seen as a definitive solution: they were only a stage before adoption or emigration.

FINDING THE CHILDREN

The reopening of the frontier with Switzerland enabled us to work in close cooperation with the Union-OSE of Geneva, whose task it was to answer requests from all over the world about the location of children. It was possible to carry out this work because first the directorate of Montpellier, then the clandestine network never ceased sending to Switzerland coded lists of hidden children, documents, identity lists,[5] and dossiers that included addresses of their relatives abroad.

A central list, carefully kept up to date, comprised all sorts of information on the hidden children. It was held in Geneva and counted more than four thousand dossiers, yet it was deemed incomplete. More than one thousand of these dossiers dealt with children who had been able to cross secretly into Switzerland and had been placed in children's homes, families, or apprenticeship centers (for adolescents). It also contained more than one thousand dossiers about children hidden in France. Apparently, nearly six thousand other dossiers had been safely stored in France, but, to my knowledge, they have never been found. Starting in January 1945, however, the OSE had re-created the itineraries of the children in its care.

Judith Hemmendiger-Feist, a young social worker who worked alongside Olga Guric at the Union-OSE of Geneva, commented that she had to record as much information as possible and also, whenever she could, to take photographs of the fifteen hundred children sheltered in Switzerland so that they could be claimed by their parents or other relatives as soon as possible. "Later," she added, "we were inundated with letters from parents coming out of hiding and looking for their children. We read each letter attentively, went through our dossiers, and when the puzzle was solved, what happiness, what emotion!"[6] Some children only knew their first names, and sometimes their native town, and we then had to conduct a veritable investigation among the people of the region. It was a matter of finding thousands of children concealed in religious institutions and with private persons, especially in the Southern Zone.

MY RETURN TO PARIS

Work at the OSE-CAR office of Chambéry came to an end in February 1945. Julien's presence had become indispensable at the main OSE office in Paris, since he traveled a great deal across the country setting up its medicosocial teams. We settled down temporarily in the apartment of an officer's wife in the rue René-Bazin, in the sixteenth *arrondissement*, an apartment that we promised to give back to her as soon as her husband, a member of the Resistance who had been deported to [the concentration camp of] Buchenwald, returned. The apartment was comfortable, but I didn't feel at ease there; everything had remained just as he had left it: clothing, mail, books. I seemed to be intruding on the intimacy of these people. I felt as if I were unwittingly prying. The birth of my second child was drawing near.

Régine did not follow us to Paris. She was entrusted to L'Hirondelle, a children's home of the OSE near Lyon. The directors of that home were none other than Nathan, Julien's brother, and his wife, Hélène. Régine was glad to be able to resume her studies, while remaining somehow part of the Samuel family. We often went to see them. Régine and Françoise always appeared to be very attached to each other.

Nathan and Hélène Samuel had spent the war at Lanteuil, a small village near Périgueux.[7] They had been miraculously spared. They decided after the war to devote themselves to the children of the OSE, whom they treated as their own. Later, when we went to see them in the home they directed at Haguenau, near Strasbourg, five-year-old Françoise, who deeply sensed the incredible love they were able to give to each person, said words that rang so true: "Mom has only three children, but Hélène has a hundred!"

On 1 January 1945, 750 children from three to eighteen years of age were regrouped into eleven homes. The OSE entrusted the organization and establishment of a home for little children to twenty-year-old Jacqueline Lévy, formerly a kindergarten teacher at Rivesaltes, on the basis of the admirable report she had submitted on these children's requirements.

During this period of reconstruction, in an atmosphere of great fraternity and relentless labor, we alternated between anguish for those who had disappeared and happiness for those who had been found.

My mother lived in a village in the Creuse. She had been there since my father's arrest, taking with her only a small amount of money, her identity card in the name of Raymonde (instead of Rachel), and a toilet kit. In the winter, she suffered from the cold in a shack open to all kinds of weather. She went into the forest every day to gather dead wood for her stove. A vegetarian, she ate mainly apples and some potatoes. On Saturdays, she went with a knapsack into the surrounding villages, walking for hours to get eggs, Gruyère cheese, onions—rich in vitamins, she said, and quite scarce. She didn't want to go back to Paris; she was waiting for the return of my father.

Moreover, our Paris apartment, whose rent my father had paid until 1943, was still occupied by refugees from the north. It took protracted legal proceedings before my mother could recover it in 1955. My sister, settled in Paris, passed her *baccalauréat.* She enrolled in medical school.

On 10 April 1945, our son was born. We called him Jean-Pierre, and Julien nicknamed him "the little prince."

We had to deal with the question of circumcision. At first I was set against it, still branded by the memory of "anatomical inspections," by the humiliation I had felt during the search of our apartment in Chambéry. But I also thought that the continuity of tradition should not be broken. Dr. Henri Nerson, my obstetrician, finally performed the operation in our Paris apartment. Françoise, like a big sister, welcomed the baby with great delight from the great height of eighteen months.

We closely followed events around the world, which followed one another in rapid succession. On Saturday, 11 April 1945, came the announcement of the death of President Roosevelt. "Deep Mourning for the Civilized World" was the headline in the new newspapers that had appeared since the liberation. On 28 April, it was the summary execution of Mussolini. One could read on the first page of the 28 April issue of *Le Monde:* "Hitler is dead, Admiral Doenitz, who succeeds him, wants 'to pursue the struggle against Bolshevism.'" We learned from the London radio that, after Hitler's suicide, Admiral Doenitz had ordered the unconditional surrender of all German forces. Yet the war with Japan continued. The American atomic bomb was dropped on Hiroshima on 6 August. Japan surrendered. The war was coming to an end. Then there began the trial of the "collaborators" and the wait for the return of the deportees.

WE WILL HAVE TO LIVE WITHOUT THEM

We waited for the return of our father. For months, I kept seeing him miraculously emerge from the exits of the Paris métro. But we were quickly given accurate information on his fate by a young man who had been held in the same prison in Limoges and then deported with him to Auschwitz. Guy Kohen, who had been twenty years old at the time of his arrest, wrote the following in a June 1945 article.

There was already a man in the room [the cell into which he was led on 1 February 1944]. Small in height, curly hair, lively eyes, a straight and firm nose, an attractive mouth, the lips well shaped as if drawn with a brush, he looked at me suspiciously. For my part, I observed him rather distrustfully. Anything could be expected from the Germans. Besides, I was in an awful state: my pants in tatters, my swollen face adorned with a black eye, one of my eyeglass lenses broken, all gave me the look of a hydrocephalic Silenius,[8] who had fallen down after many a copious libation. For fifteen minutes, we observed each other without speaking.

M. Hermann was the first to break the silence: he asked me my name, where and why I had been arrested; he certainly could tell by my answers that I was not a "fink"; from that moment on he confided in me, and we became good, true friends, brothers, it can even be said.

It was a great joy for both of us to be able to converse at length after the terrible, lugubriously silent days and the terrifying nights, when the heart beats more quickly at the slightest sound, when the jailor's boots startle you out of your sleep. Courage returns with a comrade, the beast is silent, man revives.

M. Hermann and I remained for several days in a complete intimacy; he told me about his life with an abundance of details by which he tried to demonstrate the confidence he placed in me. I was young but was nevertheless able to appreciate the value of the infinite culture of that man of unlimited knowledge, his subdued but solid philosophy, his pluck, and especially his heart. How many times, when evening came and dusk prompted us to a melancholy awareness of the coming of the night, our enemy, did we feel a bitter tear drop from our eyelashes; and this tear, we drank it, with passion, for it represented our loves, everything that mattered to us, our past. Were we not already among the living dead?

He spoke to me of his wife, his daughters, his son-in-law, of Jewish children hidden all over the place, fugitives he had helped cross into Switzerland, the secret meetings he had held, and so many things dear to him. I looked at this man and admired him.

More than anyone else, he knew that we were going to be deported. He knew the meaning of the word "Drancy," the hinge leading toward our final destination; but no one raised our morale better than he did. When we were seven in the cell that he had once occupied alone, I can say that he cut the figure of a patriarch and that we worshiped him (the word is not too strong), and we respected him as much as the Hebrews had adored and worshiped Moses. He was a great idealist, powerful and sincere; he had fought all his life for the Zionist cause; he preached the good word up to his very

130

last breath; one shared or did not share his views, but it was impossible not to be stirred by the faith that inspired this prophet of modern times.

We never became separated from each other; facing each other, we left for Drancy; next to each other, we slept in that camp; in the same wagon, always side by side, we were deported. We became separated only on the morning of 10 March, the date of our arrival in Auschwitz. I left for the slow death; he, for the quick death.[9] We might have been able to find each other again; God did not will it.

Dear M. Hermann, you who taught me so many things, from all points of view, you who were the most human of men, they killed you, as they killed millions of innocent people; but what they were not able to do, what they would never have been able to kill, is your beautiful soul, the memory that you left with us. I was the last living person to have shaken your hand, and it is for this reason that I say to you, "M. Hermann, sleep in peace. Justice has been done."

Paradoxical as it may seem, I was relieved to learn that my father had not literally entered the camp, that he, the most refined of humanists, did not live that long calvary. He was led to the gas chambers immediately upon his arrival at Auschwitz.

His name is entered in the *Mémorial de la déportation des Juifs de France* [Memorial of the Deportation of the Jews of France][10] under the name of Noël Hermann, deported from Drancy in convoy 59 of 7 March 1944.

We likewise learned that Nelly, who was pregnant, and her three children were directly led to the gas chamber on their arrival in Auschwitz and that her husband, Elie, survived only a few months before dying from exhaustion. They had been deported on 13 April 1944, in convoy 71. Annie was eight years old, Bernard six, and Jean seven. Except for Nelly's last letters, there remain for me and our children who have not known them two pages devoted to them in the *Mémorial des enfants*[11] and two photos.

As for my mother's younger brother, Isaac Spirt, it was only many years afterward that I learned the circumstances of his arrest and deportation by convoy on 6 November 1942.

THE SITUATION OF THE CHILDREN AFTER THE WAR

I often went to the main office of the OSE in the rue Spontini: the welcome there was as warm as ever. I thus participated in its immense activity. Everything had to be rebuilt. They were short of personnel, their needs were enormous, but the immediate future was secure, thanks to the technical and financial aid of the Joint.

A few numbers illustrate the situation of the Jewish children after the war.

- 11,600 Jewish children in France had been deported, all of whom perished in the camps, but 72,400 under eighteen years of age survived.
- About 62,000 were able to stay with their parents or were directly entrusted by them to institutions or to non-Jewish families.
- It was possible to save between 8,000 and 10,000 children, generally of foreign origin, thanks to Jewish organizations that helped them to emigrate overseas, to cross into Switzerland or Spain, or to be entrusted through the intervention of clandestine networks to non-Jewish families or institutions (convents, secular institutions).[12]

Although we didn't have any statistics on this point, it must be assumed that it was easier for families born in France or of French culture to shelter their children, provided that they were aware in time of the danger of "being born Jewish." It was the children of foreign families that the OSE had to take charge of and hide.

After the liberation, the OSE had no difficulty in getting back the children it had painstakingly placed in the Southern Zone. Nevertheless, some children were not ready for a new separation, since they had become attached to their foster families. They felt at home; the love of the foster families, which were often aware of their true identities, as well as the friendship of their schoolteachers and comrades, had accelerated their integration into their new lives. The social worker had said to them at the time of their placement: "Here is your new identity. For the time being you must forget the rest, and don't commit any rash acts, don't speak too much about yourself." And now they were told that they were Jewish, that they had the right to be Jewish and to live as Jews. This new separation was especially distressing to the youngest children; it was another emotional laceration just as they had found a new serenity.

Did we care enough not to traumatize the children again, especially the youngest ones, who had been placed in families that they had emotionally adopted and that hoped to keep them? When the mutual attachment was strong and the parents had not returned from deportation, we carefully studied each case to determine what was in the child's best interest, keeping in mind the parents' expressed wish to have their children raised in a Jewish setting. In some instances, we were able to keep the child in the foster family under the responsibility of the OSE and with the assurance that the child's identity would be preserved.

Of course, whenever one of the parents returned, that parent obviously recovered his or her rights to the child—but that was not always without difficulty. Separation and the ordeals that had been experienced often aggravated the conflicts that can exist even in "normal" families. The children didn't always receive the protection they had the right to expect from their parents, who often either maintained a stubborn silence about their repressed memories or made smothering emotional demands on their children, such as the need they felt to have their suffering recognized. The situation was not improved when orphans were adopted by an uncle or aunt and lived with cousins who had their "real" parents. Rightly or wrongly, the orphans felt a difference in the way the children were treated.

Paradoxically, it was possible for children raised in institutions to find differentiated, often beneficial, role models—thanks to their being surrounded by teachers of diverse political or religious allegiance, thanks to the friendship of their peers, and also thanks to the efforts made to give them the greatest opportunity possible on the material, educational, and moral planes. They shared the same past as the other children of the institution and adapted to that environment better than to families that had sheltered other children. In time, they managed to overcome their traumatic pasts.

There was also the problem of the children who had been placed in convents. Some of them were tempted to convert and even had themselves baptized. Certainly, they had been saved, and that was the essential thing. But what was one to do with the promise made to parents to raise their children as Jews? At that time, we felt obligated to keep that promise.

THE ADMINISTRATIVE IMBROGLIO

Colloquia at the OSE brought all of its personnel together. People spoke their minds freely at these meetings, and the debates illustrated the complexity of the new problems that had arisen, notably in the administrative areas. Andrée Salomon summarized them as follows: "If we were able to focus our work and effectuate the liberation of children from Rivesaltes, it is because we had the sympathy of certain administrators, the connivance of others, and the internal strength of a will that knows where it is going and where it must go—the liberation of the child. The return of peace and order brought back administrative nuisances that became intolerable."

In fact, the Emigration Service grappled with numerous complications. Affidavits had arrived from the United States confirming American relatives' desire to become the legal guardians of orphaned children, but these children of vanished parents had no legal guardian to sign the permits that would allow them to leave French territory. We had to wait for the new legislation of April 1945 dealing with the guardianship of the deportees' children. The new clauses of the law provided that the children of vanished deportees were to be entrusted to charitable societies. The OSE was then deemed to be their actual guardian, but only when a family council had been formed and a temporary guardian designated under the auspices of the Office national des pupilles de la nation [National Office of the Wards of the Nation].

The children's situation could be legalized only if proof of their identity was presented and if the dossiers first established in 1941 were brought up to date. The new dossiers had to show the date of the parents' deportation, and that date would later be accepted as the date of their death.

To obtain the restitution of property or the allocation of an allowance to which the children of German nationals who had been deported from France were entitled, recovery documents had to be provided as quickly as possible. Annelise Eisenstadt, the person in charge of that section of the dossiers, worked with the judicial service run by Else Schönberg.[13] They kept up a regular correspondence with the services in Berlin and Düsseldorf and presented the necessary arguments, case by case, for the children of Germans to recover the property taken from their parents. Paradoxically, French nationals were in a less favorable position, since the money destined for the victims of Nazism was paid by Germany to the [French] state and distributed very parsimoniously.

As for the children's addresses, if administrators needed one, the legal residence was deemed to be the last residence of the parents before their deportation. Should that address be unknown, however, children could use as their address their residence with the OSE.

Given the endless dispersals they had endured, we all took to heart the task of reuniting the children and their families, however far removed. But when the child's welfare was at stake, we had to make extensive inquiries in order to be certain that the conditions of his adoption were satisfactory.

TO REUNITE THE FAMILIES, EVEN OVERSEAS

Whenever possible, we generally encouraged the regroupings of families overseas. But difficulties arose once a decision had been taken on emigration. The immigration quotas implemented by the United States in 1890, which were rather large with respect to Englishmen and Frenchmen, were very restrictive for the natives of central and eastern Europe.[14] The problem was compounded—especially when the nationality of the children was unknown—by the variety of dossiers that had to be filled out for each child and the limited number of places available on the ships.

In November 1945, Germaine Masour and Georges Garel called on the United States consulate, requesting thirteen visas for boys who had returned from Buchenwald. Uncles and aunts were waiting for them overseas. But the consul's answer was: "We must first bring back American veterans, then we must take in the women they married in France, and only then can we think about the immigration of foreigners."[15]

The first visas did not arrive until the summer of 1946. Several ships departed for Palestine, where numerous youngsters intended to emigrate. Some countries also agreed to take in children who had lost their families, such as Canada, which welcomed a thousand children at a shelter before placing them with Jewish families. Australia took in about a hundred children, and South Africa children under the age of twelve.

The OSE was busy following up on the children who had emigrated. It remained in contact with those who had secretly left for Palestine in 1944 by the intermediary of the Agence juive [Jewish Agency]. On the other hand, it was more difficult to maintain links with the United States, for the Americans thought that the children they had taken charge of should forget their painful past and begin life anew in the United States. They thought they would be able to obtain quick results if the children agreed to cut off all contact with those who had previously played a part in their lives. Doctor Ernst Papanek, who had tracked the children in Paris and who was prevented from seeing them again in the United States, did not share this view.

> We were convinced that our former wards would be incapable of forgetting what had happened to them. How was it possible to build a new future for them and to obtain their confidence without a positive approach to the past? Is it possible to erase from their minds the guilty conscience that plagues them? Had they not abandoned those they loved to an uncertain and threatening fate? How is it possible not to feel sinful for having survived when so many others had been exterminated? The children consid-

ered us part of their past. By breaking all contact with us, did not one run the risk of having them believe that they had been rejected once again?[16]

The OSE directorate was unable to make itself heard and would be able to renew its links with these children only after many years and only upon the children's request.

THE CHILDREN OF THE CONCENTRATION CAMPS

In the camp of Buchenwald, the Americans discovered about a thousand Jewish children, boys from Poland and Hungary, collected in Barrack 66. These children had originally come from ghettoes, from which they had been deported to different camps and then regrouped in Buchenwald. Since they were without families when the camp was liberated, they could not and would not return to their country. Negotiations were then undertaken with western countries. Great Britain agreed to accept 270 of them, Switzerland 250, and France 480. The Ministry of Health and the Ministry of Foreign Affairs [in France] commandeered the *départemental* observation sanitarium of Écouis in [the *département* of] Eure and entrusted 427 boys to the OSE.

These youngsters' distress was immense, and the problems confronting the counselors/teachers were innumerable. Elie Wiesel[17] has evoked the difficult relations that sometimes existed between the "children," some of whom were eighteen years old, and their teachers: "Poor counselors! Do they think they can educate us, we who have been face to face with death? We know more about it than they do. . . . The youngest of us have undergone a much greater experience than the oldest of them has. . . . We feel sorry for them. . . . Poor fellows, they don't know." These youngsters formed their own community, with its leaders and cliques. Their slogan was, "Nothing to be done as at Buchenwald." Thus, they refused to allow portions of bread to be distributed to each person, a practice that reminded them of the hateful "bread ration;" it had to be placed in the center of the table. That, [however], did not prevent them from carefully stuffing pieces of bread in their pockets. A feeling of suspicion predominated. Ernest Jouhy, head of the teaching staff, gave examples of it:

> When they were served Camembert for the first time, a cheese they had never tasted before, they immediately claimed that we were serving them rotten food that the

136

French had thrown away. When a telegram that had been sent—thanks to us—to an uncle in America or to a relative in Australia did not bring an answer within a week, the teachers were accused of having stolen it. When long-awaited clothing did not arrive in the expected time, there was only one explanation for it: the OSE was trafficking in the goods sent to them by the Americans.[18]

They had difficulty in speaking of the past and generally preferred to hold long discussions on the future: learning a job or studying in school? leaving or staying? The great majority of them dreamed of emigrating to Palestine.

Obviously, the youngsters desperately tried to find a relative, even one from far away. The information was generally sketchy: a name, a location. People who remembered an entire address were uncommon. One of the children gave the very complicated address of his uncle; while he had been in detention, he had daily repeated it in order not to forget it. More frequently, alas, the children had only remembered scraps of information. But, thanks to lost-and-found notices circulated in the press and to the work of associations throughout the world, one child out of two found the relative he was looking for.

THE OSE CHILDREN

In 1946 Andrée Salomon announced that several thousand children remained under the responsibility of the OSE. They should be considered, she said, "as our own children," whose well-being and education we had to provide for and whose futures we had to envisage. We had to give them a renewed confidence in life.

Yet the OSE was worried that it did not have the necessary human and financial resources to pursue this work for a number of years. It gave priority to all possible solutions for providing the children with a stable future. Each dossier was studied minutely, and Andrée Salomon appealed to the instructors and social workers close to the child to help him envision his best future prospects, while taking account of his personal aspirations.

The OSE faced numerous requests for adoption. It had to examine carefully the possibility of giving the children new homes, while taking into account the obstacles and difficulties that were likely to arise. For a while sponsored children were in a privileged position. They stayed with the OSE but received the moral and financial support of persons or families that took them from time to time into their homes.

Yet this solution soon proved unsatisfactory to the children. They didn't feel at home with a family that was not their own and whose standard of living, sometimes very comfortable, contrasted too sharply with their lives in a collective.

The group "The Friends of the OSE," then in the process of being formed, was urged to attend more to the children's homes than to individual sponsorships.

Health and safety took precedence in the children's homes. The children returned to school, and the teachers were kept busy day and night. The children had choral singing, Jewish instruction, gymnastics, intensive special courses, picnics in the countryside. Georges Loinger set up the club "Sport et Joie" and organized training courses in physical education. He supervised all the sporting activities and events of the OSE and the EIF. As for Jacques Cohn, in charge of pedagogy in the children's homes, he had organized correspondence courses for the adolescents of the Limoges region during the dark days of the Occupation. A man of unusual kindness, he was totally devoted to the children and adolescents, with whom he established deep individual relationships. Once he had finished his mission, he left with his young wife, Margot, one of the prettiest young women in our group, to settle in Israel after the foundation of the Jewish state. There he busied himself with immigrant children in the *aliyah* [the emigration of Jews to Israel].

A new difficulty arose, which was the delicate one of knowing how to take the place of the family for the children in these homes. Joseph Weill later said, "Truthfully, we were not at all prepared for it. The problem was that there existed no qualified personnel at that time, and the children were frail, without much enthusiasm, unstable." From 1945 on, Ernest Jouhy kept declaring, "We need professionals." The profession of pedagogy did not yet exist, so that it was often unemployed young people without any competence or genuine motivation who spent some time at the OSE. From 1946 on, most of these improvised professionals found work, or emigrated, or rejoined their families, which needed manpower to start up a business.

Finally, people showed up whom Jacques Cohn called the "idealists," young persons from different backgrounds, not necessarily Jewish, with a calling for teaching. They sometimes came from foreign countries (the United States, Switzerland, Palestine), spent a year in France, and thus learned their job. Jacques Cohn explained that, for these young instructors, work was a "ministry." As difficult as it might have been, they had to "hold on because it concerned the future of all our young people. It was essential for the children that the structure of their lives be stable, that it constitute a dependable and reassuring landmark, and that there be

138

no large turnover of teachers." The OSE also tried to train professionals, notably women kindergarten teachers. Several young women under its charge, who had been hidden during the war, pursued such a training.

A constant worry that persisted in varying degrees throughout these years was how to enable these children to keep contact with the Judaism of their birth. The children, who had been required to keep their affiliation secret, often had great difficulty in the postwar years understanding the importance of tradition and apprenticeship. But it was also a matter of their perpetuating the teaching and religious practice of their parents. The children's homes overall encouraged the study of biblical texts and the celebration of certain holidays, without, however, making it compulsory for those who were reluctant to participate. Certain homes were particularly religious and took in those children who wanted to resume orthodox practice.

"THE IDEA OF GOD IN MALEBRANCHE"

Once again the support of our friends came to the aid of Julien and me. Dika Jefroykin lent us a splendid property in the Oise [a *département* directly north of Paris], where we settled down in the summer of 1945, after having returned the apartment in the rue Bazin to its owner.

In September we rented a furnished house at Chatou [ten miles west of Paris] from a young woman whose parents had not returned from deportation. She had just married the son of the family that had concealed her during the war. The garden of that house, our first house, was to be a haven of peace for us, the "paradise" of Françoise and Jean-Pierre and later Nicole, who was born in February 1948.

I was a "housewife" at Chatou. Life was very hard materially. Food rationing was still in effect and was to last for many more years. For heating, we had at our disposal only a small Godin stove in the living room and for fuel, only coal pellets. The children were bathed near the stove. A wash of diapers was boiling all day long in the garden. It was difficult for us to live on a single salary, but there was no question of my resuming work. A young Alsatian woman was helping me.

Bô Cohn, as he was familiarly known in accordance with the example set by the children, suggested to me over a period of two years that I organize an accelerated preparatory program at Chatou for the *baccalauréat* in French and philosophy. I therefore reconnected after five years of war with my first vocation, teaching. These work sessions in the garden were a return to normal life for those adolescents as they were for me. French was a foreign language for several of them, but they had such a thirst for learning, for making up for lost time, that the speed of their progress was impressive. Several of them subsequently went on to study at the university.

I was no longer attracted to philosophy. What did the idea of God in Male-branche[19]—the subject of my last report at the Sorbonne—matter to me? It was so-cial action that interested me, but I noticed that, despite my experience, my train-ing was incomplete. I decided to prepare myself for the state diploma in social work. My university degrees and fieldwork enabled me to benefit from an accelerated pro-gram and to obtain my diploma in a short time.

I thus had to get up at five in the morning, leave my little Nicole at home, then take the first train to Saint-Germain-en-Laye [about three miles from Chatou], where I did my internship, to give the first baths to the babies of the maternity hospital.

The courses I taught to adolescents permitted me to have meaningful discussions with them. Germaine Masour and Georges Garel, who were leaving for the United States on a fund-raising campaign, asked me to prepare a collection of monographs. I agreed to talk with the adolescents about their wartime odysseys, even if the un-spoken objective of this campaign was to move the donors to pity in order to collect money (oh so necessary!).

I therefore met with about fifty adolescents in 1946 and 1947. Each one spent a few hours at Chatou, and we held a rambling conversation. These youngsters seemed relieved and happy to be able to confide in me. It was as if a weight of si-lence had been lifted from their shoulders. After their departures, it was with a great deal of emotion that I jotted down their accounts.[20]

Encouraged by an instructor, a group of adolescents started a monthly review, en-titled *Lendemains OSE* [The OSE of Tomorrow], entirely conceived and written by the youngsters of the children's homes. All the children of the OSE were allowed to express their ideas in it. Reading it, one felt the diversity of opinions among them, for example on the subject of Jews. The tenth issue—the anniversary number—picked up anew the themes that had been broached earlier: life "in the Hosean style,"[21] the preoccupations of the day, and memories of the "painful events" that they had witnessed. However, it also included travel notes. Open to the whole world and destined to be read by everyone, without a political or ideological slant, the re-view was meant to be an example of democracy. It had rather wide circulation in

France and abroad. We see in these writings a youth emerging from a very personal nightmare.

All these initiatives helped rebuild the identity of the children and adolescents, to prepare them for a future in which they would be able to count on their own efforts.

THE OSE—AGAIN

We were still living in Chatou when I received my diploma in social work. The ADIR, an association of former members of the Resistance who had been deported and interned, offered me my first professional position in September 1950. All the women members of that association welcomed me warmly. I loved my work. I again had to use administrative strategies, this time to enable the women to obtain the status of veteran. This status entitled them to the benefits granted by the famous Article 64, notably free [health] care for diseases traceable to the deportation. I was always engaged in battle and, as at Rivesaltes, I navigated a maze of legal texts and articles in order that these women, who had suffered physically and morally, receive recognition for their struggle.

I had a great deal of love and admiration for these women. Yet the first months were very difficult for me. Because they had fought in the Resistance network, I heard them express only contempt for the "racial deportees." I had nightmares about it, but I also understood that they were possibly testing my feelings toward them. At the end of my three-month probationary period, I decided to stay.

At the beginning of 1954, Robert Job, who had become the general director of the OSE, asked me to rejoin this philanthropic society. The wartime children were leaving the children's homes little by little. Those who were arriving from North Africa and whose families were in difficulties needed urgent help.

It seemed to the OSE directorate that "given my past," I would be able to start the turnabout and make possible a harmonious cohabitation between "our" children (those without parents) and the newcomers, who were viewed by the teachers and the other children as privileged human beings.

Julien had left the OSE in 1950 to direct the Fonds social juif unifié (FSJU) [the Unified Jewish Social Fund]. I gave in to my friends' pressure. I took over as director of social services and of children's services [of the OSE]. Later on, I would take over the direction of the OSE itself. But that is another story.

9

Fifty Years Later

On the basis of the conversations I held in the years 1946–1947 with the adolescents of the OSE homes, I composed the firsthand accounts *Comme des brebis* [Like Lambs]. It fulfilled my desire to stress a precise feature of the cruel war years—the rescue of children—and also to make a clean sweep of the past by consigning it to several written sheets. When this work was finished, I presented it to publishers in 1948. It was well received, but it was explained to me that it was "too late . . . or too early." Almost relieved, I put the manuscript away and devoted myself to Nicole, who had just been born, and to the studies I was pursuing. The future was pressing. My work at the ADIR with former members of the Resistance who had been interned and deported was a kind of transitional period for me. I then carefully classified my records of the Occupation era and turned a page in my life by devoting myself wholly to my new work at the OSE, namely to help children and families in difficulties as a result of their transplantation from North Africa to postwar France. I no longer looked at any film, I no longer read any book on the deportations.

It was in the 1980s that the past abruptly burst into my life. "Oldtimers" who had settled in the United States came on a pilgrimage to France, and I welcomed them at the OSE headquarters. These men and women, about fifty years old, came to ask me, by then the director, for details on their childhood, not imagining for an instant that I would not be in a position to give them satisfaction. I again pulled out my records.

To some of them, I gave the rudiments of an answer about their personal history; to others, I was only able to put forward hypotheses, starting with their remembrances and several chronological points of reference. Whatever the case, their questions forced me to immerse myself again in everything I had tried to forget.

Some of them had extremely precise expectations, like the man who was looking for "Paulette," the child of the family that had sheltered him near Toulouse until his departure for the United States. His dossier contained no information on this foster family. Yet he insisted, and I understood, that this search mattered a great deal to him. Then, remembering the detective talents of Germaine Masour's team and the methods they had used, I advised him to put a lost-and-found notice in *La Dépêche du Midi* [the leading newspaper in southwestern France]. Several months later, he wrote me to thank me: he had found Paulette.

Whenever I expressed surprise at these belated inquiries, I always received the same answer: "We were relieved to leave Europe, but our assimilation was very difficult. It was necessary for us to learn a new language, earn a living, rebuild a family.[1] We didn't tell our children anything, we wanted to protect them; but our grandchildren asked us questions. What was I to tell them?" The search continued and brought me face to face with my own history, which I, alas, could no longer share with Julien, who had died in 1981.

Little by little the protagonists and witnesses of this period disappeared: Lazare Gurvic died in 1960, Eugène Minkowski in 1972, Georges Garel in 1979. Andrée Salomon passed away in 1985, and Joseph Weill in 1988.

The wartime archives of the OSE, which had made it possible to pick up the trail of the hidden children, had been partly scattered over the course of numerous moves. The job had to be done quickly, for the documents in the possession of private persons ran the risk of meeting the same fate in the future. As for those preserved in documentary centers, they were often inaccessible.

I thought it was important to give the OSE its memory back, that of its most difficult and darkest, but also its most combative, period. I remembered my father, at the beginning of the war, contributing to the creation of a Center of Contemporary Jewish Documentation and working to preserve these archives for future generations. That had made me indignant: "How can you think of old papers when our life is in continual danger?" Now I understood.

The restoration of the archives, undertaken in 1983 for the fiftieth anniversary of OSE-France, could be brought to a successful conclusion only after my retirement, in 1985, when I was able to devote myself entirely to that task.[2] Since 1980, however, several members of the OSE, encouraged to present their testimony, had composed writings concerning their work during the war.[3]

Since the beginning of the 1990s, many meetings have been held in France, Belgium, Israel, the United States, and elsewhere that enabled the hidden children to be discovered. Finally, a colloquium, "Mémoire et Avenir" [Memory and the Future], presided over by Simone Veil,[4] took place in December 1993 in the large amphitheater of the Sorbonne on the occasion of the eightieth anniversary of the Union-OSE. I was asked to speak of the OSE's activities during the war, but most of all it was my responsibility to present a personal account and to talk about my role [in the OSE's activities].

I was a link in a chain. It was necessary that I present my testimony in order to resurrect this formidable chain of solidarity, to pass on this history, our history. Wasn't it time to go further, to write? Who else would write this history as a firsthand witness?

I found myself confronted with confused memories that I had for a long time repressed, immersed in numerous writings that had miraculously been preserved in spite of [the ravages of] time, changes of location, oblivion. In old shoeboxes, I found, all jumbled up, photos, identity papers, letters, writings in French and English but also in Russian and Yiddish. Little by little, a linking thread emerged. I hung on to chronological points of reference, and I tried to write as if I were rewinding a ball of wool.

I came across black holes that punctuated my [chronological] route. Where had I been on 3 October 1940, the day of the promulgation of the Statute of the Jews? Did I understand what was being enacted? In those moments when I faced a loss of memory, I could no longer write. I spent hours putting my papers in order, going through books, following up a trail, until letters, passes, administrative stamps enabled me, by cross-checking, to reconstitute, as if from the outside, memories that everything told me were mine but whose traces I had lost sight of. Thus, I found in a box, along with old photos, the approval, signed by the woman director at Annel, dated Orléans, 12 October 1940, of my request for a pass to meet my parents in the Unoccupied Zone. In this way I was able to reconstruct my itinerary: Orléans, in the Occupied Zone, and Vichy. But where had I crossed the demarcation line thanks to this *Ausweis* [pass permitting the bearer to move from the German-occupied Zone to the Unoccupied Zone]? I didn't remember at all.

I was then stupefied to learn that among Professor Meyerson's papers, deposited at the Archives nationales after his death in 1983, were two writings of mine dating from October 1940, as well as ten letters from the same period. These writings failed to restore my memory. But there was no doubt that I had written them; I recognized the touch of my old typewriter. Thus, I was confronted with the certainty of not only having passed through Paris but also of having composed several writings, particularly on the Statute of the Jews [see the last two sections of chapter 2].

This loss of memory surprised me: a kind of eclipse seemed to be the only plausible explanation for these dark years. In 1992, I was invited to participate in a discussion held at Aix-en-Provence, in which two short films were shown to *classes de troisième* [equivalent to the sophomore classes in U.S. high schools] of the region: one produced by the students during their pilgrimage to Auschwitz, the other a documentary produced for *Envoyé special* [a television current event series] on skinheads. Two women who had been arrested at the age of fourteen, in January 1943, in Marseille were introduced and spoke about their deportation to Auschwitz, their separation from their mother and sisters, who were gassed upon their arrival, and their own return to France in 1945. There was a silence, a heavy silence, in the lecture hall. I was present there, I was listening, but at no moment did I make any connection with my presence at Marseille at the time of their arrest.

With the turn of a sentence, the discussion leader referred to my work at Rivesaltes. One of the two women then turned to me and asked me in a low voice whether I was familiar with the OSE. I answered her that my husband had at that time been the director of the OSE at Marseille. She then exclaimed, "I've just learned that Mme. Samuel's husband was the director of the OSE at Marseille. I want to say that I had three little brothers that the OSE snatched from deportation. When I came back [from Auschwitz], I found them again; the OSE had sheltered them and had continued to raise them." An emotional silence filled the hall. The act of rescuing children seemed, for a moment, to make up for the horror of the deportation.

But I returned to Paris ill at ease. How was it that during the discussion I kept silent, when I myself had been at Marseille at the time of the roundups in January 1943? This question haunted me and filled me with distress. I was extremely depressed, without understanding the reason for it. "I'm worn out," I said to a relation, "worn out as after childbirth. And yet," I added in a voice that arose from the depths of my unconscious, "and yet I was pregnant in Marseille in January 1943." I suddenly understood. In my own way, I had done everything not to know, to keep all this at a distance—the anxiety, the indignation, the shame—in order to be able to get through these tragic events, to continue to live, to have children. It was only at that moment that these buried feelings resurfaced.

As early as 1989, when I had returned for the first time to Rivesaltes during the filming by Bernard Mangiante of *Les Camps du silence* [The Silent Camps], I had been expected to talk about the role of the Nîmes Coordinating Committee in the camps, but I did not do so; instead, I heard myself exclaim, "I was ashamed of what men could do to other men." The words shot out all on their own, against my will.

Sometimes, too, the present awakened the past in an unexpected way. For example, when my granddaughter Barbara, Jean-Pierre's daughter, left our country home in 1973 with her maternal grandparents and I did not find her when I came back home, I was seized by a terrifying anxiety, which lasted several hours, until suddenly I understood that this anxiety was a replication of all the anxieties I had not permitted myself to feel returning home in 1943 and 1944, and when I prevented myself from imagining what could have happened to Françoise, who was then only a few months old.

Was it also the same anxiety that had revealed itself with Françoise at the age of six? She had gone to convalesce in a children's home in the mountains. Her cries, her tears, and her refusal to speak were so strong that Julien decided to fetch her. But when it came time to leave, after a day spent together, Françoise decided to stay [at the children's home]. "Now I know that you have my address," she had said. Her daughter, Judith, too, has known these fears of abandonment.[5]

In this research into the past, where I encounterd shadowy areas or unexpected eruptions, I became conscious of the weight of the transmission of sentiments and emotions long deferred. Having finished this book, isn't it time to turn a page?

The time has gone for me to be entirely absorbed with the past. Tiny indications have led me to recognize that the time for reconciliation has come. When I met the young German coproducer of Bernard Mangiante's film, I took the gravity of her silence as a sign of peace. In fact, perhaps the most difficult work for everybody from here on will be not to bring the Vichy regime once more to trial, nor to keep tirelessly bringing up the fates, no matter how tragic, that befell some human beings, but to understand better the very serious question—so decisive for the future—of indifference. I would have liked to have heard, in the postwar years, from those people who showed no reaction when tens of thousands of persons, especially children, were swallowed up in unspeakable ordeals. They should have spoken up, not to be punished but to be understood, not to be absolved but to help each of us learn to hunt down within ourselves areas of deadly indifference.

Primo Levi[6] has written: "Perhaps what took place cannot be understood, and even should not be understood, insofar as to understand is almost to justify." But we must stop believing that a wound received can be closed only by a wound inflicted.

I've decided to turn the page, not to forget but to learn from the past and to struggle against today's evils, which are the same as those of yesterday—exclusion, rejection, and intolerance.

This book has for me taken on the importance of an inheritance. Yes, this is certainly the issue: a patrimony to pass on, a history to transmit. I had to write it in order to bring its actors to life, to testify about the response necessary in the depths of the night, and to affirm—for all times and all places—the absolute primacy of life over death.

I dedicate this book to my six grandchildren: Judith, Barbara, Maia, Elie, Vincent, and Laurent.

"L'AMITIÉ CHRÉTIENNE"

ŒUVRE DE SECOURS AUX RÉFUGIÉS ÉTRANGERS

Fondée sous le haut Patronage de

S. E. le Cardinal GERLIER
Archevêque de Lyon, Primat des Gaules

M. Georges VILLIERS
Maire de Lyon

M. le Pasteur Marc BŒGNER
Président de la Fédération Protestante de France

BUREAU :

PRÉSIDENT :
J.-L. BEAUJOLIN

SECRÉTAIRE GÉNÉRAL :
Olivier de PIERREBOURG

Cette Association est établie en conformité
des prescriptions de la Loi de 1901. Elle
s'inspire avant tout des principes Chrétiens
■

SIÈGE CENTRAL : 1, Rue du Plâtre, LYON

Téléphone : B. 69-26

Lyon   Le 28 aout   1942

Je soussigné Jean Marie Soutou Directeur
de l-Amitié Chrétienne, autorise Mademoiselle
Vivette HERMANN, responsable de notre Service d'
assistance dans les camps, à percevoir les dons
en especes et en nature qui lui seront faits en
faveur de notre oeuvre.

Mademoiselle HERMANN remettra un recu
au nom de l'Amitié Chrétienne a tous les dona-
teurs.

Le Directeur

Jean Marie Soutou

A permit allowing Vivette Hermann to collect donations on behalf of Christian Friendship (From author's personal collection)

Julien Samuel, reading the Statute of the Jews (From author's personal collection)

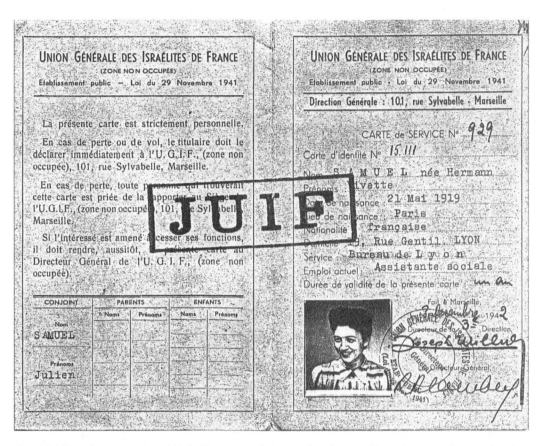

UNION GÉNÉRALE DES ISRAÉLITES DE FRANCE
(ZONE NON OCCUPÉE)
Établissement public — Loi du 29 Novembre 1941

La présente carte est strictement personnelle.

En cas de perte ou de vol, le titulaire doit le déclarer immédiatement à l'U. G. I. F., (zone non occupée), 101, rue Sylvabelle, Marseille.

En cas de perte, toute personne qui trouverait cette carte est priée de la apporter au Service l'U.G.I.F., (zone non occupée), 101, rue Sylvabelle, Marseille.

Si l'intéressé est amené à cesser ses fonctions, il doit rendre, aussitôt, la présente carte au Directeur Général de l'U. G. I. F., (zone non occupée).

CONJOINT	PARENTS		ENFANTS	
	Noms	Prénoms	Noms	Prénoms
Nom				
SAMUEL				
Prénoms				
Julien				

UNION GÉNÉRALE DES ISRAÉLITES DE FRANCE
(ZONE NON OCCUPÉE)
Établissement public · Loi du 29 Novembre 1941

Direction Générale : 101, rue Sylvabelle · Marseille

CARTE de SERVICE N° 929

Carte d'identité N° 15.111

Nom : S A M U E L née Hermann
Prénoms : Vivette
Date de naissance : 21 Mai 1919
Lieu de naissance : Paris
Nationalité : française
Domicile : 29, Rue Gentil, LYON
Service : Bureau de L y o n
Emploi actuel : Assistante sociale
Durée de validité de la présente carte : un an

Fait à Marseille,
Décembre 1942
Directeur de la 3e Direction,

Le Directeur Général,

JUIF

The card delivered to Vivette Samuel by the Union générale des israélites de France (UGIF) in December 1942 (From author's personal collection)

The wedding of Vivette and Julien Samuel at
the Couret home in October 1942 (From author's
personal collection)

Régine and Françoise at Chambéry in 1944

Georges Garel, who set up the clandestine network for the rescue of Jewish children inside the Œuvre de secours aux enfants (OSE), shown here with his son Jean-Renaud at the end of the war (Used with permission of Lili-Elise Garel)

Dr. Malkin with Dora Werzberg and Simone Weill (so-called Reinette) at Rivesaltes in 1942 (From author's personal collection)

Germaine Masour, who had a leading role in the Garel network (From author's personal collecton)

Georges Loinger in 1947 (Used with permission of Georges Loinger)

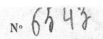

N° 6543   SÉRIE :

PRÉFECTURE DE LA HAUTE-VIENNE

Carte d'identité

Empreinte digitale :

Signature
du titulaire

Nom : Dutertre
Prénoms : Pierre Michel
Né le 19 Octobre 1910
à Asson
Département
d es Basses-Pyrénées
Nationalité Française
Domicile Limoges
31 Rue chauvelain   LIMOGES, le 10 N.. 1943

DA 15 FRANC

Le Préfet,

Signalement :

Taille : 1m 67   Nez : rect.
Cheveux : chat.   Forme générale
Moustache : blonde   du visage : IV
Yeux : bleus   Teint : clair
Signes particuliers :

The I.D. card of Pierre Dutertre,
alias Pierre Dreyfus, in 1943

Departure of the first group of immigrants
for Palestine in June 1945 (From author's
personal collection)

Photo LIMOT

An American chaplain greeting the departers on the railway platform in 1945, with Dr. Malkin facing the camera
(From author's personal collection)

Left, departure of the first group of immigrants
for Palestine, led by Armand Rein, in June 1945
(From author's personal collection)

The children of Buchenwald in
June 1945 (From author's personal collection)

The card sent by little Annie
Samuel before being deported (From author's
personal collection)

Top left, Lazare Gurvic welcoming
the children from Buchenwald in
June 1945 (From author's personal
collection)

Bottom left, Joseph Weill (on the left) with
Dr. Revel at the Andelys train station, meeting
the train that was bringing the group from
Buchenwald (From author's personal collection)

CARTE POSTALE

EXPÉDITEUR   DESTINATAIRE

COMITÉ ISRAÉLITE POUR LES ENFANTS
VENANT D'ALLEMAGNE ET DE L'EUROPE CENTRALE

RÉCEPTION - HÉBERGEMENT - ÉDUCATION
38, RUE DU MONT THABOR, PARIS (Iᵉʳ)
TÉLÉPHONE : OPÉRA 99-42

Je soussigné **W e i n e r Wolf Hersch**
(nom de famille et prénoms du père ou de la mère ou du tuteur ou du répondant)
déclare par la présente confier au "COMITÉ ISRAÉLITE POUR LES ENFANTS VENANT
D'ALLEMAGNE ET DE L'EUROPE CENTRALE" ou à tel autre organisme désigné par
cette œuvre ou éventuellement par les autorités compétentes:

l'enfant **Weiner O t t o**
(nom et prénoms)
né le **13 février 1927** à **Vienne** nationalité **allemand**
(ville et pays)
résidant actuellement à **Vienne XVI.Bachgasse 9**
(adresse complète)

enfant dont je suis : père - mère - tuteur ou (*) **XXXXXXXXXXXX**
(préciser les liens de parenté)

Ledit enfant est le fils - la fille(*) de : **XXXXX**

père   Nom de famille : **Weiner**   Prénoms : **Wolf Hersch**
Né le **10 juin 1898** à **Czudin**   Nationalité : **allemand**
(ville et pays)
Adresse actuelle : **Vienne XVI.Bachgasse 9**

Profession (diplômes et qualités) **employé**

mère   Nom de famille : **Weiner**   Prénoms **Klara**
Nom de jeune fille : **Rattin** Née le **15 mars 1900** à **Vienna**
(ville et pays)
Adresse actuelle : **Vienne XVI.Bachg.9** Nationalité : **allemand**
Profession (diplômes et qualités) **en menage**

Renseignements complémentaires sur la famille de l'enfant (santé, milieu social, situation
matérielle, etc.) : **Le père est sans travail. Le comité d'israelite
en Allemagne doit subventionnée cette famille.**

Si cette déclaration est signée par un tuteur ou par un répondant, indiquer l'adresse et la
profession de celui-ci : _____

En conséquence, la dite œuvre israélite ou tel autre organisme à lui substitué,
agissant sous le contrôle du Comité Central des Réfugiés créé par arrêté du Ministre des
Affaires étrangères en date du 29 décembre 1938, aura tous droits et pouvoirs à l'effet de
veiller à la protection de la santé et des intérêts moraux de l'enfant susdit jusqu'à l'âge
de 18 ans, étant précisé que le Comité n'encourra aucune responsabilité de ce chef et que
je l'en dégage expressément.

Le présent mandat ne pourra être annulé que dans le cas où j'obtiendrais un
domicile fixe dans un pays quelconque et où j'aurais les sommes nécessaires pour faire
venir chez moi mon enfant - mon pupille (*) et subvenir à ses besoins. Toutefois il est
bien entendu que dans ce dernier cas, je ne demanderai plus au "Comité Israélite pour
les Enfants venant d'Allemagne et de l'Europe Centrale" ou à l'organisme qui lui aurait
été substitué, de s'en charger à nouveau.

A **Vienne** , le **22 février 1939**
SIGNATURE   LÉGALISATION

der Isr. Kultusgemeinde Wien
Abteilung für Jugendfürsorge

The rescue of children was effected at the cost of filling out innumerable forms and certificates:
(1) Otto Weiner's certificate of admission to France . . .

Comi... de ...

DEMANDE D'EMIGRATION D'ENFANT

(La suite donnée à cette demande demeure réservée)

ÉTAT CIVIL

Nom : WEINER   Prénom : OTTO   Sexe : M

Né le 13-2-1927   à Vienne (Autriche)

Nationalité d'origine : autrichienne   actuelle : et - autrich.

Documents : Recipisse   Français ou Etrangers ?

Religion : israélite   Orthodoxe (oui ou non) : oui

Adresse actuelle : c/o ABBÉ GOENS   SERANON   A.M.

FAMILLE

Père :
- Nom : WEINER   Prénom : HERMAN
- Né le 10 juin 1898   à ROUMANIE   Religion : ISRAELITE
- Nationalité : autrichienne   Profession : COMMERÇANT
- Adresse actuelle : Vienne 66, Scheienplatz 4
- Date de l'entrée en France :

Mère :
- Nom de jeune fille : RATTIN   Prénom : Clara
- Née le 15 mars 1900   à Vienne   Religion : ISRAELI
- Nationalité : autrichienne   Profession :
- Adresse actuelle : idem
- Date de l'entrée en France :

	NOM	AGE	ADRESSE ACTUELLE
Frères :			
Sœurs :	ALICE WEINER	10 ans	Vienne 66, Scheienplatz 4

TUTEUR

Nom :

Adresse :

PARENTS EN FRANCE OU A L'ÉTRANGER (Sauf aux États-Unis)

NOM ET PRÉNOM	PARENTÉ	ADRESSE ACTUELLE
RATTIN HERRMAN	g'-père	Vienne même adresse

(2) Otto Weiner's request for emigration to the United States . . .

DEMANDE D'INSCRIPTION.

NOM. (en majuscules) *WEINER*   PRENOMS *Otto*

Adresse actuelle de l'enfant Institution Consuelo 37 Bd. Grosso, Nice

Nous et prénoms des parents *Wolf Hersch et Clara W.*

Adresse actuelle (ou à défaut dernière adresse) des parents, (ou à
défaut, nom et adresse du tuteur) Vienne 16, Bachgasse 2

Composition de la famille

Situation de la famille (profession ou occupation des parents)
_____ancien employé de commerce

Lieu de naissance et pays natal de l'enfant *Vienne — Autriche*

Date de naissance *13 Février 1924*

Nationalité ____ allemande

Pièces d'identité (marquez quelles sont les pièces d'identité de l'enfant, telles que : acte de naissance, carte d'identité, passe-port -
indiquez l'autorité l'ayant délivré avec lieu, date et validité

Date de l'arrivée en France 18 mars 1939 venant de Allemagne via

Donnez le nom et l'adresse de votre plus proche parent ou ami aux
Etats-Unis (ou outre-mer) et indiquez le degré de parenté s'il y a
lieu :
Nom *Mr. Joachim Parnas c/o Mr. Goldberg* Adresse *2460, Davidson Avenue Bronx,*
Degré de parenté   Nationalité   *New-York City*

Etes-vous enregistré ou avez-vous un affidavit à un Consulat américain
pour l'immigration aux Etats-Unis? Si oui, à quelle date et à quel
Consulat ?___ pas enregistré

Avez-vous demandé le transfert de votre dossier à un autre Consulat?
Si oui, au quel et à quelle date ?

Indiquez le pays natal du père Autriche ?

Observations spéciales

(3) Otto Weiner's request to the American consulate . . .

O. S. E.
Oeuvre de Secours aux Enfants
Regroupement Familial
62, rue Spontini
P A R I S - 16 °

Paris, le 23 août 1945

WEINER Otto, né le 13 février 1927 à Vienne
nation: apatr. d'orig. autrichienne

Arrivé d'Allemagne en France en mars 1939
avec un convoi d'enfants israélites et
pris en charge par l'Oeuvre de la Guerre.
A la dissolution de celle-ci en décembre
1941 recueilli par l'OSE et placé à l'
Ecole professionnelle à Nice. Parti en
Suisse en 1943 et de là au printemps 45
en Palestine.

Parents à l'étranger:
oncle Max Ruttin, 2001 University street,
New York

(4) Otto Weiner's dossier composed by the OSE in 1945 (From author's personal collection)

The Samuel family at Chatou after the war
(From author's personal collection)

Vivette Samuel typing the text of *Comme des brebis* (Like Lambs) after the war
(From author's personal collection)

10

Children's Odysseys

Immediately after the war, I composed monographs about the children, as requested by the OSE. From those that appear in the work *Comme des brebis* [Like Lambs], written in 1947, I selected [for this book] those that seemed to me to best illustrate the diversity of their experiences. Certain testimonies were collected later: that of Paul Niederman in the 1980s, that of Claude Bégué-Morhange in the 1990s, and that of Ehud Loeb in 1993.

GERDA EINBINDER: A CHILD FROM GERMANY

Gerda Einbinder was born in Breslau to a middle-class German family. Her mother was a native of Prussia; her father, who was born in Frankfurt, ran a clothing business. When I questioned her about her parents, her face tightened. She was a happy child, she said to me, proud, indomitable, a real live wire, never telling lies, returning blow for blow. One day, when she was six years old, she was slapped for having jostled a passerby with her scooter. She immediately countered with her fist. Never had anyone drawn a tear from her in public, except on 10 November 1938, and while she talked to me about it, her look hardened.

Herschel Grynzpan, a young Jew born in Poland, had killed the German diplomat Ernst von Rath in Paris. The next morning, antisemitic measures of a harshness unheard of until then were taken throughout the German Reich. Jewish apartments, stores, and synagogues were plundered and burned. History later showed that this allegedly spontaneous reaction of the German people had been meticulously prepared[1] and that the assassination of von Rath had been only a pretext. The order had been given to the police and the SS troops to attack Jews and their property everywhere.

Gerda told me, "I was asleep in my little room; the telephone suddenly rang during the night, and I woke up startled. I was afraid, very afraid."

It was a paternal uncle, whose apartment was located above his store, who told them that a troop of Hitler Youth and SS were in the midst of ransacking and plundering everything. He arrived [at Gerda's family's home] several minutes later, having succeeded in escaping. The family hid him, and Gerda went back to bed, shaking with fear. Suddenly, there was the noise of boots, knocks on the door, wild howlings, and the eruption of the pack in search of the uncle. Gerda, terror stricken, took refuge in her mother's arms. "They broke everything in front of our eyes; they tore up the books one by one, they smashed the bottles against the furniture." The mother repeated in the little girl's ear: "Du weiss es nicht: you don't know anything about it." And the child was trembling: "They'll see me blush; they'll know that I'm lying, and they'll take papa away." When there was nothing left to break, they departed, taking with them her father and the uncle, whom they had managed to find.

Life continued, while they were waiting for news. Gerda could no longer go to school. The neighbors, afraid of compromising themselves, kept their distance. The boys of the Hitler Youth threw stones at her: "But I had a strong fist." Then there were the interminable steps taken to locate her father. Her mother, who was ill, fainted when she learned that her husband was in a concentration camp. The store had to be sold, since there was no business left. Everything had been vandalized; counters and closets had been broken with axes.

After they had tried to locate him for three months, her father finally returned one evening. He entered, sat down, and, without saying a word, began to weep. He was thin, stooped over, dirty, dejected, not outraged but weighed down by the experience he had just lived through. The scared child learned about the bullying, the harassment, the endless roll calls in the rain, the absence of solidarity among the prisoners.

The family wanted to leave the country and made strenuous efforts to join up with relatives who had emigrated to the United States in 1936. Gerda was given the opportunity to leave earlier. The Jewish boarding school where she had spent several months had likewise been ransacked on the night of 10 November, and its young boarders, wearing their pajamas, had been chased across the countryside. And now the entire institution had obtained a collective entrance visa for France. Gerda's parents did not hesitate: the child would leave and wait in France for the rest of the family to make the trip with her to America.

The departure took place in March 1939. The Baroness de Rothschild welcomed the children in Paris. They learned their first French words in the train: "Merci, madame." This episode was to remain engraved on Gerda's memory as a miraculous moment: "I thought at that time that a baroness was a fairy."

The children were first led to a hospital for a three-day-long medical examination. Gerda was very unhappy there. She was devastated by her parents' absence. The new faces, the unknown language, all repelled her. The necessary discipline was hard to take: "We had to eat everything on the plate, and it wasn't good food. I was not accustomed to eating soup, and at night I had to sleep in a large hospital bed, whereas I had been accustomed to my little cozy room near my parents."

A group left on 24 March 1939 for Maubuisson in Seine-et-Oise [a *département* to the southwest of Paris, which was further divided in 1964 into three *départements*]. They found there another group that had arrived from Vienna several days earlier. Two clans were forming. The children forgot that the same events were the cause of everyone's exile. The Berlin girls scorned the excessively dolled-up Viennese girls and made fun of their accents. But, little by little, the commonality of language created a bond in this foreign land, and it was a perfectly homogeneous group that left Maubuisson on 24 April for La Guette,[2] while the children who were very devout were moved to Montmorency. "La Guette was paradise": a beautiful sunlit castle and, in front of the gate, a group of children from the Palatinate, all dressed in blue, wishing them welcome. Gerda was happy living in this community of 132 children from Germany, who learned once again how to live in a free country. Little by little, the haunting memory of the sinister November days became blurred in all their minds.

Then war came. Gerda was sheltered and until 1946 did not know anything of the fate of her parents. It was only then that she learned that they had survived the nightmare and succeeded in emigrating to Ecuador, where she rejoined them.

PAUL NIEDERMAN: "TO LEAVE" RIVESALTES

Born on 1 November 1927, in Karlsruhe, Germany, Paul Niederman was at first interned at Gurs[3] in October 1940, with his parents, grandparents, and younger brother. Nearly fifty years later, in a text he entrusted to me, Paul tells of his arrival and life at Rivesaltes.

We arrived at the camp of Rivesaltes without my grandparents. We were separated from the moment we left Gurs, and my grandparents were led to another camp located near Noé, in the [*département* of] Haute-Garonne. My grandfather died there. I learned about it only after the war. As for my grandmother, she miraculously survived everything. She was diabetic, and, as she had nothing to eat during the war, her diabetes regressed to an extraordinary degree.

When we arrived at Rivesaltes, they had us enter into the barracks, the women on one side [of the camp], the men on the other. I was able to see my mother fairly often, because I could freely move about inside the camp.

The first thing I remember is that, as I entered one of the barracks, a red, thick cloud fell from the timber of the building. They were fleas. I had never seen them anywhere else. It was absolutely unbelievable and excruciating. There were also lice, and there were bedbugs in the wood, but fleas, that's terrible, they fall down in one swoop. I would say that I spent the whole year I lived in Rivesaltes delousing myself. I can still see myself being seated with my father, at the end of summer afternoons when it was less hot, leaning against the exterior of the barrack, in the shade, and killing all the lice and fleas we could find. Of course, we had no insecticide; we had to hunt them down one by one. That kept us busy. And, because they [crawled all over] us again during the night, the job was never finished. We became very skilled in finding them; we knew where they nested in one's clothing.

Generally speaking, the camp had very serious problems with hygiene. At least the latrines were not completely in the open, as at Gurs. They had the same set-up of planks as at Gurs but provided a bit more privacy. There were also fewer epidemics. But anyone who got sick had to avoid at all costs entering the infirmary, where he was certain to catch all the illnesses that floated about. I think there were nurses and physicians there, but I didn't see any. My little brother caught the mumps. My mother immediately understood on the basis of his high fever what was wrong with him. He was swollen, but at all costs he had to be prevented from going to the infirmary, so, in the morning roll calls, my brother was hidden and I answered in his place. I then immediately left for my father's place. My brother remained with my mother all day long. He finally recovered all by himself.

People tried to escape from Rivesaltes, but they were always caught at the Perpignan railway station, through which it was necessary to pass.

It rained very heavily at Gurs, but at Rivesaltes the most painful [part of the weather] was the tramontane [wind]. Rivesaltes is on a plain at the foot of the Pyrénées. I always saw the wind at Rivesaltes the way I always saw the rain at Gurs. We had brought our little cooker made up of tin cans, but it was not easy to use it in this wind. Moreover, wood was much more difficult to procure at Rivesaltes. We were forced to cut our "beds," their lower sides, in order to make a fire. One could not make a fire inside the barracks, but human heat made up for it there.

I didn't have a good idea of the size of the camp. I was always between my father's barrack and that of my mother and brother, near the kitchen. It was there that the garbage cans were being filled. I'm convinced that many edible and good things were being brought to the camp (insofar as this was possible in wartime). But the head of the camp helped himself to them. Then it was the turn of the guards, and then of the rats. When it came to the internees' turn, there wasn't much food left. There were always Jerusalem artichokes, turnips, things I absolutely cannot stand today. When I was able to eat tomatoes, it was morning, noon, and evening, cooked in water, to the point of nausea, because the camp had bought an entire caseload that had to be disposed of. I then ate pumpkins in the same manner—for a month. What lasted the longest were globe artichokes (I had never seen them before), and we were given soups made up of their remainders, the leaves, stalks, chards, cores. That is why neither I nor my brother has been able, even forty years afterward, to bear the smell of artichokes. I never ate meat, I don't think there was any, or any floating in the soup. I dreamed of potatoes and noodles; I dreamed about them at night.

My brother and I checked the garbage cans behind the kitchen and tried to find edible things. We spent our entire time looking for lice, then for food. We were of truly skeletal thinness (I measured one meter sixty centimeters [five feet two and a half inches] and weighed thirty-five kilograms [seventy-seven pounds]).

They sometimes passed out to us a small amount of bread, minuscule portions with which one could not even make one side of a sandwich. I injured my hand while trying to make the pleasure of this piece of bread last longer. I wanted to cut slices as thin as possible so as to eat them for a longer time. One day, without realizing it, I continued to cut into the palm of my hand, and we had nothing with which to make a dressing. It left a very large scar. They put a handkerchief on it, hoping that this would stop it from becoming infected. That's all they could do. I was at first embarrassed by this handkerchief that I had to tightly hold on to, but the wound finally developed a scar.

There were devout people in the camp, who said their prayers every day. There were somewhat better organized celebrations on holidays, made possible by the presence of Jewish societies like the OSE, about which I didn't know much at that time. But my father had long before then given up practicing his religion. One could find no explanation for what was happening to us.

No one knew about the fate that awaited us. We had no information; we knew nothing. Members of the OSE, disguised, I believed, as social workers, tried to organize a semblance of a school, to give us a foundation in French, in anticipation of an eventual escape, perhaps.[4]

In the spring of 1942, a year after my arrival, my parents were contacted by the "social workers," who proposed to help their children escape, leave the camp. We were in Rivesaltes in the Unoccupied Zone (we had no idea that this zone was going to be occupied six months later), yet my parents were contacted to give their consent to our being taken away. And their reaction necessarily must have been painful but was the right one, since I am here today. They must have been thinking that this alternative would guarantee that two [people] would be saved from our group. We no longer had any news from my grandparents, and the only relative we had left [in Europe] was a distant female cousin, Martha, who had also disappeared. Hence, there were just four of us. My parents agreed to let us leave. One day in March or April 1942, I left with my brother and six or seven other children whom I did not know. They had us leave the camp by crossing the grapevines that surrounded it. All that we knew then was that we were leaving our parents. The separation was hard, we all wept, and our parents explained to us that it was better for us to leave, that they would be taken care of later. Before we left, they had us learn by heart the address of our family in the United States, an uncle and an aunt. There was no question of taking anything whatever with us (besides, we had nothing); hence we had to learn it by heart.

We left at sunrise. A social worker came to fetch us before the roll call. I presume that the guards had to be paid,[5] the Miliciens, the type of people forever with their guns, their berets, and their armbands. As for me, I did not see any uniforms on our route. I'm convinced that certain men must have been bought, because I saw, at the approaches to the camp, guys at the vines turning their backs to us as if they had not seen us. We crossed underneath the barbed wire. It was not as difficult here as at Gurs; it was easier to leave the camp. But all those who tried to escape were recaptured later, in the city or at the railroad station.

Once we were on the dirt road, we saw the arrival of a little *gazogène* [fuel derived from wood or coal] delivery van (that was the only vehicle available). I remember it well; I had never before seen one. There was a driver I didn't know and Mme. Zlatin,[6] who had a small shawl on her head and a navy blue cape (required for a Red Cross social worker, her official title). We got into this delivery van, but I don't remember the trip at all. It was closed, we could not look out, we were under wraps. I cannot tell you what places we passed by, but we finally arrived at Palavas-les-Flots. I don't know how they managed to make this trip without being arrested.

So we arrived near Montpellier, on the seacoast, in a house called the Solarium marin [Sea Solarium], which had undoubtedly been a *pension* once and was run by a stout Italian woman named Mamanita. It was she who did the cooking, who ran everything. It was an OSE home that took in children from just about everywhere. Some of them had come from Rivesaltes; others had just arrived as refugees from Belgium. Their parents had been interned or had disappeared.

After Palavas, Paul Niederman was sheltered in the children's home at Izieu, which by some miracle he left a few weeks before the April 1944 raid [ordered by Klaus Barbie, head of the Gestapo in Lyon; see note 10]; the OSE got him into Switzerland in March 1944 with other boys who were older than fourteen. His younger brother was able to join a convoy of children heading for the United States.

MARTIN OPPENHEIMER: THE ODYSSEY OF
AN INDOMITABLE PERSON

The story of Martin Oppenheimer is that of a painful journey that was also filled with courage and rebelliousness. Martin was born in Germany in 1924. When I met him in 1946, he was twenty-two years old. He was a very tall young man, whose too rapid growth seems to have taken place at the expense of his general condition. He had beautiful, somewhat dreamy, dark eyes.

Martin was only nine years old when, upon Hitler's accession to power, gangs of the SS entered the family property, ransacking everything. If by chance some of the children at school were friendly toward him, the teacher stepped in: "Aren't you ashamed to play with this Jew?" He began very early to give as good as he got and to defend himself. Brawls did not frighten him.

His family life was also hard. One of his brothers had died in 1921. His older sister was sent to France in 1933, and then to Holland. After being forcibly returned to Germany, she was finally able to leave in 1937 for the United States, where his second sister joined her later. Martin's father, a devout Jew, saw his property confiscated in 1935 to the benefit of one of his servants. The family then settled in Frankfurt, living under great tension.

Martin hired himself out as apprentice to a Jewish wood joiner and specialized in the manufacture of chests with false bottoms that were used by many emigrants eager to leave the country. Martin's father died in August 1938, and Martin was forced to support his family. He then became the owner of the joinery, which was left to him by his boss, who had left for the United States. But Martin was arrested and interned in Buchenwald. He was fourteen years old at the time.

It was a horrible experience. I'm not afraid of working. I'm skillful with my hands and well trained. But with the meager amount of food given us, the interminable roll calls in the wind, rain, and cold, my worries about my mother, I got worse each day. I was the youngest of my companions in misery, but nobody could do anything for me. What was most terrible was the brutality that came crashing down on us without rhyme or reason. I held on for six weeks until the day when, during a roll call, I wanted to help an old man (also arrested, even though he was outside the age limits), who had collapsed in the snow under the blows delivered by two guards. I was savagely beaten for this human impulse. The faces and names of those brutes haunted me afterward during sleepless nights.

I resolved to escape. I ran the risk of the death penalty if I was caught, but it was also certain death inside the camp. I decided to take a chance with a friend. We had concealed a pole at the approaches to the camp. We hid ourselves one evening by taking advantage of our going out as a group to the latrines. When surveillance was relaxed around three in the morning, we miraculously succeeded, thanks to our pole, in jumping over the high-voltage wires that surrounded the camp. I had lost thirteen kilos [twenty-nine pounds] in six weeks. I was very debilitated and had caught double pleurisy. I took refuge at my mother's place. Given my age, I was not arrested again but was given formal notice to leave Germany in four months. I worked for two months as an unskilled worker on the railroad tracks. I then obtained my official entrance visa to France and, heartbroken, had to leave my mother.

Martin then left by himself for Strasbourg [near the German border], where he was welcomed by Andrée Salomon, who was working at the Aide sociale israélite [Jewish Social Aid Society]. War began four months later. Strasbourg was evacuated, and he was now surely separated from his mother. He left for Clermont-Ferrand [a large town in central France] with a group of children. He looked for work there, and, because his nationality made it almost impossible for him to be hired, it took until March 1940 for him to find work, and then only a position as servant in a farmhouse at Moissac [about forty miles from Toulouse] in [the *département* of] Tarn-et-Garonne. Happy to be able to make a living and to be independent, he stayed there until January 1941.

The [German] occupation of a part of France and the first anti-Jewish measures made him eager to find himself again among young Jews. So he joined the first agricultural center of the EIF at Lautrec [village near Albi], which was managed by Castor [pseudonym of Robert Gamzon]. It was hard at first. Martin was the only toughened country boy in a group of youngsters for whom the return to the soil was a necessity rather than a vocation. He rose at four in the morning to take care of the

172

animals, then plowed until eight. At eleven, he worked at the carpentry shop; he was busy in the afternoon provisioning the group and then returned to the carpentry shop until seven o'clock. This regimen seriously impaired his health. When he was told by the Red Cross at the end of August 1941 that his mother, who had been deported, was dying, he suffered a nervous breakdown, followed by total amnesia, and he had to enter the hospital of Clairvivre in Strasbourg under the psychiatric care of Dr. Pfersdorf. His growing anxiety brought him to the Vauclerc asylum. The treatment and the time spent there helped him, and he stayed on as a handyman.

Thanks to Andrée Salomon, who never ceased to interest herself in his destiny, in February 1942 he joined up with the rural group of the EIF in [the *département* of] Rhône. Everything went well until July, when eight more newly liberated young people arrived from the camp of Gurs. The land was too small for all thirty-seven young people, and Martin was not satisfied with the small amount of work demanded of him.

The first roundup of foreigners in the Unoccupied Zone took place in August 1942. The members of the group scattered. Martin obtained Dr. Pfersdorf's consent to return to the hospital. He kept his true identity, however, hoping that he would succeed in emigrating to the United States.

The Germans occupied the Unoccupied Zone in November 1942 and Martin's relative security was threatened. In February 1943 he hid in a sanitarium in Toulouse, but idleness weighed heavily on him. Since he by now spoke fluent French, he changed his identity. He became Henri Martin and rejoined the farm in Tarn-et-Garonne that was run by the Sixth [Division of the Jewish Scouts].

The number of roundups was increasing, and the youngsters (even when disguised) had to be dispersed in the neighboring countryside. As a result of a denunciation, the physician responsible for this clandestine farm was arrested in his home in October 1943. Martin hired himself out to a peasant. He worked for him during the day and at night got on his bicycle and maintained contact among the boys placed in the vicinity. This lasted until 6 June 1944. After the landing of the Americans in Normandy, the youngsters decided to join the *maquis* to fight Der Führer SS company, which was terrorizing the region.

> One July evening, our little group received the order to take a gasoline depot. Four of my friends and myself immediately volunteered for the job. We used a cunning stratagem to neutralize the sentries on duty before they were able to sound the alarm. The Krauts—thirty altogether—were quickly taken prisoners by our group. When we

brought them to our encampment in the morning, I was extraordinarily surprised to recognize among the prisoners the two guards of the Buchenwald camp who had so severely beaten me five years earlier! I called them by their names. They turned around, at once worried and intrigued. They asked me how I knew them. I refreshed their memory. They grew pale and begged me to take pity on them, showing me photographs of their families. I thought of my mother, who had not been permitted to die in her bed. My heart turned to stone. I had so long dreamed of my having these brutes within my grasp one day! Should the opportunity that fate had granted me for avenging myself be allowed to slip away? I ran to tell my lieutenant of this strange encounter and asked for his advice. "Of the two of us," he answered, "is it you or me who has suffered the most? You know what you have to do." The two men were shot, and my horrible existence achieved some closure.

Martin wanted to join the regular army when France was liberated. He underwent intensive training at Castelsarrasin [city in Tarn-et-Garonne]. But, alas, some of his comrades brutally reminded him that he was Jewish and German, and he found himself involved in brawls all over again. His company supported him, which made him proud, but over the long run, these constant attacks were too painful to him. "I'll remain a dirty foreigner for a long time," he said. Then, while he was pursuing his training in Montauban [another city in Tarn-et-Garonne], his enlistment was rejected. He was demobilized.

After a short stay with the OSE, which employed him as supplier in a children's home, he joined the SNCF [the state-owned railway system] as a cabinetmaker in December 1945. He stayed there until October 1946. It was at that time that I met him. He then left France to join his married sisters in the United States. "But I will not stay there," he said as he was leaving. "I want a fatherland of my own. I want to go to Palestine, and I hope that my sisters will agree to follow me there."

Having rediscovered this testimony in 1983, I wanted to find out what had happened to Martin, and I went in search of him.

During a trip to Israel, I met Andrée Salomon, who, I knew, had been in contact with him. I learned that he had had difficulties in Israel—adjustment problems— but that he had met a woman there, a "child of the Holocaust," as he called her. I finally picked up his trail in the United States, where he had just died.

NICOLAS ROSENTHAL: A REFUSAL TO SEPARATE

Nicolas Rosenthal, as a son who had reached the age of reason, chose, of his own free will, to share his father's destiny.

Son of a German physician at Mannheim, Nicolas came to France before 1939. At the beginning of the war, he was in the ninth grade at the *lycée* of Montbéliard [near the Swiss border]. Cut off from his parents, for many months without any news from them, and without any money, Nicolas decided to apprentice himself to a hatmaker in Paris in order to be able to earn a living as fast as possible.

At the end of October 1940, he learned of the expulsion of his parents from Mannheim, their arrival in the camp of Gurs, their transfer to Rivesaltes, and, finally, the conscription of his father into a company of foreign workers near Perpignan. He was profoundly unhappy not to be able to help them. He pursued his apprenticeship until July 1942 and left Paris, forewarned on time about the extensive roundups in the offing.

He crossed the demarcation line as a young camper. He was now in the Unoccupied Zone. Where was he going to go? It had been three years since he had seen his parents. He was eager to see them again and to console them for their current misfortunes. He went directly to the company of [foreign] workers and signed up.

It was with deep emotion that the father and son embraced each other. How he had changed! Dr. Rosenthal was thinner, steeped in sorrow, in tatters, but still dignified and courageous.

The August roundups took the workers back to the camp of Rivesaltes, Nicolas included. He found his mother in the block set aside for those selected for deportation on the very day she had been chosen for deportation. Dr. Rosenthal, again working as a physician, went on the next convoy, and Nicolas, who was only sixteen years old, asked that he be allowed to accompany him.

For an entire year, father and son together endured terrible brutality and forced labor, supporting each other and both maintaining exceptionally high morale. Nicolas was then transferred to another camp and saw his father again only twelve months later, exhausted and dying. As for his mother, she had been gassed upon her arrival in Auschwitz.

The Russian offensive and victory saved Nicolas from certain death. He returned to France, miserable and demoralized by what he had experienced. He was twenty-one years old in 1947. He was a tall boy with light-colored eyes, endowed with a

175

remarkable moral conscience. His intention had been to study medicine as a vocation so that he could follow the path laid out by his father. The seven years he had
wasted after his ninth grade made it impossible for him to do so. He chose a different career.

[Nicolas Rosenthal sent a letter (in French) to Vivette Samuel in 1996. He had just
read a copy of *Sauver les enfants* that had been sent to him by Pierre Vermus, a
friend of his since 1946. An extract of that letter was sent to me (CBP) 12 June 1997
by Mme. Samuel and Mlle. Judith Elbaz, who asked me to include it in this book.]

> I've just read your book and in all sincerity I need to congratulate you for it. And to
> thank you for especially having mentioned my father. When I held the book in my
> hand, it "spontaneously" opened to the page "Nicolas Rosenthal.". . . Did you know me
> in Rivesaltes?
>
> Don't hold it against me, but the only OSE member I remember is Mme. Andrée
> Salomon, from whom I still have a wedding present, namely a *kiddush* goblet [cup
> used in the Jewish ritual blessing of wine or bread].
>
> Concerning my *curriculum vitae,* may I state the following?
>
> In actual fact, I crossed the demarcation line in 1942, forewarned—by whom?—to
> leave Paris as soon as possible. I had "real" false papers and entered the camp [of
> Rivesaltes] with my father, who came—on a weekend pass—from the Company of
> Foreign Workers [Compagnie de travailleurs étrangers (CTE); possibly intended here
> was the Foreign Labor Battalion (Groupement de travailleurs étrangers, or GTE)] in
> Barcarès [about thirteen miles from Rivesaltes] to be with mother. Soon thereafter, the
> camp was sealed off, and, with the help of the OSE, I left the camp with my father to
> join up with the CET [CTE (or GTE?)] of Barcarès, since "they" assured us that this
> way our relatives, especially mother, would not run any risk of deportation. We all
> know what such promises are worth! As for the deportation itself, all three of us were
> deported—my mother, my father, and I, plus a cousin of my father—on the same con-
> voy. You write that I left with my father of my own free will, which is true. I've never
> had any doubt on this matter. (But, let me say in passing, that if my mother had been
> deported before my father, I would certainly have left with her.) The real question is:
> if I had known where we were going, would I have acted in the same way? Or would
> my parents have agreed that I accompany them? The fact is that we knew *nothing* of
> our destination or of the Final Solution! Be that as it may, I had my "real" false papers
> and would have been able to leave the camp without difficulty. While my father and I
> were with the CET [CTE (or GTE?)] at Ille-sur-Têt [about seven miles from Perpig-
> nan], we left one day to cross the Pyrénées. But once there, we immediately realized
> that mother was in the camp, and we turned around and came back.

When we left Drancy, all four of us were in the same railway car. But at Cosel, just before the convoy arrived at Auschwitz, my father and I were separated from mother and the cousin, who continued their journey. We hadn't the slightest idea what Auschwitz was! My father was appointed physician in several camps. At the beginning, we were together. Then we were separated, [only] to find ourselves together again at the camp at Graditz, where my father had been named head physician to fight the typhus epidemic, from which he died in my arms, after I myself had been cured. I was liberated on 8 May 1945 by the [Soviet] Red Army.

Having returned to Paris, in 1948 I married a childhood friend who had survived Auschwitz and Mathausen. The wedding took place in Strasbourg. In 1952, we emigrated to Argentina, since my wife was unwilling to remain in Europe. In 1950, our daughter, Sylvie, was born in Courbevoie [seven miles west of Paris]. She is a physician specializing in infectious diseases. She has an eleven-year-old daughter, Tamara.

ROGER: THE DIFFICULTY OF LYING

Roger was born of Polish parents in 1928 in Paris. His father had left his country in 1919 and after a short stay in Germany had settled down in Paris in 1921. Five years later, established as a dealer in fancy leather goods, he married a compatriot, an exile like himself. Roger was their only child.

His education was that of any Parisian in modest circumstances. He first attended the primary school in the eighteenth *arrondissement* [the area around Montmartre] and in the fall of 1939 entered the eighth grade at the *lycée* Condorcet.

In May 1940 [after France surrendered to Germany], the family joined the general exodus [from Paris], but, once the armistice was signed, they returned to the capital.

Roger, who until then had lived outside any religious community, was quickly initiated into the "Jewish problem." The first roundups of 1941 affected friends close to the family. An unspoken anxiety pervaded his home. Bad news reached them from all sides. First it was his grandparents, who, they learned, had been interned in a Polish ghetto. Then, in June 1942, came the obligatory wearing of the yellow star. Yet Roger's life played out alongside his parents without too many changes. He removed his star at the beginning of his summer vacation and went camping with a troop of French Boy Scouts with which he had been affiliated for several years. His parents remained alone in Paris. They were both militants of the extreme Left and were forewarned about the July roundups in time. They fled toward the Unoccu-

177

pied Zone. Misfortune caught up with them at the demarcation line: they were stopped, identified as Jews, and deported on the spot.

Roger learned this sad news only upon his return from his vacation a fortnight later. With his twenty-one-year-old cousin whose parents had just met with the same fate, he immediately left Paris to take refuge in the home of the young woman's future in-laws at Saint-Rémy-de-Provence [halfway between Arles and Avignon in southeastern France]. Six months of utter idleness spent in rather cold surroundings made him feel his loss deeply.

In his precocious maturity, he tried to understand his fate and that of his parents. Were they not deported because they were Communists? And wasn't the struggle against Fascism worth any and all sacrifices?

No, he certainly felt that their battle had been lost on another level. What did it mean to be Jewish?

"I am French," he wrote later. "French is my native language, French culture is my culture. I was stirred by the epic of Vercingétorix, abhorred the noblemen who repressed the peasant revolts, detested Louis XIV, condemned and scorned the conquering Napoleon. But how I loved Robespierre, how enthusiastic I was for the Revolution![7] France is my country, my fatherland. Its history has given me confidence in its future."

His uneasiness got worse. He left his foster family to join his uncle at Roanne [a city about fifty miles from Vichy]. New disappointment: his uncle was distant and preoccupied with the fate of his own children. He himself maintained a stubborn silence that exasperated his uncle. The Sixth [Division] of the Jewish Boy Scouts of France took care of him. Since he was French, he registered under his real name as a boarder for the sophomore class at the *lycée* at Roanne. The situation worsened during 1943: all Jews henceforth ran the risk of arrest and deportation. In July and for the rest of the summer vacation, Roger was placed with a peasant, who only tried to make him work and with whom no personal contact was possible. Hence, beginning in September, he risked crossing again the demarcation line, in order to join his cousin, who in the meantime had gotten married, in Grenoble, in the Italian zone.

He was steered to the clandestine network of the OSE and placed under a false name in a little boarding school in [the *département*] of Isère. There were twelve of them, boys and girls, who every morning went by bus to the *lycée* six miles away. On Wednesdays they covered the distance by foot for lack of transportation. Roger felt very uncomfortable. The false identity bothered him like ill-fitting shoes. When he had to talk about his parents—who he said lived in Morocco—his suffering became intolerable. Why couldn't he even confide in his best friends? He was ashamed to deceive all his acquaintances in this manner and to reward with lies anyone who tried to fill his solitude.

In March 1944 they [the OSE] found a place for him in a private home near the *lycée* where he could complete the junior class in a better environment. A family of manufacturers in the city took him in during the holidays and lavished a great deal of comforting affection on him. But he had to tell lies to them as he did to the others. During the summer, he returned to a farm where the boss, a *bachelier* [someone who has passed the *baccalauréat,* which is a requirement for admission to a university] had taken a liking to him and taught him the love of the land and the beauty of farmwork. In August 1944 the FFI [Forces françaises de l'intérieur, the umbrella organization for the Resistance] occupied the farm, where, in an extraordinarily tense atmosphere, Roger awaited the end of the nightmare. He could no longer stand the tension and, in a somewhat premature outburst, dropped his role and yelled out in public: "I'm Jewish, and my name is Roger Waksman!"

EDDY SANDMAN: THE FAILURE OF A RESCUE

Eddy's history is one of those that left a tragic mark in the rescue operations of the OSE, because, in spite of all attempts, nothing was able to save him from death.

Eddy Sandman was born in Luxembourg in 1938. Having arrived in France with his parents in 1940 and after having been interned in Rivesaltes, he was hospitalized in Perpignan. The dossier, cold and terse, said: "Parents in the camp, the child in the hospital." Every week, his mother begged us to take Eddy into a day nursery.

When Eddy's health was restored in February 1942, we were finally able to get him out of the hospital. He was due to join a convoy leaving for the Creuse [the French *département* with the largest number of OSE children's homes] from the Rivesaltes railway station. His mother had obtained a special pass allowing her to see him several days earlier in Perpignan. She had to cover the eight kilometers [or five miles] on foot to find Eddy, whom she had not seen for several months. Eddy was now four years old and had forgotten how to speak [properly]: an incoherent blend of French, German, and Spanish[8] came out of his mouth. He had forgotten everything; he did not recognize her; he no longer smiled; he could hardly walk. "What have you done to him?" she asked. We then got permission for her to come to the railway station on the day of departure. The train from Perpignan stopped for three minutes at Rivesaltes. In the hubbub of the station and the departure, the mother had only three minutes to embrace her son.

Eddy's face seemed to be made up of a wax that had stayed out too long in the sun. We noticed in the train that he was suffering from a rectal prolapse. The director of [the children's home in] Chabannes hesitated before accepting him, for he needed very special care that was difficult to give within this collectivity of children.

In May 1942 we received photos of children who had left the camp, including an enlargement of Eddy's—he was unrecognizable. It was a genuine rebirth. We were told that he was happy and boisterous. He had become very handsome. His mother wept with joy.

The deportations of foreigners who had entered France after 1936 began in August 1942. Eddy's parents were deported, and we managed to remove him from being sent to join his family by transferring him to another establishment. We tried to have him emigrate to America with other children of deportees. But the U.S. entry into the war in November 1942[9] prevented the departures of convoys that were already waiting to embark in Marseille.

Children's homes were being broken up in March 1943, and Eddy was placed with a family in Indre [a *département* north of the Creuse], which sheltered him for more than a year. In May 1944 it was again necessary to transfer him as a result of "indiscretions" that put the children of Indre at risk. It was decided to send him clandestinely to Switzerland. A convoy guide took him to Lyon, where he had to spend the night before crossing the frontier, only one night before he would once again find safety. There Eddy was entrusted to a Jewish family from Algeria that had offered to shelter children. But the family was arrested that very night, as was he, and the social worker who came the [next] morning found the apartment empty. After all these displacements, ruses, hiding places, and so close to the goal, we still had not been able to save Eddy.

A terrible and guilty fear haunted me until the end of the war. If his mother, as a survivor and after all her misfortunes, were to come back to reclaim the son she had entrusted to us and whom we had not been able to save, I knew that she would not be able to endure this new tragedy, for which we had been partly responsible. Eddy and his parents, however, shared the same fate.

The name of Eddy Sandman was again brought up with a great deal of emotion during the Barbie trial.[10] One of the children of the Savarin family, which sheltered him in Indre between 1943 and 1944, had contacted Serge Klarsfeld [a French lawyer who has published the most extensive and reliable lists of Jews deported and killed by the Nazis and their allies] and then the OSE to find the trail of the little boy.

CORINNE: THE PRICE OF A RESCUE

Corinne's story is that of a daring rescue, which cost the social workers who carried it off very dearly.

Grenoble, in the Italian zone, had provided a secure shelter until September 1943. But the roundups and massive deportations began after the German occupation, and Grenoble became one of the most dangerous places for Jews to be in. It was then that M. and Mme. W. decided to get out of the city and leave Corinne, their three-month-old daughter, in a day nursery run by the Protection de l'enfance [Protection of Childhood] at Grenoble under the charge of the OSE.

M. W. was arrested by the Gestapo in January 1944 and forced to reveal the address where his daughter had been placed. The Gestapo immediately arrived to fetch the child. Realizing that it was a baby, the Germans decided to return with a nurse.

The director then alerted the OSE that a German nurse was going to take Corinne away. This led the young people in the secret network to drop everything and to take whatever action was necessary to save Corinne. It was decided to kidnap her.

A young blond woman by the name of Renée, who spoke German fluently, volunteered. She arrived at the nursery at the expected hour, provided with a document composed in German and carrying the Hitler eagle, and she ordered that the child be handed over to her. A vehicle was at her disposal. Everything was accomplished in two minutes. The bogus nurse left, carrying the little girl in her arms. The vehicle had just enough time to get away before the arrival of the Gestapo. Corinne was immediately placed in safety with a wetnurse in Savoie.

The Germans, furious at having been tricked, spent all their efforts trying to lay their hands on the perpetrators of the kidnapping. The director finally proved his good faith, but they succeeded in discovering—nobody knows how—the description and address of Mlle. Kahn, the OSE social worker. Not finding her at home, they arrested her younger sister at her workplace in reprisal. Although she was tortured, the sister did not reveal the OSE activities. She was interned at Drancy, then deported. She did not return. Once in Auschwitz, she remained with a little girl she had "adopted" at Drancy and who clung to her. They left together for the gas chamber.

Corinne's mother returned alone from Auschwitz in July 1945. She then placed Corinne in a day nursery in Perpignan and then with a non-Jewish family, the Mas family, with which she stayed for ten years. In being returned to her mother, Corinne once more suffered from being torn away from her adopted family, and serious difficulties arose in the mother–daughter relationship, which led them to consult the OSE in 1958.

Corinne got more and more involved in Jewish youth movements in Paris and made friends with the daughter of Rabbi Metzbach. A *juge des enfants* [a judge who handles cases that involve minors] named the Metzbach family Corinne's guardians. She met the person who was to become her husband, and at eighteen she left to live with him in the United States. They had two sons. After her husband's death, she left for Israel, where she busied herself with autistic children. Her sons, who are married and have children, live in the United States. Corinne has always kept in touch with Mme. Meyer, née Kahn, and with Renée, the young blond woman, both of whom saved her life.

EVA: THE TEMPTATION OF CONVERSION

Little has been said about those children who in a Christian setting were truly tempted to leave the religion in whose name they were being hounded and of their desperate search for a synthesis between Judaism and Christianity. On this issue this testimony seems to me to be of some importance.

Eva, born in Vienna in 1927, came to France in 1939. She was raised by parents who, though devout, were broad-minded. She had from her earliest years wanted to become either a rabbi's wife or a teacher of religion. [In Austria] she joined a Zionist youth movement at the age of nine and dreamed of emigrating to Palestine. But her parents, who had just lost two of their sons to illness, refused to separate from her. After the *Anschluss,* they thought of emigrating to Palestine, but the application process kept dragging on. The convoy of children with which Eva was due to leave [for Palestine] was canceled for lack of ships. She therefore left for France, where they thought she would have a better chance of emigrating. Her parents hoped to join her soon thereafter.

It is thus that Eva left [Austria] at the age of twelve. She was taken in at La Guette.[11] She was happy living there, in a community about which she had dreamt for a long time, and awaited impatiently the departure for the Promised Land. But war broke out, and Eva found herself cut off from her parents. In her childlike optimism, she could foresee only a war of short duration. She participated in civil defense work and preached the Zionist ideal to her comrades.

The children had to be evacuated in May 1940. Eva left for the residential school at Clermont-Ferrand, where she remained until November 1941, then rejoined her companions at Couret. Eva felt at ease in this [OSE] home where the [Jewish] religion was strictly observed, and she refused to find out anything about the arrests and deportations that proliferated outside its walls. She received the news of her parents' departure for "an unknown destination" with skepticism.

At that time, this denial took on for her the character of a [Girl] Scout game. Eva lived from day to day, and, because she didn't want to leave her friends once again, refused to join a convoy of children headed for Mexico. In March 1943, she left for a residential school in the south under a false identity.

She asked to be baptized in January 1944.

When I met her in 1946, I understood that this baptism had only been the outcome of an extended religious crisis. She explained to me: "To my anguished questions: 'why, why?' Christ alone had the answer. I found Christianity in the Bible. In my view, it represents the only solution to peace and universal harmony. I thought that the Christian ideal of the union of men in God was superior to that of the Jews, who more and more lose their faith and seek only to establish themselves materially in any country that will rescue them from oppression." She told me of the difficulty there might be in expressing in words "the struggle of a being who must contemplate the renunciation of all that is dear to him, to surrender himself only into the hands of God." She thus seemed to rediscover herself in the image of Christ: "Did not Christ say: 'Everyone who has left his house or brothers or sisters or father or mother for my sake will receive a hundredfold and inherit eternal life'?" [a slightly abridged version of Matthew 19:29]. Eva handed me several pages of a private note-book, written between March 1943 and January 1944. She entitled the passage "My Religious Struggle." In these lines I could sense that she was torn between "the light of Christ" and "the religion of my Fathers that is so dear to me." Thus, she wrote to the director of a children's home of the OSE, whom she called her "second mother," her "spiritual mother":

> No! your daughter cannot betray you. I suffer because, as long as I am here, I am run-ning after a certain light that I have not the slightest intention of reaching. Mama, Madame, it is you who have caused me to love God. Oh! pray to Him so that I may re-main yours, yours and my people's. . . . I repudiate nothing. I simply renounce rites that no longer have any *raison d'être* for me. I wish to be both Christian and Jewish, and, if Providence should will it, it is always to my brothers, my blood brothers, that I will try to give the best of myself.

After this period of mystical doubt, Eva at last entered Israel illegally in 1947, where she was immediately integrated into a *kibbutz* [an Israeli collective farm or settlement]. She has returned to Judaism and has three married daughters, all of whom live in Israel.

CLAUDE BÉGUÉ-MORHANGE: TO FIND HER MOTHER ONCE AGAIN

Life often remained difficult for children who were reunited with relatives who had survived deportation. In a very moving book published in the United States,[12] Claude Bégué-Morhange tells us what she, a little eight-year-old girl, who already had lost her father, felt when she once again met her physician mother, who had re-turned from Auschwitz.

> Or at least they appeared unchanged to me, her eyes, her smile, owing to which I did not notice her fearful thinness, the absence of her long blond hair, ill replaced by short unkempt tufts full of large whitish nits. But little did it matter. She was back; and I had made so many bargains with the Catholic God, waiving her smile and her good mood ahead of time provided she return, be it in a bad temper and unkind. She was back, my heart's desire . . . lying in a bed where she was to remain for a fourth part of a year, only to exchange that bed for another. But little did that matter, either. She was back, just

184

in time for my birthday, and it was I who received a gift, *The Little Prince* [the tale, half symbolic and half fairy tale, by the aviator-author Antoine de Saint-Exupéry], that I didn't like at the time, having understood neither the book's contents nor what she wrote in inscribing it to me—*After her miraculous escape from prison*—not yet having begun to listen, night after night, year after year, to those obsessional stories of daily life in a German death camp. . . . When several months later (that she had spent in a convalescent home), I both found my mother anew and, at the same time, lost her. By then she was truly out of danger, but the effects of edema had more surely destroyed the harmony of her features than had the dreadful thinness that had reduced her to a pair of eyes and a smile. Seeing her again, it took me a few seconds to recognize my mother in this lady who made happy gestures and laughed while she gazed at me. . . . The war was over. Neither of us was dead. We were living together in the same house; we loved each other. But over the course of those months I had somehow turned irrevocably into an adult. From then on, it was incumbent upon me to protect my mother, who had come close to dying and who would remain fragile for a long time, at least so we anticipated. . . . Henceforth it would be mine to listen in order to become imbued with her stories, without yet knowing that this ingestion preluded another task: that of speaking, for her and in her name, about the unspeakable that she had had the strength both to live through and to vanquish, but that she would not be able to bring herself to consign to words, . . . relying instead upon oral tradition and, for its preservation, upon this link to the future sprung from her, who has now assumed her mission.

EHUD LOEB: THE FOSTER FAMILY

Here is an excerpt from a moving testimony by Ehud Loeb that he himself presented during the eightieth anniversary of the OSE. In this colloquium, which took place in the large lecture hall of the Sorbonne in December 1993, several children from the war spoke to an audience that included several persons who had taken the same journey as they had.

Who am I? Born in a little town south of Baden-Baden in Germany, not far from Strasbourg, but on the other side of the Rhine. My names: Herbert Odenheimer, which became Hubert Odenheimer in France, then Hubert Odet, my forged name in 1943, then Herbert Loeb (after my adoption); in Israel I took the first name of Ehud; my family name is pronounced Lev in Jerusalem. Hence, I am Ehud Lev. This multitude of names reflects the stages of my odyssey. . . .

185

I was six and a half years old when we—the 6,538 Jews of the provinces of Baden and the Palatinate—were collected on 22 October 1940 and transported in a convoy of several trains to the "internment camp" of Gurs, in the first step of the "dejudaization" of the German Reich. There's no need to recall in detail this camp in which—according to survivors, researchers, and historians—there prevailed, especially during the winter of 1940–1941, absolutely inhumane conditions, a precarious sanitary and medical situation. Gurs was the antechamber of Auschwitz-Birkenau. One thousand thirty persons, including my grandmother, died there. My parents were deported to Auschwitz in August and September 1942 and gassed at Auschwitz-Birkenau.

It was only about six months ago that I dared, for the first time, to request details on my parents from a cousin living in Israel. I remember them very well, but I needed to confirm the accuracy of my memory. This cousin told me how my parents loved me and how they spoiled me; I was their only child, born after three unsuccessful pregnancies.

My father was no longer allowed to work in the printing shop and stationery store owned by his father-in-law, and from 1936 on we resided in the poorhouse maintained by the Jewish community and that supported thirty persons in all. Yet my parents did everything possible to feed me, dress me, raise me, and spoil me; I was their one and only joy. In February 1941, they must have made a difficult decision at Gurs, namely to agree to have me escape from the camp[13] and to entrust me to the OSE, to strangers. There was no way for them to know whether even one of us would survive this hell. For a year and a half, until their deaths in Auschwitz, they remained ignorant of their child's fate. It was an act of courage on the part of parents to separate themselves from their only and beloved child, without knowing who would take care of him, without knowing whether he would stay alive or whether, on the contrary, he would go to a certain death, while they themselves might perhaps be saved.

The OSE took charge of me from February 1941 to January 1946. I was taken from Gurs to the children's home at Chabannes, where I remained for several months, emaciated, sick, and, above all, heartbroken from being separated from my parents. Even today, I remember crying bitterly entire nights, and the nurses and instructors who vainly tried to console me. From there, in November 1942, the OSE tried to hide me with a Christian family in a city of the *département* of Indre. I remained there until 1944, with a brief interruption in 1943; when the danger was too great, they hid me in a small village nearby. In 1989, Jules and Jeanne Roger were acknowledged among "the Righteous of the Nations" by Yad Vashem.[14] He was a butcher; she took care of their fields and garden. Jules Roger was a member of the underground Resistance; his job entitled him to gasoline, and, naturally, his trips by car were made for other purposes. Their house was often full of wounded Resistance fighters, and plans for military operations lay all over the house. At the same time, they were hiding two little Jewish refugees. The other boy, who was younger than I, was a refugee from Poland and

Belgium who, like me, had been taken care of by the OSE and placed by them. They faced the risk of being denounced, captured, and shot on the spot. The Rogers, who were devout Catholics, never tried to convert me. I was the best student at the catechism, and, in the small village where I was hiding in 1943 (only the village priest knew I was Jewish), I played my part of choirboy with great enthusiasm. It was explained to me that once the war was over, I would meet my parents again and would be welcomed back into the bosom of my people.

The rescue of thousands of Jewish children could not have taken place in France without the active aid of hundreds of people, Jewish and non-Jewish, and of certain Christian institutions that, in full knowledge, acted in opposition to the laws decreed by the Vichy government and to the incomprehensible silence of the Holy See. Hundreds of French citizens decided to risk their lives to save these "petits refugiés juifs," that is, children, refugees, Jews. I parenthetically note the translation of these three words in German: *Jüdische Fluchtingskinder*—Jews, refugees, children. Does the character of a people influence its syntax and grammar? These saviors have remained and unfortunately will largely remain anonymous. Their files at Yad Vashem in Jerusalem, the diploma and medal they were awarded, the few publications devoted to them are insufficient to honor the enormous courage and human dignity they demonstrated. We ourselves and our children owe our lives to them.

I also wish to render homage to my adopted parents. When they took me in January 1946, I was at that very difficult age of twelve: I was a debilitated, uprooted, disoriented child, formed by years of solitude and anguish, and a total stranger to their lifestyle, to a new language. I have lived since then in a country, Switzerland, that offered me everything I lacked during my years of deprivation. My adopted parents gave me everything: their name, their affection, their love, my schooling, and my professional training. I've found a new family. And they did everything possible for me so that I would forget, but can one forget, bury the past? . . . I've realized my dream: to live in Israel and to leave behind me the lands of pogroms and of the crematoriums, and of the virulent or subtle antisemitism that is unfortunately found once more here and there. The first time one of our daughters, then hardly eight years old, left to visit her grandparents in Switzerland, I asked her, "What will you say if you're called 'a dirty Jew'?" "What!" she asked, not understanding my question. "I can't even tell him he's a dirty Christian!" I realized that our children have been able to grow up without our weighty memories, without our complexes, without our repressed silences. Strongly conscious of the past, they are free, proud, strong, and confident about the future. They are what I would have liked to have been when I was their age. . . .

Appendices
Acronyms and Abbreviations
Notes
Bibliography
Index

Appendix 1
What Happened to Them?

The history that I lived through would not have been possible had it not been for the creation of a long chain of solidarity. Here is what happened to some of the people mentioned in this book. Many others also deserve to be mentioned.

JOSÉ CARTIER-BRESSON, NÉE HERMANN

José Cartier-Bresson[1] studied medicine and practiced as a pediatrician before becoming a psychoanalyst, a profession she still practices today. She is married and has three children and three grandchildren. She was decorated with the Military Cross for her work in the Resistance.

GEORGES GAREL

Georges Garel took over the direction of the OSE in 1945 in order to complete the task undertaken [during the war] and to lead that philanthropic society in its return to legality. In 1948, deeming his mission accomplished, he resumed his job as an engineer. Replaced by Robert Job, he nevertheless remained president of the OSE until 1978. Seven children were born from his marriage to Lili Tager. Chevalier of the Legion of Honor, officer of the Order of Merit, holder of the Medal of the Resistance, he died in January 1979.

THE *ABBÉ* GLASBERG

After the war, he pursued his work on behalf of foreigners, as well as his battle against discrimination. He directed a center of orientation for foreigners and in 1946 published, with his team, *A la recherche d'une patrie* [In Search of a Fatherland], which bears witness to the experience of Christian Friendship members during the war and the Occupation. He died in the 1990s.

OLGA AND LAZARE GURVIC

After the war, Lazare and Olga Gurvic remained in the Union-OSE headquarters of Geneva. Lazare was vice-president of the Swiss branch and general secretary of the Union-OSE. He died in November 1960, and his wife survived him by only a few years.

RACHEL HERMANN

Having returned to Paris after the war, she learned, along with all of us, that her husband was not going to return [from Auschwitz]. She was only fifty-five years old. She lived modestly on a war widow's pension and an allowance from the Joint. She put up a fight to regain her apartment, but it took her ten years of legal proceedings to win her case. In the meantime, she resumed her literary activities in Yiddish and Hebrew newspapers in Paris. She traveled a great deal and visited the Soviet Union and Israel in search of family members. She died in 1979, after having finished writing an autobiography for her children and grandchildren, and thus having erected a "tomb of paper" to the memory of her husband.

GILBERT LESAGE

Only the liberation saved Gilbert Lesage from serious reprisals on the part of the Vichy authorities, who had suspected him of being a double agent. He received the Medal of the Righteous at Yad Vashem in 1985 and died in the 1990s.

GEORGES LOINGER

Bearer of the Military Cross and of the Medal of the Resistance and Chevalier of the Legion of Honor, he became director of the Israeli shipping company Choham Zim in Paris after the war and remained in that post for thirty years. Retired, he is now very active within the ARJ (Anciens Résistants juifs de France [Jewish Resistance Veterans of France]), of which he is president. Flore and Georges have two sons and two grandchildren.

GERMAINE MASOUR (ALIAS DESSONAZ)

In 1945 she headed the department of family reunion and emigration. Accompanying a group of children to the United States, she led a fund-raising campaign on behalf of the OSE children and managed the collection of funds. After her retirement in 1961 and until her death in November 1983, she continued to maintain warm and personal relations with all the children she had known, as well as with her former colleagues. She left behind a beautiful, unpublished testimony entitled *Mes vingt ans à l'OSE* [My Twenty Years with the OSE].

RÉGINE RABNER

After the war, she became instructor in the children's home that had sheltered her, then worked within Jewish philanthropic societies. Married, she had two children. She died in the 1980s.

ANDRÉE SALOMON

She left the OSE on 30 December 1947 and after the war gradually resumed her Zionist work. She waited for the retirement of her husband, Tobie, a famous chemist, to settle with him and their son, Jean, in Beersheba, Israel. Struck by a severe illness, she nonetheless continued to occupy herself with all "her" children throughout the world. From 1980 on, she participated in the restoration of the OSE archives. She had the good fortune to see her two grandchildren grow up before she died in July 1985. She forbade anyone to solicit the Legion of Honor in her behalf.

JACQUES SALON

It was with some difficulty that he recovered from the loss of his wife, Nicole Weill, who had been deported with a group of children in 1943. He made his life over again with an OSE social worker, with whom he had four children. He once again took up his post of business manager and died in 1989, leaving an important but unpublished written testimony on his and his wife Nicole's activities.

JULIEN SAMUEL

After the liberation, he assumed the direction of the medicosocial department of the OSE, which had reopened its office in Paris. He changed jobs in January 1950, at which time he was named general director of the Fonds social juif unifié (FSJU) [United Jewish Social Fund]. He died in 1981.

JOSEPH WEILL

From 1945 on, he helped provide medical assistance to camp survivors in Germany. He contributed to the restoration of the OSE services. Once his work was completed, he retired to his native Alsace with his wife and three sons and resumed the practice of medicine, all the while holding the position of president of the Consistory [executive assembly of rabbis and lay assistants] of the Bas-Rhin [leading *département* of Alsace]. In 1983 he published at his own expense a text, [Already], of more than eight hundred pages, on his multiple activities. Chevalier of the Legion of Honor, he passed away in 1988.

Appendix 2

Some Numbers

GENERAL DATA ON FRANCE

- Between 300,000 and 330,000 Jews in France in 1939[1]
- Between 18,000 and 20,000 interned in camps at the beginning of the war
- About 100,000 Jews on the routes of the exodus after June 1940
- 75 percent of the Jews survived extermination (of whom 86.2 percent were children, who were better protected than the adults)
- 72,400 Jewish children (under eighteen years of age) survived, and 11,600 were killed

NUMBERS CONCERNING THE ACTIONS TAKEN BY THE OSE

Between January and June 1942

- 816 children were sheltered in the children's homes of the OSE
- 578 were placed with foster families
- 206 children were liberated from the [French] camps (623 if those liberated in 1941 are included)
- 4,500 adults were given assistance in the camps
- 3,412 families, including 2,373 children, were followed up on and given assistance
- 46 children were sent to the United States[2]

At the end of 1944, the French branch of the OSE had 5,700 dossiers on children who had been placed in children's homes or in foster families.

Appendix 3
Chronology

1939

23 August	The German–Soviet nonaggression pact
3 September	[Great Britain's and France's] declaration of war against Germany
September	Internment of "enemies of the nation" in [French] camps

1940

4 May	The construction of Auschwitz
17 May	Marshal Pétain named vice-president of the Cabinet
12 June	Breach of the French lines of battle
14 June	The Germans' entry into Paris
17 June	Formation of a new [French] government and Marshal Pétain's speech requesting an armistice
18 June	General de Gaulle's call from London for continued resistance
22 June	Signing of the armistice
10 July	Marshal Pétain made head of state
27 September	German statute on the census of Jews in the Occupied Zone
3 October	Promulgation of the Statute of the Jews by the Vichy government
4 October	Law authorizing the internment of "foreigners of the Jewish race" in special camps
7 October	Algerian Jews deprived of their French nationality
18 October	German law providing for the census of Jewish businesses and assigning them trustees
22 October–7 November	Addition of the word "Jew" on identity cards in the Northern Zone, as requested by the Germans

October	Transfer of seven thousand Jews from the provinces of Baden and the Palatinate to the [French] camp of Gurs

1941

23 March	Creation of the Commissariat-General for Jewish Affairs
14 May	Arrest of thousands of foreign Jews by the French police and their internment in the camps of Pithiviers and Beaune-la-Rolande
2 June	The second Statute of the Jews, forbidding them access to the professions, as well as to higher education
June	Census of Jews in the Unoccupied Zone
13 August	Confiscation of radios from Jews in the Northern Zone
21 August	Creation of the camp of Drancy
3 September	First massive gassing at Auschwitz
29 November	Establishment of the UGIF
8 December	U.S. entry into the war

1942

20 January	Wannsee Conference: the "Final Solution" to the Jewish issue decided by the Nazis
7 February	Imposition of a curfew on Jews between 8 P.M. and 6 A.M.
27 March	First deportations of one thousand Jews arrested in December 1941
16 April	Return of Pierre Laval as head of government
16 May	Replacement of Xavier Vallat by Louis Darquier de Pellepoix at the Commissariat-General for Jewish Affairs
1 June	Jews in the Northern Zone required to wear the yellow star
8 July	Drastic restriction on Jews' freedom; restaurants, theaters, parks, and similar facilities barred to them in the Northern Zone
16 July	Roundup of the Vel' d'hiv' in Paris
August	First roundup of Jews in the Southern Zone
4 September	Establishment of the STO [Service du travail obligatoire]
8 November	American landing in North Africa
11 November	Occupation of the Southern Zone by the Germans and the Italians
26 November	Scuttling of the French fleet at Toulon
11 December	Pierre Laval's decree requiring Jews in all of France to add the word "Jew" to their identity cards

1943

January	Establishment of the Milice by Joseph Darnand
24 July	Fall of Mussolini
3 September	Italian capitulation and the signing of the armistice
9 September	German occupation of the former Italian zone

1944

6 June	Allied landing in Normandy
25 August	Entry of the Second French Armored Division into Paris and German capitulation, but continuation of fighting in eastern France

1945

27 January	Liberation of Auschwitz
11 April	Liberation of Buchenwald
8 May	Signing of the armistice [ending World War II in Europe]
14 November	Opening of the Nuremberg trials

PARIS
Committee of the
OSE directed
by Doctor Eugène Minkowski

CHABANNES
CHAUMONT
USSAC MASGELIER
BROUT-VERNET
LE COURET MONTINTIN
MAS-JAMBOT CROCQ
POULOUZAT
LIMOGES
(boarding school) (nursery)

MIRIBEL
SAINT-PAUL-EN-CHABLAIS
MOUTIERS-SALINS

ESPERE
SAINT-RAPHAEL
PALAVAS-LES-FLOTS
(villa Mariana)

■— Children's homes

▲— Children's homes
of strict religious observance

Children's homes of the OSE from the end of 1939 to February 1944

Acronyms and Abbreviations

ADIR   Association des déportées et internées de la Résistance [Association of Deported and Interned Women of the Resistance]

AIU   Alliance israélite universelle [Universal Jewish Alliance]

CAR   Comité d'aide aux réfugiés [Committee for Assistance to Refugees]

CCOJA   Commission centrale des organisations juives d'assistance [Central Committee of Jewish Aid Societies]

CIMADE   Comité intermouvements d'aide aux évacuées [Committee of Societies for Aid to Evacuated People]

EIF   Éclaireurs israélites de France [Jewish Boy Scouts of France]

GTE   Groupement de travailleurs étrangers [Foreign Labor Battalion]

HICEM   Association d'aide à l'émigration juive [Mutual Aid Society on Jewish Emigration]

Joint   American Jewish Joint Distribution Committee

ORT   Organisation-Reconstruction-Travail [Organization-Reconstruction-Work]

OSE   Œuvre de secours aux enfants [Society for Assistance to Children]

SSAE   Service social d'aide aux emigrants [Social Service for Aid to Emigrants]

STO   Service du travail obligatoire [Service of Obligatory Labor]

UGIF   Union générale des israélites de France [General Union of the Jews of France]

YMCA   Young Men's Christian Association

Notes

INTRODUCTION

Note: The epigraph is taken from Lucien Lazare, *Rescue as Resistance: How Jewish Organizations Fought the Holocaust in France,* trans. Jeffrey M. Green (New York: Columbia University Press, 1996), 134. Unless indicated otherwise, the notes are the translator's.

1. Marion Michel Oliner, review of *Sauver les enfants, Martyrdom and Resistance* (March–April and May–June 1996).

2. H. R. Kedward, *Occupied France: Collaboration and Resistance, 1940–1944* (Oxford: Basil Blackwell, 1985), 4.

3. In *The Courage to Care: Rescuers of Jews during the Holocaust,* eds. Carol Rittner and Sondra Meyers (New York: New York University Press, 1986), 67–68.

4. Kedward, *Occupied France,* 55.

5. *Martyrdom and Resistance* (May–June 1996).

6. In *The Courage to Care,* 125.

CHAPTER 1. ODESSA TO PARIS

1. World War I, in which Russia and the Turkish Empire fought on opposite sides.

2. A traditional Jewish academy devoted essentially to the study of the Talmud and the rabbinical literature. [Vivette Samuel, henceforth indicated as V. S.]

3. One of the *grandes écoles,* the prestigious state schools of higher education.

4. "Patriots" undoubtedly refers to some citizens of Alsace and Lorraine, which were taken over by the Germans during the Franco-Prussian War of 1870–1871 and returned to France at the end of World War I.

5. The name given at that period to the senior year in the *lycée;* the term is no longer used.

6. The Rhineland, not the Ruhr, was reoccupied by Germany in 1936 in direct violation of the Treaty of Versailles, which declared the region west of the Rhine a demilitarized zone.

7. In an attempt to avoid war, Prime Ministers Chamberlain of Great Britain and Daladier of France met with Hitler and Mussolini in Munich, Germany, to discuss the issue of the

Sudetenland, and they gave Hitler a free hand to take over the Czech territory in exchange for a guaranteeing that the integrity of the remainder of Czechoslovakia would be respected. Germany, however, invaded and occupied that country in March 1939. Ever since that time, the phrase "Munich Pact" has become synonymous with appeasement and abject surrender in international affairs.

8. The legislative achievements of the Popular Front include the forty-hour work week and the first paid vacations for workers.

9. Jacques Prévert (1900–1977), a French poet and scenarist for films; Jean Giono (1895–1970), a French novelist.

CHAPTER 2. WAR, EXODUS, AND OCCUPATION

1. A pact signed between Germany and the Soviet Union, in which each party agreed to remain neutral if the other were attacked by a third power. The secret clause of the pact providing for the division of Poland into zones of influence was put into effect when Poland was invaded by Germany on 1 September and by the Soviet Union on 17 September.

2. On 27 September, the Axis powers of Germany, Japan, and Italy concluded a ten-year-long military and economic alliance.

3. The British expeditionary force of about two hundred thousand men, as well as 140,000 French, were caught in the Dunkirk salient on the Channel, from which they were evacuated to England on 14 June.

4. This was the definition of "foreigners in surplus in the national economy," meaning, those who had no regular work. [V. S.]

5. See the testimony of Gerda Einbinder in the chapter "Children's Odysseys." [V. S.]

6. See "The OSE and Its History" in chapter 3. [V. S.]

7. Each of the *départements* making up metropolitan France was governed by a *préfet* responsible to the Ministry of the Interior in either zone. Algeria was at that time an integral part of France, and its Christians and Jews were granted special privileges.

8. In 1940 the United States, the Soviet Union, Spain, and Greece were not at war with Germany. On 26 June 1940, the Soviet Union took Bessarabia and northern Bukovina from Romania, and, on 21 July 1940, it annexed the three Baltic states of Estonia, Latvia, and Lithuania.

9. It is by referring to the essays she wrote at that time that the author was able to compose this part of the testimony on the "Statute of the Jews" and on Paris under the Occupation. They were rediscovered in the papers of Professor Meyerson, deceased in 1983 (Archives nationales 521 AP 58. Ten manuscript letters; a typed letter of July 1939; an essay signed Vivette Hermann on the persecutions and anti-Jewish measures taken by the French authorities; eight typed pages dated 11 November 1940). [V. S.]

10. *Gleichschalten* literally means "to normalize," "to bring into step with," "to make uniform." [V. S.]

11. The forerunner of the yellow star. [V. S.] Throughout occupied Europe, the German government required all Jews to wear in public a yellow star sewn on their outer garments.

12. A *concours de l'agrégation* is a competitive examination for posts on the teaching staff of *lycées* and universities; a *professeur agrégé* is a teacher who has passed the *agrégation* exam.

13. See the photograph on p. 61. [V. S]

14. Jacques Doriot, one-time Communist mayor of Saint-Denis, turned Nazi collaborator and formed the Légion des volontaires contre le bolshévisme (Anti-Bolshevik Legion), which was made up of French volunteers who fought in German uniform on the Russian front after the summer of 1941. Doriot was killed when his car was strafed by an Allied plane in 1945.

15. Jean Jaurès (1859–1914), historian, orator, and the leader of the Socialist party in France. A militant pacifist, he was assassinated by an ultranationalist on the eve of World War I (on 31 July 1914), a war that he had tried to prevent with all the powers and eloquence at his command.

CHAPTER 3. TO BE COMMITTED AT THE AGE OF TWENTY

1. *Le Figaro* was, and is, a leading French newspaper. Lons-le-Saulnier is the capital of the *département* of Jura, near the Swiss border.

2. Organizations, formed by the Vichy government, of twenty-year-old men who worked in forest work camps.

3. "A flower on the hat, a song in the mouth. . . ."

4. Clara Goldschmidt (1897–1982), a Jewish-German intellectual, was married in 1921 to André Malraux (1901–1976), novelist, aesthetician, pilot, and politician. They were divorced in 1930.

5. The American Jewish Joint Distribution Committee. Founded in 1914 to help Jews in Palestine who were facing starvation, it remained in existence and continued to extend aid to Jews throughout the world. It is the main philanthropic organization that represents American Jews. [V. S.]

6. One aspect of the program of the Vichy regime "'declared war on the world of money' and longed to revive a preindustrial world in which 'the fields were plowed, sown, planted and harvested. . . .'"(Emmanuel Mounier, "Programme pour le mouvement de jeunesse français," *Esprit*, 9e année, no. 96 [January 1941]: 152–167); Jean Giono, *Ides et calendes* (Paris, 1942), both quoted in Robert O. Paxton, *Vichy France* (New York: Columbia University Press, 1972), 141.

7. Agde was an internment camp in the *département* of Hérault, near the Mediterranean Sea.

8. Comité d'intermouvements d'aide aux évacués [Committee of Societies for Aid to Evacuees], a merger of various Protestant youth organizations. [V. S.]

9. Obstechestvo Zdvavooberaney Evrei: Society for the Medical Protection of Jewish Populations. [V. S.]

10. The state ministry in charge of maintaining order within France.

11. Joseph Weill, *Contribution à l'histoire des camps d'internement dans l'Anti-France* (Paris: Editions du Centre, 1946). [V. S.]

12. And, in July 1941, the OSE obtained the necessary funds from the Joint of New York to fit out children's homes. [V. S.]

13. A third convoy of children left in May 1942. The last one was stopped in November 1942 because of the German invasion of the Southern Zone. [V. S.]

14. For the location of all the children's homes run by the OSE during World War II, please see the map on p. 199.

15. The capital of the *département* of Pyrénées-Orientales and only six miles from the internment or concentration camp of Rivesaltes.

CHAPTER 4. RIVESALTES

1. The tramontane is a strong cold wind blowing for most of the year, forcing us children to walk bent over when we were outside.

2. I distinctly remember the toilets being made up of raised, doorless platforms, into whose floors had been cut holes, below which stood metal tubs or cans. These tubs were emptied by crews of male internees.

3. The Spanish Republicans who lost the war against the insurgent pro-Franco forces.

4. Extract of a report presented in May 1941 to the Nîmes Coordinating Committee by Dr. Joseph Weill. This text is produced in *extenso* in his book *Contribution à l'histoire des camps d'internement dans l'Anti-France.* [V. S.]

5. "Ubuesque" is an adjective meaning repulsive and grotesque. It is derived from "le Père Ubu," the main character of *Ubu Roi* (1896), a satirical farce by the Symbolist writer Alfred Jarry (1873–1907).

6. Kristallnacht, or "the night of broken glass," 9–10 November 1938, climaxed the issuance of a series of Nazi edicts that persecuted and discriminated against Jews in Germany and deprived them of their citizenship. In retaliation for the murder of a German diplomat in Paris by a young Jewish man, the Nazi government during Kristallnacht orchestrated well-organized attacks upon synagogues and Jewish property throughout the Reich, levied an enormous fine upon the Jewish community, and interned many Jews in concentration camps.

7. This was actually a German organization; only the name was Jewish. [V. S.]

8. No Spanish child was deported. [V. S.]

9. Formed by the Vichy government on 27 September 1940, they were under the authority of the Service des étrangers [Assistance to Foreigners] [V. S.]

10. After the war, she emigrated to the United States, where she married. [V. S.]

11. A festive eight-day Jewish holiday that is celebrated in December to commemorate the rededication of the Second Temple in Jerusalem in the second century B.C.

12. A candlestick with seven branches. [V. S.]

13. See the testimony of Paul Niederman, a child rescued from the camp of Rivesaltes, in the chapter "Children's Odysseys." [V. S.]

14. Eclaireurs israélites de France [Jewish Boy Scouts of France]. They took an important part in the rescue of adolescents. Edouard and Shatta Simon directed the home at Moissac. [V. S.]

15. Moissac and Charry were EIF centers, and Vic-sur-Cère, run by a director of the OSE, Henriette Malkin (wife of Dr. Malkin) belonged to Christian Friendship. See the testimony of Martin Oppenheimer in the chapter "Children's Odysseys." [V. S.]

16. OSE archival report, reproduced *in extenso* in the work *Au secours des enfants du siècle,* under the direction of Martine Lemalet, Nil Editions, 193. [V. S.]

17. See the testimony of Gerda Einbinder in the chapter "Children's Odysseys." [V. S.]

18. My sister was one of these adolescents, since at the time of her liberation from the camp in the spring of 1942 she was sixteen and a half years old.

19. It should be noted that, if it was difficult to communicate between the two zones, one could accomplish it through overseas countries via Switzerland, Spain, and Portugal, at least until November 1942, when the Germans occupied the Southern Zone. [V. S.]

CHAPTER 5. AT THE TIME OF THE DEPORTATIONS

1. In February 1941 Lesage assumed command of the Social Service of Foreigners at Vichy. He had infiltrated Vichy's services in order to divulge certain pieces of information to the Resistance and to act as a buffer between them. [V. S.]

2. Raon-l'Étape is a small town in the Vosges, a mountain range that separates Alsace from Lorraine.

3. The manner of applying the Final Solution had been decided by the Nazis at the Wannsee Conference in January 1942. [V. S.]

4. This was three months before Germany occupied the Southern Zone on 11 November 1942 (except for some southeastern *départements* to be occupied by Italy).

5. My two parents should be counted among these deportees.

6. Before being regrouped in camps from which the deportation convoys later departed. [V. S.]

7. Eventually all Jews would be affected, even Frenchmen and the wives of prisoners of war who had heretofore been exempt. [V. S.]

8. Testimony drawn up in 1946 by Andrée Salomon for Vivette Samuel's work *Comme les brebis* [Like Lambs], deposited with AIU (Alliance israélite universelle [Universal Jewish Alliance]) in Paris. [V. S.]

9. It is thus that for the second time the OSE saved my sister's and my life.

10. The commission that undertook to study the exemptions to the deportations. [V. S.]

11. See "August 1942: The Night of Vénissieux,"in this chapter. [V. S.].

12. That is, the "L" stamped by the camp commander in the children's exit pass.

13. René Bousquet, chief of police of the Vichy regime.

14. In July 1993, while I participated in Jerusalem in an international reunion of children who had been hidden in France, a woman in her sixties stood up and addressed me while I was at the speaker's platform. She introduced herself as one of the girls of Couret. There were eleven of them in the audience and they all asked to be photographed with me. In the emotion that we then shared, I felt what the marriage must have meant to them at a time when, without knowing it, they were undoubtedly orphans already. I also understood what one of them meant to say to me by these words: "I've had four children, I have twelve grandchildren, that's my revenge on Hitler." [V. S.]

15. The wife of Professor Meyerson, who had directed my thesis. [V. S.]

16. The official function of that organization was to represent Jews to the public authorities. It was directly subordinated to the authority of the Commissariat aux questions juives (Commissionership on Jewish Matters), directed by Xavier Vallat. Its role was very controversial, at that moment and subsequently. [V. S.]

17. This was the legitimation card that was passed out to officials of the UGIF: those who carried this card were protected from roundups for a period of time. See the photograph on p. 151. [V. S.]

18. There was a widespread belief, encouraged by the Vichy regime itself, that its head, Marshal Pétain, was playing a double game. That game was overtly collaborating with Nazi Germany while covertly working with the French Resistance movement, within and outside of France and officially headed after 1942 by General de Gaulle in London. There was never any truth to the belief in Pétain as a double agent.

CHAPTER 6. THE HUNT FOR THE CHILDREN

1. The text they had to sign was a declaration of "surrender of the rights of guardianship and paternal authority to the UGIF," according to the terms of the 1889 law. See the photograph on p. 68. [V. S.]

2. Limoges is the capital of the *département* of Haute-Vienne, which is flanked on the eastern side by the *département* of Creuse.

3. Or the third floor, if we count in the American manner.

4. The Vichy regime replaced the motto Liberté, Égalité, Fraternité of the Third Republic with the motto Travail, Famille, Patrie [Work, Family, Fatherland].

5. "Françoise" is the old French word for "Frenchwoman."

6. See "August 1942: The Night of Vénissieux," in chapter 5. [V. S.]

7. The European center of the Joint was located in Lisbon. [V. S.]

8. Germaine Masour, *Mes vingt ans à l'OSE* [My Twenty Years with the OSE], written in 1984 and deposited at the Alliance israëlite universelle. [V. S.]

9. The transmission *Les Français parlent aux Français* [The French Are Speaking to the French] and its slogan Radio-Paris Ment, Radio-Paris Est Allemand [Radio-Paris Tells Lies, Radio-Paris Is German] were listened to despite the danger of being denounced and arrested. [V. S.] The penalty for this "crime" was either death or deportation to a German camp.

10. The Allied invasion first of North Africa, then of Sicily and the Italian mainland.

11. Specifically, the Calvinist church, the dominant Protestant church in France.

12. See the remarkable film *Weapons of the Spirit,* written in 1990 by a man who had been sheltered as a child in Chambon-sur-Lignon. A commune is the smallest administrative unit in France.

13. A mountainous and poor region of south central France, known for a Protestant insurrection against Louis XIV's policy that forbade the French from practicing the Protestant faith.

14. Clandestine section of the Jewish Scouts. [V. S.]

15. These lists made it possible after the liberation of France for my sister to find my address in Switzerland, to which I had escaped in March 1944.

16. Germaine Masour, *Mes vingt ans à l'OSE.* [V. S.]

17. Allied bombings of military installations, factories, railroads, and other military targets in France intensified in the months preceding the Normandy invasion of June 1944.

18. In Spain he would have joined a convoy to bring him to his uncle in Palestine.

19. Other meanings of the word in the original text, *égarement,* are "aberration," "deviation," and "wildness."

20. See his testimony in the chapter "Children's Odysseys." [V. S.]

21. For the recording of births, deaths, weddings, and similar occasions.

22. Testimony written in 1947 for Vivette Samuel by Georges Loinger, who had been in charge of the clandestine crossings into Switzerland. [V. S.]

23. A narrative transmitted to Vivette Samuel by Elizabeth Hirsch. [V. S.]

CHAPTER 7. GOING UNDERGROUND

1. Soon after the Italian capitulation in September 1943, that zone was occupied by the Germans. The special commando unit led by Aloïs Brunner arrived in Nice on 10 September; 1,819 Jews were arrested and deported. [V. S.]

2. The Académie française, founded in 1635, consists of forty members, most of whom are well-known writers. Its main function is to uphold the standards of the French language. The League of the Rights of Man was founded by the politician Georges Clemenceau at the height of the Dreyfus Affair at the end of the nineteenth century to protect the individual's liberties against such embodiments of "Caesarism" as the state and the army. M. Régnier's

gesture, though well intentioned, was futile and ridiculous, because it had no power whatever in a France occupied by Nazi Germany and officially ruled by the authoritarian Vichy regime.

3. By January 1944, Soviet troops had expelled the Germans from most of their territory and were at the borders of prewar Poland. Meanwhile, the Germans were secretly working on the V-1 rocket, which carried an eight-hundred-kilogram warhead. These weapons were first used in large quantities against London on 13 June 1944.

4. In exchange for workers who left for Germany, certain prisoners—fathers of large families—were liberated. [V. S.]

CHAPTER 8. COMING OUT OF THE WAR

1. A plateau near Grenoble in southeastern France, on which, during the summer of 1944, about thirty-five hundred members of the French Resistance fought the Germans, lost, and were subjected to bloody reprisals.

2. On 15 August 1944, a second Allied landing took place in France, on the Mediterranean coast between Nice and Marseille. These Allied troops very soon were able to join up with the other Allied armies in northeastern France.

3. Dr. Eugène Minkowski had not left Paris and had worked with a very small team to rescue children in the Northern Zone in collaboration with other organizations. The [OSE] presidency was subsequently assumed by Senator Justin Godart, then by Georges Garel. In January 1945, the OSE officially resumed the title of association it had held under the 1901 law. [V. S.]

4. Before the diffusion of television sets in the 1950s, movie houses ran short newsreels before presenting their main feature films.

5. The coded alphabetical lists referred to other lists that contained names camouflaged with new addresses. Several types of information were entered on these lists: identity, history, portrait, school level reached, the child's family connections abroad, and so on. [V. S.] Mme. Samuel was kind enough to send me photocopies of documents pertaining to my sister and me.

6. Testimony cited in *Notre mémoire,* deposited with the Alliance israélite universelle in Paris in 1993. [V. S.]

7. Périgueux is about half way between Limoges and Bordeaux.

8. The mythological creature, half man and half horse (neither a centaur nor a satyr), who raised the god Dionysius.

9. Because Nahum Hermann was fifty-five years old, he was immediately gassed; hence he died a quick death. Guy Kohen, being young and able bodied, was required to perform very hard labor and, had he not been liberated, would have suffered a slow death from exhaustion.

10. This refers to the alphabetical and chronological (by convoy) lists of Jews deported from France, published in 1978 by Beate and Serge Klarsfeld. [V. S.]

11. Serge Klarsfeld, *Mémorial des enfants juifs déportés de France* [Memorial of Jewish Children Deported from France], published by the *Association des fils et filles de déportés juifs de France* [Association of Sons and Daughters of Jews Deported from France] and by the Beate Klarsfeld Foundation, Paris, 1994. [V. S.]

12. Annette Wieviorka, *Déportation et génocide* (Paris: Plon, 1992); Lucien Lazare, *Rescue as Resistance: How Jewish Organizations Fought the Holocaust in France* (New York: Columbia University Press, 1996); Serge Klarsfeld, *Mémorial de la déportation des juifs de France* and *Mémorial des enfants.* [V. S.]

13. Both natives of Germany, they had been interned in the camp of Gurs. [V. S.]

14. Following the huge immigration of Italians and eastern Europeans into the United States between 1890 and 1920, the U.S. Congress in 1924 passed a law that as of 1929 set the annual immigration for all foreigners at 150,000. In addition, to maintain an ethnic preponderance of northern and western Europeans in the U.S. population, the same law divided the immigration quota in proportion to the relative size of the various ethnic groups present in the U.S. population in 1920. This 1924 law was not fundamentally repealed until 1965.

15. This sequence was twice applied to the group of children (including myself) and adults who had left Switzerland with the intention of sailing from Antwerp, Belgium, to the United States in March 1946. Largely because of the priority extended to returning American veterans and their war brides, I did not leave Europe until 1 May, and then not from Antwerp but from Le Havre, France. When we arrived in New York City on 8 May, the order of debarkation and customs inspection followed the same sequence of priority.

16. Testimony cited in *Notre mémoire*, 1993. Likewise see Ernst Papenek, *Out of the Fire* (New York: William Morrow, 1975). [V. S.]

17. *Tous les fleuves vont à la mer* [All the Rivers Flow to the Sea] (Paris: Le Seuil, 1994). Elie Wiesel was one of the youngsters sheltered by the OSE at Écouis. [V. S.] Wiesel is a Nobel Prize laureate in peace, who has written many profound and eloquent books on Judaism and the concentration camp experience.

18. "Le Problème pédagogique des jeunes de Buchenwald" [The Pedagogical Problem of the Youngsters of Buchenwald], in *Les Enfants de Buchenwald* [The Children of Buchenwald] (Geneva: Union-OSE, 1946). [V. S.]

19. A French philosopher (1638–1715), known for his philosophy of Occasionalism, in which he tried to reconcile Cartesianism and Christian theology.

20. For these testimonies, see the chapter "Children's Odysseys." [V. S.]

21. Presumably a reference to Hosea, an eighth-century B.C.E. Hebrew prophet of the Kingdom of Israel, which was conquered by the Assyrians during his lifetime. The main theme of the Book of Hosea is God's compassion for His people, who will overcome the disasters that befall them.

CHAPTER 9. FIFTY YEARS LATER

1. In my case, the United States was the fourth country of residence and English, the fourth language I learned to speak. Moreover, since my relatives in the United States were unable to finance my higher education, it was only thanks to the Korean War G.I. Bill, some academic grants, and more than two dozen part-time and full-time jobs in three states that I was able to receive my doctorate at the late age of thirty-five.

2. The archives have been deposited at the AIU in Paris and can be consulted by researchers and historians. [V. S.]

3. *Mes vingt ans à l'OSE* [My Twenty Years at the OSE], by Germaine Masour, in 1983; an autobiographical essay by Joseph Weill, *Déjà* [Already], in 1988; several accounts by Jacques Salon concerning his young wife, Nicole Weill, deported in 1944, and their work in the Italian-occupied zone; accounts and testimonies by Ruth Lambert, Madeleine Dreyfus, and Fanny Loinger, summarized in *Notre mémoire* [Our Memory], in December 1993. All these typescripts were deposited at the AIU. [V. S.]

4. Veil was a former French Minister of Health (1974–1979) and a former president of the European Assembly (1979–1983).

5. See Judith Elbaz's reminiscence.

6. An Italian of Jewish ancestry, Levi was deported to Auschwitz, where he worked as a chemist. After the war, he wrote about the Nazi concentration camps but at first could not find a publisher. He committed suicide in 1987.

CHAPTER 10. CHILDREN'S ODYSSEYS

1. This is the Crystal Night [Kristallnacht] [V. S.]

2. The children from La Guette were transferred to the Unoccupied Zone under the responsibility of their director, Flore Loinger, and then dispersed. [V. S.]

3. He was one of the people expelled from the States of Baden and Palatinate. [V. S.]

4. This is how many children saw us—and were thinking of escape—while at that time (June 1942), the liberation of children under the age of fifteen was done within the law and with the parents' permission. [V. S.]

5. This was not the case, and the camp guards were not armed. What we have here is a conglomeration of memories from different periods. [V. S.]

6. I often met Mme. Zlatin on the platform of the Montpellier railroad station. She had come to "sign in" the children in order to accompany them to Palavas-les-Flots. [V. S.] With her husband, she subsequently managed the children's home at Izieu in the Ain, whose children were arrested by Klaus Barbie, head of the Gestapo in Lyon, and deported (Vivette Samuel's letter of 12 June 1997; see note 10).

7. Vercingétorix (72–46 B.C.) was a Gallic general who led an unsuccessful coalition of

tribes in an attempt to prevent the Roman general Julius Caesar from conquering Gaul (later called France). Louis XIV was the longest ruling monarch (1643–1715) in French history and in many ways the most splendid, expensive, and absolute. Napoleon Bonaparte took power illegally in 1799, made himself emperor in 1804, and waged war for more than fourteen years all over the European continent and the Middle East, in Haiti, and on the high seas. Robespierre was one of the most radical leaders of the French Revolution of 1789–1799.

8. The languages of the Duchy of Luxembourg are French and German; many people in Rivesaltes, Perpignan, and the surrounding countryside spoke Spanish.

9. Although the United States had been at war after the Japanese bombing of Pearl Harbor on 7 December 1941, it maintained diplomatic relations with Vichy France until the Allied invasion of French North Africa in November 1942.

10. Klaus Barbie, the former head of the Gestapo in Lyon, was tried and convicted in a French court in 1987 for crimes against humanity, especially the raid he himself led in 1944 on the Jewish orphanage of Izieu, where he captured forty-one children and ten adults, who were then deported to Drancy and on to their deaths.

11. A residence that belonged to the Baronness de Rothschild. [V. S.]

12. Claude Bégué-Morhange, *Chamberet—Recollections from an Ordinary Childhood* (Marlboro, Vermont: Marlboro Press, 1987). [V. S.] The excerpt in the preceding section is taken from that remarkable work.

13. See note 4 above. [V. S.]

14. The Yad Vashem memorial center in Jerusalem has honored thousands of Righteous Gentiles who—at the peril of their own and their families' lives—saved, usually by concealment, one or more (sometimes thousands of) Jews from death or deportation by the Nazis. See, for example, Eric Silver, *The Book of the Just: The Unsung Heroes Who Rescued Jews from Hitler* (New York: Grove Press, 1992).

APPENDIX 1

1. Her husband is the brother of the famous photographer Henri Cartier-Bresson (13 October 1996 communication by Judith Elbaz).

APPENDIX 2

1. That figure represented 0.75 percent of the total French population of forty-two million.

2. For the most part, these numbers [in both of the preceding lists] were extracted from the articles by Annette Wieviorka and Renée Poznanski, as well as from an OSE report included in *Au secours des enfants du siècle* [To the Aid of the Children of Our Time]. [V. S.]

Bibliography

This brief bibliography is far from exhaustive, since many titles have not been included.

WORKS IN FRENCH

Bauman, Denise. *La Mémoire des oubliés: Grandir après Auschwitz.* Paris: Albin Michel, 1988.

Brauner, Alfred. *Ces enfants ont vécu la guerre.* Paris: Editions sociales françaises, 1946.

Caen, Simon. *Georges Garel.* Grenoble: Université des sciences sociales, 1988–1989.

Delpard, Raphaël. *Les Enfants cachés.* Paris: Jean-Claude Lattès, 1993.

Fayol, Pierre. *Le Chambon-sur-Lignon sous l'occupation.* Paris: L'Harmattan, 1990.

Grynberg, Anne. *Les Camps de la honte: Les Internés juifs des camps français, 1939–1944.* Paris: La Découverte, 1991.

Gurvic, Lazare. *L'OSE, ses buts et ses activités pendant la période 1912–1945.* Geneva: Union-OSE, 1947.

Klarsfeld, Serge. *Le Mémorial des enfants juifs déportés de France.* Edited and published by the *Association des fils et filles de déportés juifs de France* and by the Beate Klarsfeld Foundation. Paris, 1994.

Knout, David. *Contribution à l'histoire de la Résistance juive en France, 1940–1944.* Paris: Editions du Centre, 1947.

Lemalet, Martine, ed. *Au secours des enfants du siècle—Regards croisés sur l'OSE.* Paris: Nils, 1993.

Poznanski, Renée. *Être juif en France pendant la Seconde Guerre mondiale.* Paris: Hachette, 1994.

Weill, Joseph. *Contribution à l'histoire des camps d'internement dans l'Anti-France.* Paris: Editions du Centre, 1946.

Wieviorka, Annette. *Déportation et génocide: Entre la mémorie et l'oubli.* Paris: Plon, 1992.

Zeitoun, Sabine. *Ces enfants qu'il fallait sauver.* Paris: Albin Michel, 1989.

Zeitoun, Sabine. *L'Œuvre de secours aux enfants (OSE) sous l'occupation en France.* Paris: L'Harmattan, 1990.

COLLECTIVE WORKS

L'Activité des organisations juives en France sous l'occupation. Paris: CDJC, 1947, 1983.

Les Enfants de Buchenwald. Geneva: Union-OSE, 1946.

L'Étoile jaune—Hommage à Eugène Minkowski. Geneva: Union-OSE, 1972.

Lazare Gurvic. In Memoriam. Paris: Union mondiale-OSE, 1961.

"Le Procès Barbie." *Les Nouveaux Cahiers* 76 (spring 1984).

"Le Sauvetage des enfants juifs de 1940 à 1944." Colloquium, *Le Monde juif* 136 (1989).

WORKS IN ENGLISH

Bégué-Morhange, Claude. *Chamberet—Recollections from an Ordinary Childhood.* Translated by Austryn Wainhouse. Marlboro, Vermont: Marlboro Press, 1987.

Conan, Eric, and Henry Rousso. *Vichy: An Ever-Present Past.* Translated by Nathan Bracher. Hanover, N.H.: University Press of New England, 1998.

Hemmendinger, Judith. *Survivors: Children of the Holocaust.* Translated from the French. Bethesda, Md.: National Press, 1986.

In Fight for the Health of the Jewish People—50 Years of OSE. New York: World Union-OSE, 1968.

Kieval, Hillel J. "Legality and Resistance in Vichy France: The Rescue of Jewish Children." *Proceedings of the American Philosophical Society* 124, no. 5 (October 1980), 339–366.

Latour, Amy. *The Jewish Resistance in France (1940–1944).* Translated by Irene Ilton. New York: Holocaust Library, 1981.

Lazare, Lucien. *Rescue as Resistance: How Jewish Organizations Fought the Holocaust in France.* Translated by Jeffrey M. Green. New York: Columbia University Press, 1996.

Papanek, Ernst. *Out of the Fire.* New York: William Morrow, 1975.

Vegh, Claudine. *I Didn't Say Goodbye.* Translated by Ros Schwartz. New York: E. P. Dutton, 1984.

Wolf, Jacqueline. *"Take Care of Josette": A Memoir in Defense of Occupied France.* New York: Franklin Watts, 1981.

Zuccotti, Susan. *The Holocaust, the French, and the Jews.* New York: Basic Books, 1993.

TRANSLATOR'S SUGGESTED ADDITIONAL RESOURCES

Block, Gay, and Malka Drucker. *Rescuers: Portraits of Moral Courage in the Holocaust.* New York: Holmes and Meier, 1991.

Gossels, Lisa, and Dean Wetherell. *The Children of Chabannes.* 1999 (film).

Hallie, Philip. *Lest Innocent Blood Be Shed.* New York: Harper and Row, 1979.

Josephs, Jeremy. *Swastika over Paris.* Foreword by Serge Klarsfeld. New York: Arcade, 1989.

Kedward, H. R. *Occupied France: Collaboration and Resistance, 1940–1944.* Oxford: Basil Blackwell, 1985.

Klarsfeld, Serge. *The Children of Izieu: A Human Tragedy.* Translated by Kenneth Jacobson. New York: Abrams, 1985.

Lowrie, Donald Alexander. *The Hunted Children.* New York: W. W. Norton, 1963.

Marrus, Michael, and Robert O. Paxton. *Vichy France and the Jews.* New York: Basic Books, 1981.

Rittner, Carol, and Sondra Myers, eds. *The Courage to Care: Rescuers of Jews during the Holocaust.* New York: New York University Press, 1986.

Silver, Eric. *The Book of the Just: The Unsung Heroes Who Rescued Jews from Hitler.* New York: Grove Press, 1992.

Webster, Paul. *Pétain's Crime: The Full Story of French Collaboration in the Holocaust.* Chicago: Ivan R. Dee, 1991.

Wiesel, Elie. *All Rivers Run to the Sea: Memoirs.* New York: Alfred A. Knopf, 1995.

Index